Management:
The Basic Concepts

MANAGEMENT:
The Basic Concepts

By
Henry H. Albers
Chairman, Department of Management
University of Nebraska, Lincoln, Nebraska

John Wiley & Sons, Inc.
New York • London • Sydney • Toronto

42,646

PREFACE

This textbook presents the basic concepts that relate to the practice of management in all kinds of organized endeavor. The subject matter is presented within the process framework originally formulated by Henri Fayol. The elements of managerial action are assumed to include planning, organizing, directing, and controlling. Organizing is defined to include staffing and related personnel functions, which follows Fayol's approach. The problem of coordination is not given separate status because it is involved in all the functions of the process.

This book is directed toward undergraduate students in business administration, industrial engineering, public administration, hospital administration, military science, and the arts and sciences. It can also provide a basic background for graduate courses and a foundation for management development programs in business and other fields.

I contend that the basic management concepts are the same for different kinds of organization (business, hospitals, government, the military), for different functional fields (production, marketing, personnel, and finance), and at different levels of management. These concepts can be used in small as well as large organizations and are important to those who wish to form their own enterprise.

I have attempted to blend the best from the traditional knowledge with such modern developments as operations research and computer technology. The perspective is always that of the manager instead of that of the specialist.

I have tried to serve the needs of students in two-year and four-year colleges and technical schools as well as those in universities. I do not assume that students will necessarily become associated with a large or even a medium-sized corporation; smaller enterprises are not neglected in this presentation.

I would like to express a special thanks to a number of people. Professor John D. Minch of Cabrillo College, Aptos, California, read the entire manuscript and made many constructive comments and helpful suggestions. His ideas were highly instrumental in shaping the content of this book. Important contributions were also made by the following individuals. Professor Marc D. Roberts, Department of Business, Skyline College, San Bruno, California; Professor Walter Weintraub, Chairman, Department of Business, Kingsborough Community College, Brooklyn, New York; and Professor Irving Wechsler, Borough of Manhattan Community College, New York, N. Y.

My thanks to Carmen Mattes for her editorial assistance and administrative support, to Jeanne Maynard for her organizational talents, and to Jane Pokrant for typing and proofing the manuscript.

Saipan, Mariana Islands

June 1971   **Henry H. Albers**

CONTENTS

PART I

Management: Past and Present

1

INTRODUCTION

This book presents the basic principles that relate to the practice of management in business and other kinds of organization. These principles can be applied in performing the managerial task in enterprises that employ a small number of people as well as those with thousands of employees.

Early Examples of the Practice of Management

Although the systematic study of management has a recent origin, the practice of management is as old as human society. The history of man is full of evidence of organizational activity that indicates a knowledge of many of the ideas later expressed by the pioneers of scientific management. Archaeology has unearthed extensive accumulations of relics from past civilizations that reflect elaborate organizational achievements. The mammoth walls of ancient Babylon, the pyramids of the Pharaohs, and the temples of the Aztecs rival the accomplishments of modern industrial civilization, considering the then existing state of technology. Hannibal's crossing of the Alps in 218 B.C. with troops and equipment was a remarkable organizational feat.

THE ROMAN EMPIRE

The glory that was Rome must be credited in great part to superior organizational abilities. The Roman legions conquered an empire that in the second century of the Christian era "comprehended the fairest part of the earth, and the most civilised portion of mankind."[1] This vast domain was linked together

[1]Edward Gibbon, *The Decline and Fall of the Roman Empire*, Vol. I (New York: The Modern Library, 1932), p. 1. Gibbon's classic study of Rome contains some excellent descriptions of Roman organization and accomplishments.

by an elaborate system of roads that reached from Rome into the outlying provinces. Relay stations with a supply of horses were established to facilitate rapid communication throughout the empire in the manner of the pony express of the American West. A short distance from the capital, the great port of Ostia sent ships to the provinces beyond the Mediterranean. Commerce extended overland to the shores of the Baltic and by sea to ports that supplied Rome with the riches of Asia. These accomplishments with a technology that must be considered primitive by modern standards give emphatic testimony to the genius of Roman organizers. Furthermore, Roman administrators were successful in making the organizational changes necessitated by the growth of a small city into a world empire.[2] The modern business corporation has had to contend with a similar situation. The Romans solved the matter in a way that would not be at all foreign to the executives of today. They had a clear understanding of the problems associated with decentralization, delegation, and coordination. Their success in solving these problems is adequately attested to by the fact that the Roman Republic and later the Empire spanned centuries.

THE ROMAN CATHOLIC CHURCH

The Roman Catholic Church successfully solved the organizational problems of large size long before today's industrial giants came into being. It developed organizational practices that made possible comprehensive control over the religious lives of more than half a billion people in every corner of the world. The central administrative organization of the Catholic Church, known as the Curia Romana, corresponds to the top levels of complex governmental and military organizations. Two American business executives from General Motors and Remington Rand came to the following conclusion in a historical study of organization: "It can be said in general of the Curia Romana that as an example of efficient departmentalization and executive coordination it is perhaps without a parallel in the entire realm of organization."[3] The Catholic Church followed a geographical pattern in its basic departmentation, but it also developed a highly effective functional approach to problems that can be better handled on this basis. The staff concept is utilized at all levels of the organization to permit specialized and subordinate participation in the decisional process without destroying unity of command.

THE ARSENAL OF VENICE

An outstanding example of the application of many of the ideas later advanced by the pioneers of scientific management is found in the famous Ar-

---

[2]James D. Mooney and Alan C. Reiley, *Onward Industry!* (New York: Harper & Brothers Publishers, 1931), pp. 109–144; Mooney, *The Principles of Organization* (New York: Harper & Brothers Publishers, 1947), pp. 62–72.

[3]Ibid., p. 241.

senal of Venice. The Arsenal anticipated the direct line production of the modern meat packing and automobile assembly plants. This fact is indicated by the Spanish traveler, Pero Tafur, who in 1436 described what he saw at the Arsenal in the following words.

"And as one enters the gate there is a great street on either hand with the sea in the middle, and on one side are windows opening out of the houses of the arsenal, and the same on the other side, and out came a galley towed by a boat, and from the windows they handed out to them, from one the cordage, from another the bread, from another the arms, and from another the balistas and mortars, and so from all sides everything which was required, and when the galley had reached the end of the street all the men required were on board, together with the complement of oars, and she was equipped from end to end. In this manner there came out ten galleys, fully armed, between the hours of three and nine."[4]

The Arsenal was probably the largest industrial establishment of the fifteenth century, covering sixty acres of ground and water and employing between one and two thousand workers.[5] See Figure 1-1. It had a threefold task: the manufacture of galleys, arms, and equipment; the storage of these items; and assembly and refitting. The work of the Arsenal was divided into several functional departments with a foreman in charge of each department. Shipbuilding was divided into three stages of production and was carefully preplanned. The first step was the building of the frame by the ship carpenters. Then the planking was fastened and the cabins and superstructures were built. Both carpenters and caulkers participated in this work. The final stage of production was completed when the ship was called into service. All the departments of the Arsenal participated in this final assembly stage. The ship's seams were filled with tow and pitch, and the hull was covered with tar or grease. Then came the launching of the ship, after which the deck fixings were fastened in place. Finally the ship was provided with the rigging, moorings, and oars and arms for the crew. The efficiency attained in this stage of production is indicated by the assembly, launching, and arming of a vessel in less than one hour during a visit by Henry III, King of France, in 1574.

THE INDUSTRIAL REVOLUTION

History books are filled with glowing accounts of the technological innovations of the industrial revolution in Great Britain and the United States. Relatively little is known about the management methods and techniques that helped make this progress possible. As Urwick and Brech point out in their

[4]Malcolm Letts (editor and translator), Pero Tafur, *Travels and Adventures, 1435–1439* (London: George Routledge & Sons, Ltd., 1926), p. 170.
[5]Frederic Chapin Lane, *Venetian Ships and Shipbuilders of the Renaissance* (Baltimore: The Johns Hopkins Press, 1934), pp. 129–175.

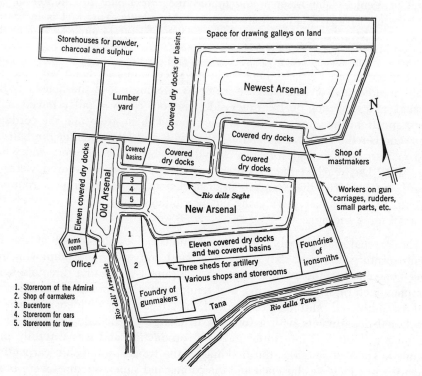

FIGURE 1-1. The Arsenal of Venice about 1560. (Reproduced with permission from Frederic Chapin Lane, *Venetian Ships and Shipbuilders of the Renaissance*. Baltimore: The Johns Hopkins Press, 1934).

study of the development of scientific management, it seems highly unlikely that Great Britain could have made the industrial progress of the nineteenth century without a foundation of successful management.[6] A comprehensive study of the management practices of the Birmingham (England) plant of the Boulton and Watt Company is one bit of evidence to support this view.[7] The following observation is made in the introduction of this study.

"Neither Taylor, Ford, nor other modern experts devised anything in the way of plan that cannot be discovered at Soho [the Birmingham factory of Boulton and Watt] before 1805; and the Soho system of costing is superior to that employed in very many successful concerns to-day. This earliest engineering

[6]L. Urwick and E.F.L. Brech, *The Making of Scientific Management*, Vol. II (London: Management Publications Trust, 1946), p. 7.

[7]Erich Roll, *An Early Experiment in Industrial Organisation* (London: Longmans, Green and Co., 1930). A summary of this study is found in Urwick and Brech, *The Making of Scientific Management*, pp. 24–39.

factory, therefore, possessed an organisation on the management side which was not excelled even by the technical skill of the craftsmen it produced."[8]

As the name of the firm implies, one of the original participants in the organization was James Watt, whose developmental work on the steam engine supplied the power of the industrial revolution. The evidence presented in the Boulton and Watt study points to the development of managerial methods that equal the progress made in the purely technical areas. For example, an incentive system for cylinder borers was devised by determining the average time necessary for different size and type cylinders. A list of machines required in the production process with data on machine speeds was found in one of the company documents. A complete list of all subassemblies and components with full details of operation sequences was found. A detailed list of jobs assigned to individuals and groups of workers indicates a fixed standard job. Forecasting was used as a basis for production planning, and elaborate cost control records were maintained by the company.

The Background of Modern Management

THE FACTORY SYSTEM

The ascendancy of the factory as the primary mode of production and the tremendous rise in the volume of production after the industrial revolution created a need for large numbers of managers. Factory organization brought about a more complete differentiation between management and nonmanagement functions and between managers and workers. It also enlarged the scope of the management function.

The factory system may be distinguished from other modes of production by the following characteristics. (1) Workers, raw material, machinery, and equipment are concentrated in a building or a group of buildings used exclusively for production. Before the advent of the factory system a great deal of production was performed in the home by a single or a small group of craft workers. (2) The factory system brought centralized control of raw material, production, and output. The earlier merchant-employer or putting-out system lacked such unified control. The merchant furnished the raw materials and provided the markets; production was generally controlled by the craft workers. (3) The ultimate development of the factory system brought a clear distinction between the employer and the employed. Under earlier forms of craft organization, the master was more a fellow worker than an employer. An elaborate complex of customs and traditions governed the relationship between master and worker.

The industrial revolution was a major contributing factor in the rapid development of the factory system. It furnished both the power and the machines

[8]Ibid., p. xv.

for large-scale production. The specialized machine performing one operation in a total sequence of hundreds of operations required the concentration of many workers to produce the final product. Large amounts of capital were required to finance the mechanized factories which shifted the control of production to the capitalist. The craft worker who lacked the resources to buy the machine or to compete with it assumed the role of an employee.

The factory required more planning and supervision than the smaller and simpler handicraft production units. The function of work division became more important and complex. The worker's part in the production process became ever more minute. His perspective became the specialized job. The task of integrating his job with other jobs passed to the manager. The relationship between the employer and the worker became more impersonal and the problem of motivation became more difficult. The customs and traditions of craft production had played an important role in promoting cooperation. Pride of craftmanship and the social status that evolved from craft status were also important factors. The worker in the evolving factories no longer felt that he was an organic part of the enterprise. His interest in the enterprise rested in its ability to pay him a wage with which to nurture his body and soul. The difficulty of achieving cooperation in factory organization is indicated by the effort of the pioneers of scientific management to devise improved wage systems. The importance of the noneconomic motivations of the early craft organizations is emphasized by the attention now being given to the social system in organization and the attempts to reproduce smaller scale production units through decentralization.

The examples of the previous section show that the practice of successful management preceded the factory system and the industrial revolution. Many of the problems that evolved from the rise of the factory as the dominant mode of production existed in preindustrial revolution factories, such as the Arsenal of Venice. The functions of management were important in these early organizations, and fragmentary historical accounts indicate that they were often well performed. But industrial production in factories was not quantitatively significant during earlier periods. Agriculture and craft production in small shops or homes were the dominant forms of economic activity. The industrial revolution greatly magnified industrial production in factories and at the same time created a managerial class. With the factory system came larger and more complex organizations in other areas of endeavor, which further expanded the need for management and managers.

THE RISE OF A MANAGERIAL CLASS

Corporations constitute the legal framework within which the organizations of modern industrial civilization have developed. The corporate form of organization overcame certain limitations imposed by a private control of property. It provided the means whereby the property of innumerable individuals could be combined and brought under unified control. In a world in which the life-span of the personal property holder is limited, the corporation provided a greater continuity in time.

With the development of capitalism, the control of the enterprise passed to the property owner or the capitalist. But the age of the capitalist was soon to become the age of the manager. Control has in great part shifted from the property owner to a nonpropertied managerial class. This shift in control has been expressed by such terms as "the managerial revolution" and "managerialism." It has resulted in a change in the manner of speaking. As Peter Drucker has noted, we now talk about the "responsibilities of management" rather than the "responsibilities of capital."[9] The term "management and labor" has generally replaced "capital and labor" in the vocabulary.

The rise of large corporations brought into being a large class of hired managers. The property owners could at best assume only a few top-management positions; the middle and lower ranks of management were filled with professional managers. Frequently the property owners were more interested in finance than in the active management of industrial organizations, which gave many top-management positions to the nonpropertied professional. Simultaneously, the managerial class began to assume more complete control of the corporation. Management control was facilitated by a number of factors that evolved from the nature of corporate organization and its ultimate development. A wide dispersion of stock ownership occurred in many corporations—in some cases the largest stockholder held only a fraction of one percent of the controlling stock. Stockholders began to view stock ownership primarily as a financial investment instead of as an instrument of control. So long as a reasonable financial return was forthcoming, little difficulty was experienced by management in obtaining a sufficient number of proxies to control. In other instances the use of nonvoting stock made possible legal control with a relatively small investment. Even though unqualified legal control requires a majority of the voting stock, actual control can be obtained by minority stockholders if the remaining stock is well dispersed. Through these and other devices a clear differentiation between property and control began to appear in many corporations. The capitalistic system began to give way to the managerial system.

Similar developments occurred in other fields. In government, the professional public administrator has replaced the politician in many areas. University and college administrators have taken away many of the functions formerly performed by the professor and in some cases have taken active control of the curricula.

[9]Peter F. Drucker, *The Practice of Management* (New York: Harper & Brothers Publishers, 1954), p. 3.

TRADE UNIONISM

The development of industry on a large scale has been followed by a trade union movement in every democratic society. A number of explanations have been advanced for this phenomenon. The radicals have viewed trade unionism as one aspect of a class-conscious revolt of the proletarian worker against the capitalist, which they assumed to be the ultimate consequence of the new industrial system. The realization of this prophecy has been repudiated by the events of history. Industrial workers did not become the proletariat. The long-run consequence of the new industrial system was a higher standard of living than ever before experienced by the large masses of people. Anachronistically, the dictatorship of the proletariat was initially established in a nation that had not developed industry or capitalism on a significant scale.

The workers of the Western industrial nations have generally repudiated the ideas of the radicals. They have not been interested in destroying the basic institutions of capitalism. They sought higher wages and better conditions of work by extending control over the supply of labor through trade union organization. They rejected the views of the radicals and accepted the market mechanism of the private enterprise system.[10]

Beginning with small craft unions of carpenters, printers, and shoemakers in the early 1800s, the American trade union movement has resulted in the organization of 17 million workers in some 185 national and international unions. These unions range in size from 200 members for the smallest to well over a million for the largest. Some of these unions are craft unions including only workers in a particular craft, such as painters or bricklayers. The industrial unions, as the name implies, have organized workers in a particular industry. A number of the larger unions are actually multicraft-industrial unions because they have members in a number of crafts or industries or both.

American trade unions have generally accepted the philosophy that the best way to promote the welfare of the worker is through collective bargaining with the employer for wages, hours, and conditions of work. The nature of collective bargaining involves a union challenge to management control.[11] Collective bargaining is joint union-management action about certain matters. Contract negotiation results in important decisions about wages, hours, and conditions of employment, which are formally set forth in a trade agreement. Joint decision making is also involved in the procedure generally established in the trade agreement to resolve difficulties that arise in the administration of the agreement. What is the proper dividing line between the subject matter

---

[10]One account of the philosophy of American trade unionism is found in Selig Perlman, *A Theory of the Labor Movement* (New York: The Macmillan Company, 1928).

[11]Neil W. Chamberlain has made an outstanding contribution to a better understanding of this problem in *The Union Challenge to Management Control* (New York: Harper & Brothers Publishers, 1948).

of collective bargaining and those areas that remain the exclusive domain of management? Management has generally conceded that unions have a right to participate in matters that directly affect the interest of the worker. But they have opposed attempts of unions to expand beyond this point. The management argument is that they are legally responsible to the stockholder and that they can assume this responsibility only if they are given a free hand in managing the enterprise. Union leaders argue that they represent the worker and should have a voice in any matter that directly concerns the interests of the worker.

Government Regulation of Business

The manner in which government intervention in the economic sphere has affected decision making by private business leaders is now considered.[12] Some government activity is designed to promote the exercise of private business leadership. The protection of property rights and the development of contract and corporation law are examples of this form of government intervention. This type of government control is usually taken for granted by business leaders. Of greater concern have been government activities that restrict the action of business leadership.

THE IDEAL OF COMPETITION

The American attitude toward the role of government in a private enterprise system has been greatly influenced by Adam Smith's *Wealth of Nations* and the Classical School of economists who promulgated his basic philosophical premises.[13] The fundamental thesis of the classical economists was that government intervention in the economic sphere should be minimized and that the

[12]Many of the ideas in this section were originally presented by Robert A. Gordon in *Business Leadership in the Large Corporation* (Washington, D.C.: The Brookings Institution, 1945), pp. 222–245.

[13]Adam Smith was particularly concerned with the government restrictions recommended by some of the mercantilists in the field of foreign trade. In the following oft-quoted passage he recommends *laissez faire* as a better policy: "As every individual, therefore, endeavours as much as he can both to employ his capital in the support of domestic industry, and so to direct that industry that its produce may be of the greatest value; every individual necessarily labours to render the annual revenue of the society as great as he can. He generally, indeed, neither intends to promote the public interest, nor knows how much he is promoting it. By preferring the support of domestic to that of foreign industry, he intends only his own security; and by directing that industry in such a manner as its produce may be of the greatest value, he intends only his own gain, and he is in this, as in many other cases, led by an invisible hand to promote an end which was no part of his intention. Nor is it always the worse for the society that it was no part of it. By pursuing his own interest he frequently promotes that of the society more effectually than when he really intends to promote it." Adam Smith, *The Wealth of Nations*, Cannan edition (New York: The Modern Library, 1937), p. 423. Originally published in 1776.

pursuit of self-interest and competition would promote the greatest social welfare. Ironically, this doctrine of *laissez faire* and competition laid the initial basis for government intervention in the activity of businessmen. This intervention proceeded on the assumption that competition is good and that any attempts by business firms to become monopolistic had to be controlled. The businessman was given the freedom to control the destiny of his enterprise with one important exception: he could not engage in activities that threatened the survival of competition. Another important postulate of early government intervention was that competition should be fair and constructive. Originally enforced by the common law, this policy was soon enunciated by the statute law. The first legislation designed to promote competition was the Sherman Anti-Trust Act of 1890, which prohibited combinations in restraint of commerce. The Sherman Act was followed by the Clayton Act (1914), which prohibited local price discrimination, tying contracts, and interlocking directorates.[14] The Federal Trade Commission, an administrative agency, was created in 1914 to enforce statutory provisions against unfair competition. Additional amendments to the statutory law governing unfair competition were made in the Robinson-Patman Act of 1936. These and other federal statutes, the administrative rulings of the Federal Trade Commission, the common law on the subject, and state legislation provide a voluminous body of rules within which the business leader must operate. The fact that enforcement has not always been stringent does not alter the basic idea that business decision making must take into account the fact or possibility of governmental action.

OTHER FORMS OF GOVERNMENT INTERVENTION

Federal labor laws have resulted in a comprehensive body of law governing the relationship between management and unions in industries engaged in interstate commerce. The Wagner Act (1935) with the amendments and additions made by the Taft-Hartley Act (1947) makes recognition of a union mandatory if the majority of employees in the bargaining unit vote for the union. The employer is also required to bargain in good faith with a union certified under the law. Although the law does not force the employer to come to an agreement with a union, the practical exigencies of the relationships created by the law have led to the establishment of joint union-management decision making about a number of important issues.

The Fair Labor Standards Act (1938) set a minimum wage and required the payment of time-and-one-half for work beyond 40 hours per week. Legislation passed in the early 1930s forbade certain practices in the securities mar-

---

[14]An example of local price discrimination is price reduction by a local branch of a large firm to drive out independent merchants. Tying contracts were often used to force a buyer to purchase an entire line of goods produced by the manufacturer. An interlocking directorate exists when an individual is a director in two or more supposedly competing firms.

ket and created the Securities Exchange Commission to administer the law. Railroads, telephone companies, electric light and power companies, and other public utilities were excluded from the regulatory efforts to enforce competition. Public policy in this field has been guided by the idea that the absence of competition necessitated more comprehensive government regulation. Administrative agencies, such as the Interstate Commerce Commission and the Federal Communications Commission, have placed severe restrictions on management decision making.

Although not expressly designed to regulate business, social security legislation (such as the Social Security Act) makes necessary accounting procedures and reports beyond the ordinary requirements of business. Corporation and personal income taxes have imposed similar responsibilities and also influence business decisions in a wide area. The requirements of national security have increased government participation in private decision making in numerous ways. Government contracts generally involve a great deal of such participation. The experiences of World War II and Korea indicate the extent to which government controls can be imposed in a private enterprise system when the national security demands it.

The role of government in a private enterprise system has been and will be the subject of a great deal of debate. A private enterprise system is founded on the idea of private rather than government decision making in the primary areas of economic activity. The principal form of government intervention has been regulation instead of government ownership. This regulation has placed limits on private decision making and also frequently involves the transfer of decision making to a government agency, such as the Interstate Commerce Commission and the National Labor Relations Board. The pursuit of self-interest is also a fundamental premise of a private enterprise system. The question of when the pursuit of private self-interest begins to interfere with the public welfare frequently presents a difficult problem. Some of the policy problems in this area involve the rights of one economic group relative to another. The tariff question, for example, often leads to controversy between exporters and domestic producers over what is proper public policy.

The Pioneers of Scientific Management

This chapter has provided various points of departure for the study of management. The chapter that follows will be concerned with the pioneers of scientific management and the manner in which their contributions relate to the development of management knowledge.

2

TOWARD SCIENTIFIC MANAGEMENT

Few publications on the subject of management were available before the beginning of this century. Fragmentary accounts of what might be called principles of management can be found in the writings of early historians, church officials, and military and political leaders. A few treatises in the fields of military and political organization are antecedent to the modern book on management.[1] An early contribution came from Charles Babbage as a result of his ideas for an automatic computer.[2] Babbage visited many British and French factories and workshops in search of the technical capacities to construct an automatic computer. A by-product of this activity was a book in which he presented "some principles that seemed to pervade many establishments."[3] He dealt with such problems as work division and specialization, better methods for doing work, the utilization of machines and tools, and the maintenance of cost records.

[1]One of the oldest military treatises is *The Art of War*, written about 500 B.C. by Sun Tzu Wu (Harrisburg: The Military Service Publishing Company, 1944). Other well-known classics in the field of military organization and strategy are Karl von Clausewitz's *On War* (Washington, D.C.: The Infantry Journal Press, 1950); Maurice de Saxe's *Reveries on the Art of War* (Harrisburg: The Military Service Publishing Company, 1944); and Frederick the Great's *Instructions for His Generals* (Harrisburg: The Military Service Publishing Company, 1944). Early examples from the field of political organization and policy are Plato's *Republic* and Machiavelli's *The Prince*.

[2]Charles Babbage, *On the Economy of Machinery and Manufactures* (Philadelphia: Carey and Lea, 1832).

[3]Ibid., p. vii.

Scientific Management: Frederick W. Taylor and His Lieutenants

The development of scientific management in the United States is generally considered to have begun with the experiments of Frederick W. Taylor at the Midvale Steel Company in the early 1880s. Taylor was born in Germantown, Pennsylvania, in 1856.[4] During his early youth he attended school in France and Germany and traveled extensively in Europe. In the fall of 1872 Taylor entered the Phillips Exeter Academy to prepare for Harvard College. The high scholastic standards at Exeter severely taxed Taylor's already poor eyesight. Although he passed the Harvard entrance examinations with "honors," he was not able to continue his academic pursuits. Late in the year 1874, at the age of 18, he decided to learn the pattern maker and machinist trades in the shop of a small Philadelphia pump manufacturing company owned by friends of his family.

THE MIDVALE EXPERIENCE

In 1878 Taylor went to work at the Midvale Steel Company as a laborer because employment was difficult to find in the machinist trade. A short time later he was given a machinist job with the lathe gang and within two months became the gang boss. His promotion at Midvale was rapid. In six years he rose from gang boss to foreman of the machine shop, to master mechanic in charge of all repairs and maintenance in the works, to chief draftsman, and finally to chief engineer. To facilitate his advancement in industry Taylor took correspondence courses in mathematics and physics from Harvard professors and then through home study completed the requirements for the M.E. degree at Stevens Institute.

A factor in Taylor's promotion to gang boss was his good production record as a machinist. He knew that greater output was easily possible and that workers were engaged in what he termed "systematic soldiering." When he became gang boss and later foreman, he was determined to do something about the problem. The solution, he thought, was a careful study by management as to what constituted a proper day's work. The company granted him money to conduct experiments to find the time required for various kinds of work. Time study was begun in the machine shop in 1881, and after two years of preliminary experimentation, a full-time man was hired. Taylor considered the Midvale studies the beginning of the "profession" of time study.

THE BETHLEHEM EXPERIMENTS: PIG IRON HANDLING

In 1898 Taylor was hired by the Bethlehem Steel Company to increase the output of one of the larger machine shops, which had been a serious produc-

---

[4]The "official" Taylor biography was written by Frank Barkley Copley, *Frederick W. Taylor, Father of Scientific Management*, Vols. I and II (New York: Harper & Brothers Publishers, 1923). The biographical material in this section is drawn from this source.

tion bottleneck. Taylor's most noted achievements at Bethlehem were his studies of pig iron handling and shoveling and his metal-cutting experiments.[5] These studies are good illustrations of the practice of scientific management during the formative period.

The product of Bethlehem's five blast furnaces was handled by a gang of about 75 men. A railroad switch paralleled the piles of pig iron in the yards. Pig iron handling consisted of picking up a pig of iron (about 92 pounds in weight), carrying it up an inclined plank, and dropping it into a railroad car. Before Taylor began his study each man moved about 12½ long tons per day. A fourfold increase in output resulted from a scientific study of pig iron handling, a better selection of workmen, and training workers in the improved method.

To find the best method for handling pig iron, Taylor conducted a series of experiments. These experiments showed that a man should be able to handle 47½ long tons per day. In order to handle this much pig iron, research results indicated that the man would have to rest about 57 percent of the time. This amount of rest was made necessary by the heavy load that the workman had to carry all day long. With a lighter load the amount of work time could be increased.

The next step in the project was to select a man and train him to handle the amount of pig iron that the experiments indicated was possible. A man, to whom Taylor gave the pseudonym of Schmidt in his writings, was trained to work in accordance with the methods derived by experimentation. Schmidt was told when to work and when to rest, and by 5:30 of the first afternoon he had loaded 47½ tons. He rarely failed in meeting this standard during the time that Taylor spent at Bethlehem. After the success with Schmidt, other men were trained to work at the 47½ ton rate until all pig iron was handled at this rate. Wages under a new task system averaged $1.85 per day compared with $1.15 previously paid on a day basis.

THE SHOVELING EXPERIMENTS

The Bethlehem yards employed a large crew of men to shovel iron ore and rice coal. The shoveling experiment began with a systematic study of shoveling. What is the best shovel load for a given type of material? When Taylor came to Bethlehem each worker brought his own shovel. A worker would shovel rice coal, which gave him a shovel load of 3½ pounds, and then use the same shovel for iron ore, which involved a load of 38 pounds. Taylor selected several first-class shovelers, and paid them extra for following his direc-

[5]Taylor's account of his work at Bethlehem can be found in his book, *The Principles of Scientific Management* (New York: Harper & Brothers Publishers, 1915), pp. 42–48, 58–77, 97–115.

tions. His experimentation indicated that an average load of 21 pounds gave the best results.

A large tool room was built to stock different-sized shovels designed to give a 21-pound shovel load for various types of material handled in the yards. The tool room also stocked other implements, such as picks and crowbars, designed and standardized for particular jobs. A detailed system of work assignment was developed. Two slips of paper were placed in a pigeonhole assigned to each worker, one indicating the implements he would have to use and where he was to work that day and the other reporting output and earnings of the previous day. When output was below par, a yellow slip served as a warning to improve, and a failure to meet the standard meant transfer to other types of work if available. The work was planned in advance, and workers were moved around the yard by clerks in the labor office. Elaborate maps and diagrams of the yard were used for this purpose, and telephone and messenger services were established to facilitate communication.

Studies were also conducted to determine the best way to shovel various types of material. For example, the best method for forcing the shovel into iron ore or bituminous coal was to hold the shovel so that the weight of the body could be used. This method takes less energy than when the arms are used alone. Workers were trained to use the new methods and were checked periodically to see whether they were using them.

The results of the shoveling experiments were phenomenal. The number of yard laborers was reduced from between 400 and 600 to 140. The average number of tons handled by each man per day increased from 16 to 59; handling cost per ton decreased from 7.2 to 3.3 cents. The cost included the office and tool-room expenses, the wages paid to foremen, clerks, and time study men, and an increase in wages from $1.15 per day to $1.88.

THE METAL-CUTTING EXPERIMENTS

Taylor continued a study of cutting metals that he had begun at Midvale. This experimentation was carried on over a period of 26 years. Over 30,000 experiments were recorded, more than 800,000 pounds of iron and steel were cut into chips by experimental tools, and the total cost was estimated to exceed $150,000. One result was the discovery (by Taylor and Maunsel White) of high-speed steel which greatly increased the output of metal-cutting machinery. Another was information about the proper speed and feed for lathes, planers, drill presses, milling machines, and related equipment. The achievements of the metal-cutting experiments were in many respects more important than Taylor's other contributions. They represented a major breakthrough in American industrial development. High-speed and precision cutting tools are an essential ingredient of large-scale production.

THE TAYLOR DIFFERENTIAL PIECEWORK PLAN

Taylor developed an incentive piecework plan that made use of standards developed through time study. The plan called for high wage rates for performance above the standard and relatively low rates for work below standard. It did not guarantee a basic day wage as did later plans.

PUBLICATIONS ON SCIENTIFIC MANAGEMENT

After 1903, Taylor spent most of his time writing and lecturing on scientific management. In his paper "Shop Management," presented to the American Society of Mechanical Engineers in 1903, Taylor outlined the essential features of his system.[6] In 1907, he presented the results of his metal-cutting experiments.[7] In 1911, *The American Magazine* published a series of three articles by Taylor, which were later combined in book form as *The Principles of Scientific Management*.[8] *Shop Management,* originally published in the *Transactions of the American Society of Mechanical Engineers,* was also brought out in a more popular format.[9]

THE EASTERN RAILROADS RATE HEARINGS

Taylor had gained considerable fame from his metal-cutting and mechanical achievements at Bethlehem. But few people were familiar with his ideas on management. Wilfred Lewis, president of the Tabor Company, had asked Taylor to help his company out of a bad financial situation. Taylor announced that he would help only if his system of management was adopted. Lewis made the following comment about this stipulation: "We were only too glad to do this without having any conception of what it was."[10] A few years later editors of popular magazines were flocking to Taylor's home to learn about scientific management. The reason for this sudden popularity was a hearing before the Interstate Commerce Commission involving a request by eastern railroads for a rate increase. A number of engineering consultants and business executives testified that the lack of net income about which the railroads were complaining could be corrected by the techniques of scientific management. The press headlined this testimony and introduced the term "scientific management" into the homes of the average American.

TAYLOR'S LIEUTENANTS

The contributions of a number of other individuals were as important in the development of scientific management as those of Taylor. The names of Henry

[6]Frederick W. Taylor, "Shop Management," *Transactions of the American Society of Mechanical Engineers,* Vol. 24, June 1903, pp. 1337–1480.

[7]Frederick W. Taylor, "On the Art of Cutting Metals," *Transactions of the American Society of Mechanical Engineers,* Vol. 28, 1907, pp. 31–350.

[8]New York: Harper & Brothers Publishers, 1915.

[9]New York: Harper & Brothers Publishers, 1919.

[10]Copley, *Frederick W. Taylor,* Vol. II, p. 176.

L. Gantt, Morris L. Cooke, and Frank and Lillian Gilbreth must be placed high on the list of original contributors. Gantt first came into contact with Taylor's work at Midvale and later played a part in the Bethlehem experiments.[11] He developed a wage incentive system that proved superior to Taylor's and devised a planning and control technique, the Gantt Chart, which is still extensively used in the United States and abroad. He applied scientific management techniques in more than 50 companies and achieved results as impressive as those of the shoveling and pig iron handling experiments. Morris L. Cooke adapted scientific management to the problems of university and municipal administration.[12] His tenure as the Director of the Department of Public Works in Philadelphia from 1912 to 1916 increased departmental efficiency and reduced costs by large margins.[13] Frank B. Gilbreth is best known for his work in motion study, but he also developed a comprehensive body of planning and control techniques for the construction industry.[14] Lillian M. Gilbreth collaborated in many of her husband's research and writing ventures and, after his death in 1924, independently developed and applied scientific management techniques. Many others can be categorized as pioneers of the scientific management movement. The scrolls of history have accorded them a better fate than they suffer here.

Toward Systematic Organization and Management Principles

Frederick W. Taylor and his lieutenants were primarily concerned with problems at the operating level. They did not emphasize managerial organization and processes. This section discusses those contributors who systematized the work of the managers.

[11]L. P. Alford, *Henry Laurence Gantt* (New York: The American Society of Mechanical Engineers, 1934); Alex W. Rathe (editor), *Gantt on Management* (New York: American Management Association and the American Society of Mechanical Engineers, 1960).

[12]Morris L. Cooke, *Academic and Industrial Efficiency* (New York: The Carnegie Foundation for the Advancement of Teaching, Bulletin No. 5, 1910).

[13]Cooke's experiences in this capacity are described in his book, *Our Cities Awake* (Garden City, N.Y.: Doubleday, Page & Co., 1918).

[14]Frank B. Gilbreth, *Field System* (New York: The Myron C. Clark Publishing Company, 1908). This book deserves more attention than it has received in the literature of management history. It represents the application of scientific management techniques to a complete organization. It sets forth standard practices and procedures for all phases of construction including the paperwork necessary for efficient field and home office operations. It was used as early as 1902 as a "confidential" company manual. The effectiveness of the system is indicated by a number of outstanding construction accomplishments of the Gilbreth Company and the fact that competitors frequently attempted to obtain a copy by dubious means.

THE CONTRIBUTIONS OF HENRI FAYOL

A major contribution to the development of management science was made by Henri Fayol, a French executive and mining engineer. Fayol first presented his ideas on management at the International Mining and Metallurgical Congress held in 1900. He continued to play an active part in the French management movement until his death in 1925. His basic contribution was that management should be viewed as a process consisting of the following activities: (1) planning, (2) organization, (3) command, (4) coordination, and (5) control.[15]

Fayol thought that planning was the most important and difficult managerial responsibility and that a failure to plan properly leads to "hesitation, false steps, untimely changes in direction, which are so many causes of weakness, if not of disaster, in business."[16] After a discussion of the problem of structural design, Fayol gave particular attention to the human aspects of organizing. He believed that when an organization is formed, the function of command is necessary in order to execute the plans previously formulated. Coordination is necessary to make sure everyone is working together, and control ascertains whether everything is proceeding according to plan. Much of management knowledge, including the content of this book, follows the basic framework of Fayol's management process concept.

MAX WEBER'S THEORY OF BUREAUCRACY

The contributions of Max Weber, the German sociologist, have also been long neglected in American management circles. Weber thought bureaucratic organization to be "the most rational known means of carrying out imperative control over human beings."[17] Although he recognized the importance of personal (charismatic) leadership, Weber concluded that bureaucratic leadership was indispensable for the mass administration required in a modern society.

Weber set forth his conception of the attributes of a model bureaucratic structure.[18] The organization of positions follows the principle of hierarchy, each lower office being subject to the control of a higher one. There is a sys-

[15]English translations of Fayol's writings can be found in the following sources: Henri Fayol (J. A. Coubrough, translator), *Industrial and General Administration* (Geneva: International Management Institute, 1929); Fayol (Constance Storrs, translator), *General and Industrial Management* (Geneva: International Management Institute, 1929); Fayol, "The Administrative Theory in the State," *Papers on the Science of Administration* (New York: Institute of Public Administration, 1937), pp. 99–114.

[16]Fayol, *General and Industrial Management*, p. 44.

[17]Max Weber (translated by A. M. Henderson and Talcott Parsons), *The Theory of Social and Economic Organizations* (New York: Oxford University Press, 1947), p. 337.

[18]Ibid., pp. 329–341; *From Max Weber: Essay in Sociology*, translated and edited by H. H. Gerth and C. Wright Mills (New York: Oxford University Press, 1946), pp. 196–198.

tematic division of labor; each office has a clearly defined sphere of responsibilities. The occupants of the offices are selected on the basis of technical qualifications. The office should be the sole or primary occupation of the occupant and should constitute a career with promotion based on seniority, achievement or both. Official activity should be considered as something apart from the private sphere.

The bureaucratic model presented by Weber corresponds to what many management people call the formal organization. It incorporated the primary functional properties of a bureaucratic system, but it did not recognize the importance of informal organization. Weber was correct about the necessity for bureaucratic organization in modern society. His principles of bureaucratic structure were similar in many respects to those developed by early organization theorists from the business field.

OTHER IMPORTANT CONTRIBUTIONS

Much of the credit for the development of a systematic approach to managerial organizations must be given to practicing executives. The contributions of Alfred P. Sloan, Jr. were particularly important in this respect. Sloan prepared a comprehensive organizational plan for the General Motors Corporation, which established decentralized operating divisions (such as Chevrolet, Oldsmobile, and Buick) within a framework of centralized policy making and control. This model has been followed by large numbers of medium-sized and large corporations.

An early contributor to organization theory was Russel Robb, who in 1910 gave a series of lectures on organization at Harvard University.[19] Robb felt that there is no "royal road" or easy formula for effective organization. He warned against particular approaches to organization, such as functional specialization, and pointed to the danger of too many records and statistics.

Much of the American literature on organization followed Robb's contribution by almost two decades. A book on the basic principles of organization and their historical origins by two executives, from General Motors and Remington Rand, was published in 1931.[20] A New England industrialist, Henry S. Dennison, came out in the same year with a book on structural and human problems in organizations.[21] An important contribution was made in 1938 by

---

[19]Russel Robb, *Lectures on Organization* (privately printed, 1910); reprinted in: Catheryn Seckler-Hudson (editor), *Processes of Organization and Management* (Washington, D.C.: Public Affairs Press, 1948), pp. 99–124, 269–281; a portion of this work is found in: Harwood F. Merrill (editor), *Classics in Management* (New York: American Management Association, 1960), pp. 161–175.

[20]James D .Mooney and Alan C. Reiley, *Onward Industry!* (New York: Harper & Brothers Publishers, 1931).

[21]Henry Dennison, *Organization Engineering* (New York: McGraw-Hill Book Company, Inc., 1931).

Chester I. Barnard, former president of the New Jersey Bell Telephone Company, with the publication of *The Functions of the Executive*.[22] Barnard emphasized the sociopsychological and ethical aspects of managerial organization and functions.

Professors of industrial management began to approach their subject from an organizational perspective in the 1920s. Such early contributors as Richard H. Lansburgh (1923) and Ralph C. Davis (1928) gave attention to the importance of organizational structure and such basic management functions as planning and control.[23]

Oliver Sheldon, a British management consultant, made a contribution in *The Philosophy of Management* published in 1923.[24] Sheldon approached the problems of industrial management from the broader perspective of organization, administration (top policy making), and management (execution of policy). He also gave emphasis to the social responsibilities of management and the need to develop ethical as well as scientific principles.

A New Light from Hawthorne

The first intensive study of human behavior in an industrial situation was made at the Hawthorne Works of the Western Electric Company, which produces telephone and electrical equipment for the telephone industry.[25]

THE ILLUMINATION EXPERIMENTS

The experiments at Hawthorne were begun in November, 1924, with a study of the "relation of quality and quantity of illumination to efficiency in industry."[26] The illumination studies were conducted with the usual controls of scientific experimentation. The original assumption was that there was a correlation between the intensity of illumination and worker output. Workers

[22]Chester I. Barnard, *The Functions of the Executive* (Cambridge: Harvard University Press, 1938).

[23]Richard H. Lansburgh, *Industrial Management* (New York: John Wiley & Sons, Inc., 1923); Ralph C. Davis, *The Principles of Factory Organization and Management* (New York: Harper & Brothers Publishers, 1928).

[24]Oliver Sheldon, *The Philosophy of Management* (London: Sir Isaac Pitman & Sons, Ltd., 1923). An American edition (Englewood Cliffs, N.J.: Prentice-Hall, Inc.) came out in the same year.

[25]A comprehensive account of the Hawthorne experiments is found in: F. J. Roethlisberger and William J. Dickson, *Management and the Worker* (Cambridge: Harvard University Press, 1939). See also George C. Homans, "The Western Electric Researches," in S. D. Hoslett (editor), *Human Factors in Management* (New York: Harper and Brothers Publishers, 1951), pp. 210–241; Henry A. Landsberger, *Hawthorne Revisited* (Ithaca: Cornell University Press, 1958).

[26]The original illumination experiments are reported in Roethlisberger and Dickson, *Management and the Worker*, pp. 14–18.

were divided into a test room, with varied illumination, and a control room, with constant conditions. Output increased in the test room, but it also increased in the control room. Illumination was then cut, in one case to an amount of light equivalent to moonlight, with no appreciable decline in output. The results were all negative.

The researchers also experimented with rest periods, shorter working days, and wage inventives; and they tested the influence of fatigue and monotony on output. They began to realize that they "had not been studying an ordinary shop situation but a socially contrived situation of their own making."[27] In the words of Roethlisberger and Dickson:

"The experiment they had planned to conduct was quite different from the experiment they had actually performed. They had not studied the relation between output and fatigue, monotony, etc., so much as they had performed a most interesting psychological and sociological experiment. In the process of setting the conditions for the test, they had altered completely the social situation of the operators and their customary attitudes and interpersonal relations."[28]

After this point the investigators discontinued testing the effects of single variables and turned to a study of the sociopsychological factors that seemed to exert a greater influence than changes in rest periods, wages, hours of work, and the like.

THE INTERVIEW PROGRAM

Thousands of interviews were conducted to determine employee attitudes on a variety of matters. The first interviews sought to determine the worker's attitude toward the company, supervision, insurance plans, promotion, and wages. It soon became clear that this method resulted in comments on the subject considered important by the interviewer instead of what was important to the employee. The interviewing method was changed to a nondirective approach with the interviewer assuming a passive role. The worker was no longer guided along predetermined lines but was permitted to talk about anything that came into his mind. The problems that bothered him were not as logical or as easily identified as was originally assumed. Many of the responses were founded in nonlogical sentiments.

A SOCIOLOGICAL PERSPECTIVE

Although the interview program gave valuable insight into the nature of human behavior in organization, it was not completely satisfactory. The social situation that had played an important role in the responses that employees

[27]Ibid., p. 183.
[28]Ibid.

gave in the interviews seemed to require further attention. A detailed study of a shop situation was begun in order to develop new research methods and to find out something about the behavior of people in small groups.

The Bank Wiring Observation Room

The Bank Wiring Observation Room group was composed of 14 workers engaged in wiring, soldering, and inspecting equipment used in telephone exchanges.[29] The physical layout, the tools and equipment, and the operating methods were planned by the use of scientific techniques. The workers were under a group piecework wage plan that conformed to the basic precepts developed by Taylor, Gantt, Emerson, and others. The research results showed that the actual behavior of the group departed in a marked degree from the behavior planned by the company.

Systematic Soldiering

Systematic soldiering or output restriction caused Taylor difficulty when he became gang boss at the Midvale Steel Company. The research people at Hawthorne also found that workers gave a great deal of attention to output. Out of the 32 men interviewed before the group study began, 22 discussed output rates. The observations of the group observer led to the conclusion that "there existed a group norm in terms of which the behavior of different individuals was in some sense being regulated."[30] In view of the comments made by Taylor on the importance of the group in restricting output,[31] this conclusion was not particularly original. What was significant was that output restriction occurs even when the techniques recommended by Taylor are utilized. The Hawthorne researchers did not assume that the problem could be solved by time study and wage incentives. They sought a solution through a better understanding of group dynamics.

A Group Output Norm

Each individual in the group was restricting his output a significant amount below the company standard of 7312 terminals per day. The group seemed to agree that two equipments constituted a "proper" day's work. An output of two equipments required 6600 terminal connections for connector equipments and 6000 for selector equipments. Operators would frequently stop working before the official stopping time when they had met the group standard. Each individual seemed to know how much he had accomplished at a given time and, also, how much his neighbors were producing. One wireman was able to

[29]For more detailed information about this aspect of the Hawthorne research: Ibid., pp. 379–548. The material that follows is indebted to this source.
[30]Ibid., p. 423.
[31]Frederick W. Taylor, *Principles*, pp. 50–52.

tell the time within two minutes by computing the amount he had wired that morning. Workers who attempted to exceed the group output norm were generally looked on with disfavor, and group pressure was directed against them.

Why Restrict Output?

Why did the group restrict output? Some of the following reasons were given by individuals in the group. One thought that working at the rate set by the company would result in unemployment for one out of four people and another that higher output "would mean that somebody would be out of a job."[32] Still another thought that the "bogey would be raised, and then we would just be turning out more work for the same money."[33] Others thought that the supervisor "might 'bawl out' the slower men,"[34] and most of the workers seemed to agree that something would happen.

Who Set the Norm?

How did two equipments come to be the output norm of the group? The investigators were not able to find a satisfactory explanation. Fatigue did not seem to be a limiting factor, and there was no evidence that the foreman or his assistants originated the norm, even though the foreman agreed that, if a man did more than 6600 connections a day, "he would wear his fingers out."[35] The supervisors generally felt that the norm represented a satisfactory day's work. Another possible explanation for the norm is that the workers could finish two equipments, but not three, and therefore might prefer to stop with two instead of leaving a partially completed equipment for the next day. This explanation is discounted by the fact that they frequently stopped work during the wiring of an equipment. Another factor that probably influenced the group's thinking about the norm was indicated by one worker. "I turn out 6600 regularly. . . . Of course you could make out less and get by, *but it's safer to turn out about 6600.*"[36] In other words, the norm seemed to satisfy supervision and higher management. A lower norm might, in the opinion of the group, cause "something to happen"; a higher norm might also bring bad consequences. It caused no difficulties—why risk the possible consequences of change.

Although the logic of either output restriction or the norm of two equipments cannot be completely explained, the fact that individuals seemed more concerned about the group norm than the company standard indicates that the

[32]Roethlisberger and Dickson, *Management and the Worker*, p. 419.
[33]Ibid., p. 418. The bogey was a psychological incentive and was not related to the amount of pay the worker received.
[34]Ibid., p. 417.
[35]Ibid., p. 455.
[36]Ibid., p. 413 (italics added).

social consequences of not conforming played an important role in their output behavior. How important was scientific management in the output situation at the Hawthorne plant? The methods work of the company industrial engineers and the scientifically derived output standards were undoubtedly important variables. Actual output and the output norm developed by the group would probably have been lower in the absence of scientific management. As it was, the norm of two equipments and also the output of the group seemed satisfactory to the company. Output had increased over a period of years, and the group was turning out considerably more than workers in other companies.

Regulated Output Patterns

The fact that the group norm set forth two equipments as a "proper" day's work did not mean that all individuals produced this number of equipments.[37] There were significant differences in the actual output of different individuals in the group. However, the weekly average output of individuals showed little change from week to week. They felt that, if their output was not reasonably constant, "something might happen." Too high an output would indicate that they could do better; low output might cause supervisors to "bawl them out." They resorted to subterfuge to prevent undue fluctuation in individual output records. One technique was to underreport or overreport actual output; another was to control the output rates by reporting a greater amount of daywork, which increased the output *rate* because output was divided by a smaller amount of time. Daywork allowances were permitted only for a number of specific reasons, such as material shortages and defective wire, but they were frequently used to control the recorded output rate.

Psychological Testing

A seemingly logical explanation for the differences in the output of individuals was that it reflected differences in ability. To test this hypothesis, each person in the group was given dexterity and intelligence tests. The three slowest wiremen scored higher on the dexterity test than did the three fastest men, and the lowest producer ranked first in intelligence and third in the dexterity tests. This relationship between the test results and actual output suggests the importance of the group to these workers. An individual could by increasing his output receive a larger share of the total group "wage fund" and also reduce the possibilities of unemployment. But these material rewards had a penalty in the form of group censorship.

[37]Orvis Collins, Melville Dalton, and Donald Roy, "Restriction of Output and Social Cleavage in Industry," *Applied Anthropology* (now *Human Organization*), Vol. 5, No. 3, Summer 1946, pp. 1–14; Donald Roy, "Quota Restriction and Goldbricking in a Machine Shop," *American Journal of Sociology*, Vol. 57, No. 5, March 1952, pp. 427–442.

Job Trading and Helping

The company rule against job trading expressed the logic of greater efficiency through specialization. The assumption was that a worker could become a more proficient wireman, solderer, or inspector by concentrating his attention on one type of work. Workers were not supposed to trade jobs, but they frequently did. They were permitted to help a fellow worker only when conditions prevented them from working on their own equipment. A shortage of parts, for example, would be a valid reason for helping someone until parts could be obtained. Most of the helping that occurred during the study could not be justified on this basis. Everyone in the group, except inspectors, participated in this practice, but the helping hand was not extended equally to all. Friendship increased willingness to help one another, and those who received help were expected to return the favor. An informal leader, who was popular with the group, received the most help even though he did not actually need it. One of the faster wiremen, who showed a great desire for leadership, helped the most, but his help was rarely returned.

Other Social Activities

Almost everyone in the group participated in games, such as matching coins, shooting craps, card games, pools on horse races, baseball and quality records, and "binging,"[38] which were played during lulls in the work and lunch periods. Financial gain was not the primary consideration in the games of chance —the winnings ranged from one to ten cents. A great deal of controversy occurred about whether windows should be open or closed. The subject of group conversations ranged from arguments about religion to a discussion of a shapely woman. They talked about the possibility of war and the role that they would play. One worker liked to imitate "Popeye the Sailor" and tell long yarns about his virility. There were many off-color stories and much good-humored kidding. One of the solderers was the "clown" of the group and frequently entertained the group with his comments. An inspector with three years of college liked to impress the group with his superior knowledge; he once walked over to a worker and told him he was going to test his vocabulary.

Group Norms

The Bank Wiring Observation Room group responded to norms that they themselves made about their behavior. Some norms had reference to output;

[38]"Binging" was a game that involved hitting someone as hard as possible. The person who was hit had the privilege of returning one "bing" or hit. An object of the game was to see who could hit the hardest, but it was also used to restrain high-output individuals. Roethlisberger and Dickson, *Management and the Worker*, p. 421.

others involved personal conduct.[39] The following norms seemed to influence behavior.

1. You should not turn out too much work. If you do, you are a "ratebuster."
2. You should not turn out too little work. If you do, you are a "chiseler."
3. You should not tell a supervisor anything that will react to the detriment of an associate. If you do, you are a "squealer."
4. You should not attempt to maintain social distance or act officious. If you are an inspector, for example, you should not act like one.
5. You should not be noisy, self-assertive, and anxious for leadership.

These norms were enforced by such social sanctions as binging, ridicule, and ostracism from social activities. A relationship was found between conformity to these norms and standing in the group. The best-liked worker in the group conformed closely to the group norms. Although his actual production was generally higher than the group norm, he underreported his output and also claimed less daywork, which would have increased his hourly output rate. Another worker respected the output norm of the group, but he was not as well liked because he violated the norms that related to personal conduct. One of the most disliked persons in the group had an acceptable output record, but he "squealed" to the foreman, an extremely serious offense in the eyes of the group.

PAST CONTRIBUTIONS IN PERSPECTIVE

Scientific management involved the application of scientific methods to such operating problems as plant and office layout, operating standards, methods and procedures, and material storage and movement. Many planning functions formerly performed by supervisors and workers were shifted to specialists in personnel, purchasing, production engineering, quality control, and other areas. An important assumption of Taylor and many of his lieutenants was that the primary interest of management and workers is economic gain in the form of lower labor costs and higher wages. Although the existence of groups was recognized, people were assumed to be essentially "individualistic" in their quest for economic welfare.

The Hawthorne Study gave emphasis to the idea that worker attitudes can affect productivity as much as improved procedures and methods. It applied sociopsychological techniques to managerial problems and gave impetus to the development of a theory of human behavior in organization. The importance of "group dynamics" and social forces was stressed, and earlier misconceptions about cooperative behavior were corrected.

[39]The first four norms listed here were originated by Roethlisberger and Dickson, *ibid.*, p. 522; the fifth norm was added by George C. Homans, *The Human Group* (New York: Harcourt, Brace & Co., Inc., 1950), p. 79. Norms are what people think behavior ought to be.

The management process concept of Henri Fayol and Max Weber's theory of bureaucracy have continued to be of importance in the management field. The contribution of Chester I. Barnard noted earlier as well as the Hawthorne Study and subsequent behavioral research have elaborated on these earlier contributions through a greater emphasis on informal organization. Much attention has been given in recent years to the manner in which informal processes can affect the bureaucratic structure and the management process.

THE COMPUTER REVOLUTION

The most significant modern contributions to management science have centered around the electronic computer. The high speed and the logical capacities of the computer have made possible much more efficient data processing and problem solving. The systematic approaches to management developed by the pioneers noted above have been carried a step forward through the more complex and comprehensive models made possible by the computer.

TOWARD A PROFESSION OF MANAGEMENT

The contributions of the pioneers and more recent developments have given rise to a comprehensive body of management knowledge. The significance of the management process in systematizing this knowledge is considered in the next chapter beginning with a description of the management process and the basic functions that comprise the process. Emphasis is then given to the idea that management is a universal process that can be found in all kinds of organized endeavors. A final section will be devoted to the problems related to the development of a management profession.

3

THE MANAGEMENT PROCESS

This chapter is concerned with the basic functions performed by managers, and the manner in which they are interrelated in the management process. These functions form the basis for a systematic approach to management education and professional development.

NATURE OF THE MANAGEMENT PROCESS

The management process assumes that the totality of what managers do can be divided into a set of interrelated functions. Henri Fayol, who has been called the father of the process concept, included planning, organization, command, coordination, and control in his list of administrative or managerial functions.[1] Since this pioneering effort many different lists of functions have been formulated by proponents of the process approach. However, the differences are generally not as great as they appear, and not infrequently, the same thing is said in a different way.

In this book, the management process involves the following basic management functions: (1) planning, (2) organizing, (3) directing, and (4) controlling. These functions may be defined as follows:

Planning is concerned with the determination of organizational objectives and the procedures and methods that will be necessary to achieve them. The result is policies designed to channel the behavior of managerial and other personnel in particular directions.

Organizing involves the development of a structure of interrelated managerial

---

[1] Henri Fayol, *General and Industrial Management* (London: Sir Isaac Pitman & Sons, Ltd., 1949), p. 3.

positions in accord with the requirements of planning. Planned responsibilities are allocated to the persons who occupy these positions. Coordination is facilitated through the authority relationships and the communication channels that result from the organizing function. An important aspect of the organizing function is management development, which is concerned with the education, training, recruitment, and promotion of managerial personnel.

Directing is concerned with carrying out the policies that result from planning. Important in this respect are the authority relationship, the communication process, and the problem of motivation.

Controlling determines whether everything is going in accordance with the policies developed through the planning process. The purpose of control is to find mistakes, to correct them, and to prevent them in the future.

The logic of the management process is that particular management functions are performed in a sequence through time. Planning comes first, then organizing, which are followed by directing, and controlling. One function is assumed to lead logically to the next. Thus, planning provides the basis for organizing, which in turn sets the stage for the remaining functions. There may be significant departures from this sequence idea in actual practice. There are generally many different plans that give the appearance that managers are performing their functions out of order. But aside from such a fusion of functions, the sequence may begin with different functions and come to an end without completing the entire process cycle. Changes in the organizational structure are often made without regard to particular plans. Past management development can lead to planning instead of the other way around. For example, companies with an excess of managerial personnel resulting from reduced product demand may plan new programs rather than lay off personnel. Directing may simultaneously involve several or all plans (including future plans) instead of a specific plan. Organizing may be constantly carried on to strengthen the organization in a general sense.

The management process provides a good framework for management knowledge. It emphasizes the fact that effective management involves the successful practice of the skills (such as planning and organizing) defined by the functions that make up the management process. These functions have become the basis for specialized research and teaching. Such specialization is a sound development. It indicates that management has taken a long step toward professionalization.

The Universality of the Management Process

The management process is a necessary feature of all organized activity. Although the purposes of organizations differ, the management process remains constant.[2] It is present in factories, banks, retail establishments, government, the military, churches, universities, and hospitals. Figure 3-1 shows the

Man-agement Process	Kinds of Organization				
	Business	Political	Military	Religious	Education
Planning Organizing Directing Controlling					

FIGURE 3–1. The relationship between kinds of organized endeavor and the management process.

nature of this relationship. The management process is also a common denominator that pervades such basic business functions as production, marketing, finance, personnel, and procurement. This relationship is noted in Figure 3-2.

Man-agement Process	Business Functions				
	Production	Marketing	Finance	Personnel	Procurement
Planning Organizing Directing Controlling					

FIGURE 3-2. The relationship between selected business functions and the management process.

The important point is that the management process (planning, organizing, directing, and controlling) is concerned with knowledge and skills that have universal applicability. The management process becomes the basis for effective management in a large variety of situations.

A FUSION OF FUNCTIONS

A distinction should be made between managerial and other functions performed by the people who occupy managerial positions. Most managers are

[2]Oliver Sheldon has this to say on this subject: "It is because management is the one inherent necessity in the conduct of any enterprise that it is possible to conceive of it as a profession. Whether capital be supplied by individuals or by the State, whether labour be by hand or by machine, whether the workers assume a wide control over industry or are subjected to the most autocratic power, the function of management remains constant." *The Philosophy of Management* (London: Sir Isaac Pitman & Sons, Ltd., 1923), p. 48.

part-time managers and part-time something else. The head of an accounting department, for example, is often engaged in accounting activities in addition to managing his subordinates. The president of a steel company employs both a knowledge of management principles and the technology of steel producing and marketing in performing his duties. The director of an art museum combines a knowledge of art with his management tasks. A university dean makes use of his teaching and research experiences in performing managerial functions.

A HIGH DEGREE OF SUBSTITUTION

The common properties of the managerial process make possible a high degree of substitution among managers in different kinds of endeavor. Army officers have become successful university administrators and business executives. Governmental posts have been filled by business executives with a large measure of success. Executives in one kind of business, such as retailing, have successfully moved to industries with radically different technologies, such as manufacturing or publishing. Equally important in this respect are transfers from one area of functional specialization to another. A vice-president of finance or advertising often becomes the chief executive of a manufacturing concern.

MANAGEMENT AS PROCESS AND PEOPLE

A distinction should be noted between management as a process and the use of that word to denote the people who perform the function.When the word "management" is used to mean people, it is often restricted to those who manage business and industrial organizations. The management process has a broader scope than this usage implies. It includes the activities of anyone who manages the affairs of any kind of formally organized endeavor.

A Profession of Management

Can management be categorized as a profession? The answer to this question partly depends on the definition of a profession.

THE NATURE OF A PROFESSION

The terms "profession" and "professional" have been given a variety of meanings.[3] They may be broadly used to refer to any occupation by which a

[3]The entire issue of *The Annals of the American Academy of Political and Social Science*, Vol. 297, January 1955, is devoted to problems relating to professional status, standards, and conduct in such vocations as accounting, engineering, medicine, business, and architecture. Of particular interest for present purposes are the articles by Morris L. Cogan, "The Problem of Defining a Profession," pp. 105–111, and Howard R. Bowen, "Business Management: A Profession?" pp. 112–117. The problems of professionalization in the area of business are also considered in: Robert A. Gordon and James E. Howell, *Higher Educa-*

person earns a livelihood. They may also be used in a restricted sense to include only "the three learned professions" of theology, law, and medicine. The majority of definitions fall somewhere between these two extremes. The conditions that seem to be most often used to differentiate a profession from an ordinary vocation are: (1) the learning of a systematic body of knowledge together with the skills necessary for application and (2) conformity to an established body of standards governing professional and personal behavior. Other factors (some of which are related to the above) that have assumed varying degrees of importance in this respect are the existence of an association, such as the American Medical Association or the American Institute of Accountants; a relationship of responsibility toward patients or clients; legal or other restrictions to entry into the profession, or both; an oath, such as the Hippocratic Oath of the physician; and a high degree of altruistic motivation. The nature of educational requirements and social status also seem to have importance. Some unionized crafts meet many of the conditions cited above, but they are not usually categorized as a profession.

THE EXECUTIVE AS A PROFESSIONAL

The executive role seems to satisfy at least some of the conditions that make a vocation a profession. Executives require knowledge and skills which can be acquired through formal education or experience or both. The problem of executive development is much like that of medicine, law, and other fields, where some knowledge and skills can be acquired through formal education and some through practical experience. The physician or lawyer is not a "finished product" on graduation from medical or law school. A similar statement can be made about the executives produced by university executive development programs. Much of the knowledge and skill that make for professional competence is gained after a long period of practical experience.

Executives have given some attention to the development of professional standards, but such standards have by no means been systematized or universally accepted or applied.[4] There is no Hippocratic Oath or Engineer's Vow of Service to which an executive must testify before he practices his "vocation." A number of management associations, chambers of commerce, and better business bureaus do set forth various norms of behavior, but they do not enforce them in the manner of the American Medical Association. However, such associations may represent the basis for more complete professionalization in the future.

The traditional professions of law and medicine have generally involved a

---

tion for Business (New York: Columbia University Press, 1959), pp. 69–73; and Frank C. Pierson et al., The Education of American Businessmen (New York: McGraw-Hill Book Company, Inc., 1959), pp. 16–33.

[4] The attitudes of executives toward ethical standards and the nature of such standards are indicated in: Stewart Thompson, Management Creeds and Philosophies, Research Study No. 32 (New York: American Management Association, Inc., 1958).

personal relationship between practitioners and clients or patients.[5] The Principles of Medical Ethics of the American Medical Association, for example, stress the personal role of the family physician. The relationship between executives and customers, stockholders, suppliers, creditors, and labor is generally impersonal. This difference, however, would not seem to preclude professional status since large specialized medical clinics and hospitals have significantly reduced the importance of the family physician without a marked "deprofessionalization" of medicine in the public mind. A high degree of altruistic motivation has been given a great deal of emphasis in the traditional professions. It is generally assumed that executives qualify least with respect to this quality. Yet, physicians are not completely immune to the quest for money, and executives have been known to make great personal sacrifice in the interests of organization. There are many "organization men" who are dedicated to their responsibilities within the meaning of the Oath of Hippocrates. The executive "profession" does not control entry in the manner of many of the traditional professions, but the educational requirements of the future may well provide a similar consequence.

Professional status for executives and their work should not be viewed as a matter of definition or nomenclature. Some of the techniques employed by the traditional professions to enhance the quality of practitioners would seem to apply to executives. The basic elements of professionalization are important irrespective of whether they lead to formal professional status. The development of skill in executive work through education or experience is a primary consideration in executive development. Appropriate motives for effectiveness in the executive role should also have a high place in the scheme of things. Some of the other conditions that make for professionalization may also be important in that they provide means to control standards relating to skills and motives.

KNOWLEDGE AND SKILLS FOR PROFESSIONAL DEVELOPMENT

A systematic body of management knowledge that can be used for professional development has evolved during the past 60 years. An important argument for the accumulation of knowledge about management is the need to develop large numbers of executives. Even though such knowledge is limited, the student can be given some significant insights into the nature of the management problem. A university cannot train "finished" executives. It can only provide a useful point of departure for further executive development through experience. The same is true for professional pursuits such as medicine, law, engineering, and the military.

The management process provides the basic framework for this book. Each of the functions that make up the process will be given comprehensive consideration. The chapters in Part II are concerned with the planning function and the manner in which it relates to the totality of managerial action.

[5]Bowen, op cit., p. 114.

PART II

Planning

4

THE PLANNING ENVIRONMENT

The economic, political, social, and technical environments play important parts in planning the program of business and other organizations. Organizational objectives evolve from responses to environmental forces and from attempts by organizations to change and to control these forces. Executives spend a great deal of time surveying the environment in search of opportunities for their organizations. They also look for obstacles that may impede the achievement of organizational objectives. A complete evaluation of all of the factors that are pertinent in a particular situation is obviously impossible; the problems of every organization are unique in some or many respects. The purpose here and in subsequent chapters is not to provide specialized knowledge in such fields as economics, political science, labor economics, market research, procurement, and finance but to promote a better understanding of the manner in which such subject matter relates to the planning problem.

Market Forecasting and Analysis

The importance of market forecasting in planning for the future can hardly be overestimated. Such forecasts make possible planned adjustments to economic change. The adverse effects of a recession can often be mitigated by such prior changes as reductions in inventories, changes in the product line, and more aggressive merchandising. The opportunities made possible by favorable market trends can also be better exploited if time is available for adequate planning. Long-range market projections provide the basis for a systematic instead of haphazard approach to secular growth and development. Such projections are particularly important in coordinating short-run and long-run planning.

Some market forecasts, if indeed they can be called forecasts, are little more than hunches or guesses by executives, whereas others involve simple projections of the experience of the recent past into the future. There is also a tendency to go along with whatever the prevailing consensus on the economic future may happen to be. However, there seems to be a trend toward a more objective approach to the problem of forecasting. One reason is that greater objectivity has been made possible by more reliable business and economic statistics and improved forecasting techniques. Another is the realization that survival in a dynamic economic environment can be enhanced by the use of such information.

DEMAND DETERMINANTS

The practical forecaster generally restricts his analysis to a few important demand determinants such as personal income, population growth, inventory levels, steel output, and the cost of living. Although accurate forecasts sometimes result, the executive should recognize that such forecasts involve some rather broad assumptions about the general state of the economy. Thus, highly accurate forecasts of the demand for a product may result from a correlation with personal income during a relatively stable economic period, but a failure on the part of the forecaster to anticipate a forthcoming economic recession will upset the whole scheme. The accuracy of demand forecasts is closely related to an ability to forecast such dynamic phenomena as cyclical fluctuations, inflation, structural changes, and secular growth and development.

ECONOMIC AND SALES FORECASTING

The forecasting problem is generally viewed as a process that begins with forecasts of general economic conditions and ends with a forecast of the sales prospects for a given company. However, a relatively small number of business organizations are actively engaged in economic forecasting. Even those who profess to make such forecasts are greatly dependent on outside economic prognostication. The cost of a full-fledged economic forecast is prohibitive for all except some of the larger companies. The attitude of executives seems to be, "Why spend a lot of money trying to forecast general business conditions when good forecasts are available at practically no cost?" Many companies use the market and economic information found in industry, trade, business, and government publications. These forecasts are generally prepared by people who make a business of forecasting, and there is little reason to believe that they are any less reliable than those prepared by company staffs. However, they may not be completely applicable to the needs of a particular company. For this reason some companies employ consultants to interpret and to modify the data.

The importance of economic forecasts in formulating sales objectives varies from company to company. Some companies feel that such forecasts are highly significant. Others express an opposite point of view. This diversity of opinion can be partly attributed to the degree of correlation that exists between general economic and industry data and the sales of a particular company. A lack of correlation would tend to reduce the value of external data. Furthermore, sales objectives are not entirely determined by external market factors. For example, a company may fail to maximize its sales potential because it lacks plant capacity or fears government antitrust intervention.

Many companies use the economic forecasts only as a general guide for officers and executives. Thus, the influence that an economic forecast may have on planning cannot be entirely expressed in objective terms. Much of it enters the decisional process through the subjective judgments of executives. Economic factors tend to be blended with a wide variety of other considerations.

The demand for a given product or service is defined in terms of both quantity and price. How many units will be purchased at a given price, or how much will be purchased at different prices? Some forecasting is concerned only with the sales potential of a particular company. A more general approach is to forecast the total industry demand which is then used to project the revenue potential for the firm.

MARKET FORECASTING TECHNIQUES

Companies generally use a combination of different methods in making a market forecast. The most widely used forecasting techniques include the projection of past sales behavior (trend-cycle analysis), correlation analysis, and a variety of survey, interview, and judgment techniques.

Trend-Cycle Analysis

This technique assumes that there is a high degree of continuity between past and future demand or sales behavior. Historical sales data are studied to determine seasonal, cyclical, and secular patterns of behavior. A projection of these data forms the basis for forecasting future sales. Such projections may be highly reliable in forecasting seasonal and secular sales patterns, but the technique is not very dependable in forecasting cyclical variations because of the lack of regularity in such movements.

Correlation Analysis

This method is frequently used if a relationship can be found between sales and other economic and noneconomic phenomena, such as the national income, defense expenditures, population growth, and the weather. Thus, if the national income and sales have moved together in the past, a forecast can be derived from national income data. Such forecasts are generally concerned with the sales volume for the entire industry. The forecaster arrives at a company forecast by estimating the company's share of total industry demand. The basic logic of correlation analysis is that the variables used (such as national income or building construction expenditures) can be forecasted more accurately than sales. However, if the forecaster is fortunate enough to find a sufficient lag between movements in a variable and sales, he can forecast directly from historical data. A six-month lag between a decline in national income and reduced sales illustrates such a situation. One difficulty with correlation analysis is that a past relationship may not continue into the future. Correlation techniques are most reliable when a causal relationship can be established between the variables and sales. However, there is always the possibility that factors other than those used in forecasting may significantly change the outcome.

Correlation techniques have been used to develop *demand functions* for a number of products, such as furniture, refrigerators, and automobiles. Thus, the demand for furniture is a function of disposable personal income per household, the value of private residential construction per household, and the ratio of the furniture price index to the Consumer Price Index.[1] Some demand functions show a close correlation between actual and calculated demand over a relatively long period of time. But, like more simple types of correlation analysis, forecasting the variables used in the equation is a major problem. To paraphrase a market research specialist, it might be guessed that the errors in forecasting several variables would add up to a greater total than those of a straight "judgment" estimate of demand.[2]

Survey and Interview Techniques

Such techniques are used to obtain information about sales prospects from purchasers, the sales force, company executives, and others. A survey of purchaser intentions would seem to provide a useful source of data about future sales potential. The difficulties are that purchaser planning is based on a variety of economic and noneconomic expectations and that many individuals, institutions, and business firms are not engaged in systematic forward planning.

Survey techniques can also provide historical and current sales data that may be useful for forecasting purposes. For example, information about consumer and dealer inventories may be helpful in many instances. Data on current purchasing provide a basis for predicting future purchases of wholesalers and retailers. Companies frequently turn to sales personnel for assistance in forecasting because they have information about local conditions. However,

[1] Walter Jacobs and Clement Winston, "The Postwar Furniture Market and the Factors Determining Demand," *Survey of Current Business*, May 1950, pp. 8–11.

[2] C. M. Crawford, Market Research Department, Mead Johnson and Company, *Sales Forecasting Methods of Selected Firms* (Urbana: Bureau of Economic and Business Research, College of Commerce and Business Administration, University of Illinois, 1955), p. 49.

salesmen sometimes fail to see the forest for the trees and flavor their reports with too much optimism or pessimism. Also, the possibility that sales quotas may be derived from the sales forecast may tinge the estimates somewhat. Some sales forecasters find that interviews and conferences with company executives can frequently supply pertinent information about industry and intraorganizational matters. The forecaster may also obtain useful information from interviews with jobbers, wholesalers, retailers, and others in the industry.

NEW AND CHANGED PRODUCTS

Forecasting the demand for new products and services is complicated by the lack of historical data. The television and aircraft industries faced this problem during the initial phase of development. Changes in an established product present a similar difficulty because, even though a historical record is available, the data do not provide information about the possible influence of styling, technological, and other innovations on future sales. Next year's automobiles, washers, refrigerators, television sets, and fountain pens may differ significantly from those sold last year or five years ago.

A number of techniques have been developed to contend with these problems. One is to use past sales of an existing product as a basis for forecasting new product sales. For example, the sales potential for automatic washers may be derived from the sales history of wringer washing machines. An entirely new product may be viewed as a substitute for an established product or service. Overseas air and passenger ship travel illustrates such a relationship. An estimate of the rate of growth and ultimate demand potential for a new product can sometimes be inferred from an analysis of the growth curves of established products. The marketing history of a variety of household appliances may thus provide an empirical growth curve that can be used to forecast the potential market for a new appliance.

Another approach is to experiment in a restricted market, such as a metropolitan area or a chain of stores, in order to gauge the national or regional sales potential of the product. Consumer acceptance can also be tested by survey and interview techniques. A difficulty with this approach is that the consumer has limited knowledge of the product. However, this problem can sometimes be overcome by trial demonstrations in the home, office, and plant.

THE HAZARDS OF FORECASTING

The hazards of forecasting are almost too obvious to mention. Forecasting seems most successful when there is nothing much to forecast. A successful forecast is something of a miracle and often occurs for the wrong reasons. The forecasting problem indicates the difficulties of developing a science of management. However, it should not lead to the assumption that nothing has been accomplished. There are good "rule of thumb" forecasts. A part of the problem is that too much is expected from forecasting. People want more precise answers than are possible in an environment characterized by uncertainty.

A number of factors help mitigate the consequences of inadequate forecasting. One is that all of the firms in an industry frequently respond to similar economic data in determining their objectives. The errors that are made will affect them in the same direction with essentially equal burdens or benefits. Another factor is that competition is by no means perfect, and this discrepancy supplies some margin for forecasting errors. Still another is that forecasters often bury their mistakes. For example, an automobile manufacturer decides to produce body design X instead of Y for his new model. The resulting profit of 6 percent would seem to denote a good decision. But the profit might well have been 9 percent with body design Y.

SHORT-RUN AND LONG-RUN FORECASTS

A forecast is generally classified as a long-run forecast if it extends beyond one year. Although such forecasting is less prevalent than short-run forecasting, many companies have recognized the importance of a longer-range perspective, so that three-, five-, and ten-year forecasts are not at all uncommon. Long-range forecasts may afford vital information for decisions about capital outlay, plant location, executive development, and research programs. The forecasting problem changes as the time period of the forecast is lengthened. The vagaries of cyclical fluctuations become relatively less important, but basic structural and cultural changes in the economy become more significant. Demographic factors, such as population growth, age and sex distribution, and geographic distribution become more important in long-range forecasting. Fundamental changes may also occur in the size and distribution of real income, the state of technology, and sociopsychological patterns of behavior.

The Markets for Productive Resources

The markets for productive resources are subject to forces that are for the most part beyond the control of the individual enterprise. The prices of raw materials, equipment, plants and buildings, money, and personnel are important cost determinants. The supply of resources available to a particular enterprise is another planning factor. Although the problem of scarcity is generally solved by the price mechanism, an absolute scarcity may be present with respect to some resources.

FINANCIAL MARKETS

The revenues from consumers are used to compensate those who contribute productive resources to the firm. A company cannot long meet its financial obligations without sales receipts. However, current receipts are not always sufficient to match current expenditures even when the enterprise is operating under profit conditions. Some cash is needed to compensate for variations in the relative magnitude of expenditure and income flows. Companies must either possess the necessary cash or acquire funds in the money market. A money demand may also arise from investment in such current assets as inventories, work in process, supplies, and consumer receivables. The replacement and expansion of plant facilities, equipment, and other fixed assets require large amounts of money.

Where do companies obtain the money required for such purposes? A distinction is generally made between internal and external financing. The primary internal sources are depreciation allowances and retained earnings. External sources include the organized securities markets, insurance companies, banks, suppliers, and private individuals. Such funds have generally played a smaller quantitative role than funds accumulated internally. During the last few decades external sources have probably accounted for about 35 percent of the total required for all kinds of capital expenditures. However, such factors as the age and size of the company, type of business, and economic conditions make for considerable variation from norm. A survey of small- and medium-sized businesses indicated that smaller companies were on the whole less interested in obtaining capital from outside sources than were the larger companies in the sample.[3]

Internal financing mitigates the impact of changes in the money markets on business planning, but it does not by any means eliminate interest rates and money scarcity as strategic planning factors. A considerable diversity of opinion can be found on the importance of interest rates in business planning.[4] Interest rates should not be viewed apart from the many other factors that may influence planning, such as consumer demand, wage rates, raw material prices, and construction costs. A 1 percent increase in the interest rate may have a negligible effect when profit expectations are high.[5] A 1 percent decline may likewise have little effect if profit expectations fall to zero or below. But this polarity fails to take into account the many circumstances under which a change in interest rates might be important. Companies have modified their financial plans when interest rates advance. Although such actions generally evolve from a combination of economic factors, it seems reasonable to assert that the interest rate is sometimes the straw that breaks the camel's back.

Interest rates reflect in some degree at least the supply and demand conditions in particular money markets. However, it cannot be assumed that higher

[3]Loughlin F. McHugh and Jack N. Ciaccio, "External Financing of Small- and Medium-sized Business," *Survey of Current Business*, October 1955, p. 18.

[4]An excellent summary of the interest rate-investment argument is found in: Jan Tinbergen and J. J. Polak, *The Dynamics of Business Cycles* (Chicago: The University of Chicago Press, 1950), pp. 167–171. This study is based on statistical and econometric research by Professor Tinbergen over a period of 15 years.

[5]Since such expectations are frequently based on high profits in the past, the impact of the external money market is further mitigated by greater internal financing.

interest rates will always bring forth an adequate supply of money. The lending agent assumes a more strategic role during periods of short supply. The available funds tend to go to those who have relatively better financial standings and profit expectations, while otherwise good credit risks may experience financial difficulties because the more affluent companies are at the front of the line. Larger concerns are usually more successful than small businesses in obtaining outside money. Newly established companies are particularly vulnerable in this respect. However, even the largest and most successful corporations can be plagued by troubles in the money market. The high interest rates of the early 1970s had a significant effect on business and private expenditure. The money market can become a highly strategic planning factor under certain economic conditions. The plans of enterprising executives often go astray because a banker frowned and uttered nay.

THE LABOR MARKETS

A glance at the want ad section of a newspaper or trade publication gives testimony to the importance of the labor market in planning. Every company experiences a continuous inflow and outflow of executive, professional, technical, and operating personnel over a period of time. Retirement, death, and discharge create a constant demand for replacement. The addition of a new plant, a large cutback in output, and changes in the nature of operations are also important in this respect.

The availability of labor is sometimes a critical factor in planning the company program. The supply of certain kinds of labor is inelastic in the short run. A great deal of time is required to develop such skilled and educated personnel as engineers, chemists, mathematicians, and tool and die makers. Regional variations in supply may also create planning difficulties. Labor is sometimes highly immobile and cannot always be attracted by higher wages. Companies requiring particular kinds of labor may find that some areas are better than others. Furthermore, such factors as local labor laws and union conditions can affect the situation.

A lack of knowledge of economic opportunity and the prevalence of non-economic motives make actual labor markets less than fully competitive. Companies can sometimes take advantage of market imperfections[6] and can maintain their labor force with lower wages than are being paid by others in a particular market area. Regional wage differentials make possible movement from one market area to another to reduce labor costs. However, labor unions and collective bargaining have removed some of the opportunities afforded by such conditions. Many of the differentials within given market delineations have been wiped out by union efforts to achieve equalization in the level of

---

[6]Imperfections in the sense that actual markets do not correspond to the abstract models of competitive markets portrayed in economic theory.

wages. This kind of equalization may create difficulties for companies operating under higher cost conditions than others in the same line of business. The ability of companies in different types of endeavor to pay the same level of wages is partly related to the elasticities of product demand. Companies with inelastic demand curves for their products have a greater opportunity to pass on higher wage costs to the consumer than those with elastic product demand curves.

The relationship between general wage and price levels has an important bearing on the cost-revenue problem. Wages and salaries tend to increase less rapidly than prices during a strong inflationary trend. However, wage reopening and escalator clauses in collective bargaining agreements have probably taken some of the slack out of the lag. Unions also take anticipated price rises into consideration in making wage demands. On the other hand, wages generally lag behind downward swings in the general level of prices, so that the result is often a price-cost squeeze with serious consequences for companies with insufficient financial resources. A sound long-run business venture cannot always remain solvent in the short run.

PLANT AND EQUIPMENT

A company sinks money into plant and equipment because it expects a positive rate of return over cost. The total return over the life-span of such assets must be sufficient to cover the original money investment, implicit or explicit interest on that money, other operating costs, and enough profit to satisfy the businessman. The greater the original cost of an asset, the lower the rate of profit with given revenue expectations. However, revenue expectations are not constant and may rise as much as or more than costs. Business expenditure for plant and equipment continued at a high level during the postwar years in spite of a large rise in construction and other costs. The reason was that businessmen were generally optimistic about future revenue potential. Greater uncertainty in this respect would tend to make the cost of plant and equipment a much more strategic planning factor.

The cost of plant and equipment is determined by a variety of market factors and conditions. Contracts for the construction of plants and other facilities are often awarded on a competitive bid basis. However, the size and nature of a construction project frequently limits the number of potential contractors. Only one or a few construction companies may possess the required financial means or have the specialized personnel and equipment for a particular project. It cannot be assumed that there is a going market price for the construction of plant facilities. Every plant is somewhat or significantly different from every other plant. The final price generally results from a great deal of bargaining between the company and the contractor or contractors about specifications and estimated cost data. Companies have an advantage when more than one qualified contractor is actively interested in the project. The contractor is often willing to cut his profit margin and take greater risks in his cost estimates during a recession period; a construction boom generally results in opposite propensities. However, the cost of the materials and labor required for construction tends to place minimax limits on this kind of flexibility. A construction company, like any other company, can find itself in a price-cost squeeze induced by price rises in markets over which it has little control. The whole process of cost determination can be traced back through a maze of markets to the original raw materials.

Some plant acquisitions result from the purchase of existing facilities that are either adequate for the intended purpose or adapted by construction. The cost of such facilities may range from nothing or almost nothing to an amount that is as high or higher than new construction. Communities often offer plant facilities as an inducement to companies seeking new locations. The sale of war surplus plants after World War II provided some real bargains. However, locational factors, the urgency of need, and construction material scarcities may raise the price of "used" plants to a high level. Plant facilities may also be acquired by a lease-back and other rental arrangements; such practices are particularly common in the merchandising field.

Many equipment items are purchased in the same manner that a consumer buys a hammer in a hardware store. However, a company can often gain important price concessions by quantity purchases. Specialized equipment and tooling are frequently purchased through the same procedures used in placing construction contracts. The sellers of such items can sometimes make a "monopoly profit" by virtue of patents and trade secrets. On the other hand, a company may gain advantages if it is the sole or a major purchaser from a particular supplier. The possibility of producing instead of purchasing such items as tooling may also be a bargaining element. Some specialized and complicated equipment, such as an electronic computing machine, is acquired through lease.

RAW MATERIALS, MERCHANDISE, AND SUPPLIES

A large percentage of company revenues is paid to other business firms. A manufacturing concern requires a continuous flow of raw material and parts from outside vendors. A retail establishment buys merchandise inventories for sale to consumers. Business firms also purchase supplies and services not directly used in the production process or sold to consumers. The amount spent for raw materials, merchandise, and supplies relative to other expenditures varies from industry to industry. Expenditures for these items may account for 25 percent of the sales dollar for a railroad, 50 percent for a manufacturing company, and as high as 80 percent for a retailer. The number of firms supplying a company may range from a score into the thousands.

The economist has categorized market behavior by such analytical concepts as pure competition, monopolistic competition, oligopoly, monopoly, monopsony, oligopsony, and bilateral monopoly. These concepts afford some insight into the nature of the market forces that may be involved in buying goods and services. Thus, a manufacturer who buys steel is faced with a different price and supply situation than a meat packer who buys in the livestock market. The ability of a company to influence the price of the goods and services it buys may vary a great deal. A competitive market offers little opportunity to gain a price advantage relative to other buyers. On the other hand, significant price concessions may be granted a monopsonist (one buyer) or an oligopsonist (one of a few buyers). Monopoly power on the part of both buyer and seller may lead to a number of possible bargaining solutions. A variety of institutional and structural relationships makes for an almost infinite number of market situations.

Although price is an important factor, it is by no means the only consideration. Also important are such factors as quality, technical efficiency, the availability of parts, servicing, and advertising. For example, a furnace manufacturer may install a more expensive control device primarily because it is better advertised than another equally good device. The ability of a vendor to supply parts or raw material at a given rate is sometimes a vital factor. An automobile manufacturer, for example, might experience considerable difficulty if a supplier failed to deliver a sufficient number of spark plugs. Public and community relations may cause a company to buy from a local firm in spite of price or other disadvantages.

An important consideration in planning purchase programs is the possibility of price fluctuations. A rise in prices can result in large inventory profits; a price decline may lead to irreparable losses. Specific shifts in the overall price level and the prices of particular commodities cannot generally be forecasted with a high degree of accuracy. Companies sometimes attempt to avoid the speculation involved in purchasing inventories of raw materials, merchandise, and supplies by hedging in the futures markets. A flour miller buying wheat can hedge by selling an equivalent amount of wheat for future delivery. However, the large majority of purchases cannot be hedged either directly or indirectly. The uncertainty of general or particular price changes cannot be entirely eliminated in a dynamic economy.

Shortages in the supply of materials may seriously disrupt company planning. Companies may also have difficulties finding a source of supply for unique and specialized items. Purchasing is not always a matter of sitting back and waiting for salesmen to arrive in the outer lobby. A company should develop a well-planned purchasing strategy. Such a strategy can bring about significantly lower costs and higher profits.

NATURAL AND LAND RESOURCES

The product of industry can ultimately be traced back to the contributions of nature. The economic development of nations has been greatly influenced by the amount of agricultural land, mineral deposits, and fuel and power resources found within their borders. The United States has been more fortunate than most nations in this respect. Yet, the attrition of two world wars and high levels of capital formation and consumption have reduced or depleted the supplies of some vital resources. Large amounts of iron ore, titanium, manganese, copper, bauxite, and other minerals have to be imported from abroad.

The adequacy of mineral and fuel resources may become a strategic planning factor for companies requiring such resources in the production process. Private companies have played a major role in the discovery and development of domestic and foreign sources of petroleum, iron, and other resources. Steel-producing companies, for example, have spent millions of dollars to develop large iron ore deposits in Canada, Venezuela, and Liberia. They have also devised techniques that make possible the utilization of lower-grade domestic deposits of coal and iron. The petroleum industry has extended its exploration and development activities to the oil-rich countries of the Middle East. Chemical companies import large quantities of barite, bauxite, chromium ore, and other minerals from abroad. The development and importation of foreign sources of raw materials may involve highly complex international political and economic factors. Trade restrictions imposed by foreign governments, a rising tide of nationalism in some areas, diplomatic moves and countermoves, and the specter of communistic imperialism can play havoc with company plans and programs.

Companies also have to contend with scarcities imposed by the institution of private property and the market system. Thus, although the domestic supply of coal is more than adequate to meet industrial needs, a mining venture may have to stop operations because it cannot acquire additional coal properties. A similar eventuality may face companies requiring mineral and fuel resources in the production process. An important reason for vertical integration[7] is to insure an adequate supply of raw materials. The United States Steel Corporation was undoubtedly motivated by this consideration in extending ownership control over large iron ore and coal deposits. But, at the same time, such control over basic raw materials may preclude entry by other firms. Companies who purchase mineral and fuel resources are faced with market forces similar to those that determine other prices. A possible difference is that the supply of some natural resources is highly inelastic. A period of rising demand can bring about exorbitant prices or absolute scarcities at a given price.

Except for firms engaged in agricultural pursuits, the acquisition of land is primarily a problem of location. The value of land is closely related to the factors that determine the location of company production and marketing facilities, such as nearness to raw material supplies, availability of labor, trans-

[7]Vertical integration means control of various steps in the production and marketing process.

portation facilities, market proximity, power resources, and community and other services. The price of land partly depends on the extent to which companies seek the locational advantages offered by a given site. Another determinant is the availability of other sites with the same or similar inducements.

Government and Business Planning

Business planning may be influenced directly or indirectly by government action. Antitrust policies, the regulation of competitive practices, government spending, and taxation are particularly important in this respect.

FEDERAL ANTITRUST LAWS

The hand of government may point an accusing finger at any business practice or activity that violates a vast body of antitrust laws and regulations. Business planning must contend with the possibility that something planned today may become unlawful in the future. The best corporation lawyers cannot accurately forecast the manner in which a court may interpret the many laws designed to restrain monopoly and enforce fair competitive practices. The public utilities find themselves in a somewhat different category with respect to government intervention. They are given certain monopolistic prerogatives, but their rates and operating practices are subject to regulation by governmental agencies.

GOVERNMENTAL PURCHASES

Federal, state, and local government expenditure is an important source of revenue for some business concerns. A decline in government spending can induce a general business recession if expenditure in the private sector is not increased by a sufficient amount.[8] Equally important is the impact of changes in the type of government expenditure on the revenues of particular companies. Reductions in governmental expenditures for defense and space projects can significantly reduce the sales of some companies. The uncertainties involved in gleaning revenues from government purchases are much the same as those experienced in the consumer markets. It is most difficult to forecast the actions that may be taken by politicians and administrators in Washington, D.C., Lincoln, Nebraska, or Belle Plaine, Iowa.

BUSINESS TAXES

Company profit margins can be significantly affected by income and other taxes. Indirect business taxes can reduce profit margins by increasing the cost of business operations. Income or profit taxes transfer an appreciable portion

---

[8]If reduced government spending brings about lower taxes, consumer and business spending may rise. Lower public expenditure is sometimes necessary to ease inflationary pressure during a hyperprosperity period.

of business earnings to government. However, the impact of taxes on company planning is not limited to such direct revenue and cost consequences. Thus, although a corporate income tax may reduce the money available for investment, it may also tend to stimulate investment if accelerated amortization is permitted. A good example is the tax write-off program designed to increase capital expansion during the Korean War. Companies producing certain products were allowed to deduct the cost of new plant and equipment from income over a five-year period instead of the normal life of the asset. Much of the money that would otherwise have to be paid as income taxes could be used to purchase capital goods. Accelerated amortization of a capital asset increases expense and reduces profit. Since a large percentage of the greater profit without such amortization would have to be paid in taxes, the actual cost of plant and equipment may only be a fraction of the market cost. Corporate profits taxes can influence company planning and expenditures in other respects. The high excess-profit tax rates of the postwar years caused some companies to increase advertising budgets and permit more liberal expense accounts. With a tax rate of 85 percent on the last increment of profit, the actual cost of an additional dollar spent for such purposes amounts to only 15 cents.

OTHER EXAMPLES

There are many other ways in which government action may directly or indirectly influence business planning. Labor legislation has undoubtedly given impetus to the development of the "human relations" emphasis in management. Agricultural price support programs have an effect on costs in such industries as meat packing and grain processing. The activities of the Federal Reserve System may cause changes in the supply and price of funds in the money markets. International trade agreements and import duties have a bearing on company price policies, foreign sales opportunities, and the amount of competition. Zoning ordinances and parking restrictions may become important locational factors.

Innovation as an Environmental Factor

The term "innovation" is used here to mean the introduction of new ideas and techniques that result in higher productivity, lower costs, or increased revenues. The executive must be constantly alert to innovations that relate to his field of endeavor. He must keep pace with innovations made by competitors if his firm is to prosper and survive. The process of innovation is characterized by a relatively continuous sequence of major and minor developments. Some innovations are revolutionary in their impact on business operations and existing economic interrelationships. Others are like drops of rain, individually minute, but collectively of great magnitude.

MANAGERIAL AND OPERATING EFFICIENCY

A primary precept of a competitive system is that greater productive efficiency enhances the survival power of a company. The literature of management is replete with accounts of innovations that have increased productivity in a small or large measure. The development of line production, the self-service market, decentralized management, and automation expresses the innovation process in its most revolutionary form. The solution of some fundamental problem frequently gives rise to a number of related innovations in a short period of time. Such innovations as automation actually involve a cluster of major and minor innovations that form a systematic whole. A revolutionary sequence of innovations within a given area may be followed by a long evolutionary period involving relatively routine improvements in technique. However, not all innovation should be considered as a part of some major achievement. A great deal of progress is made by a series of small changes, such as an improved sequence of operations for producing a gasket or a better procedure for hiring employees. The importance of innovations outside the mechanical arts and sciences should not be neglected. The development of a better organizational technique or a more accurate employee testing program is sometimes more important than an improved production process.

The relationship between innovation and productivity may be difficult to measure. Some of the recently developed "human relations" techniques can be placed in this category. The oft-expressed idea that these techniques have improved morale does not necessarily lead to the further conclusion that productivity has been favorably affected. Many such conclusions are more the product of fairy tales than the hard realities of production economics. The hiring of preachers or psychologists as employee counselors, for example, has probably resulted in less inhibited workers, but there is little concrete evidence that output has been increased. However, improved human relations tend to have a more indirect relationship to productivity than other kinds of innovation. Thus, a company may experience fewer strikes in the long run than a competitor who uses the stick instead of the carrot to motivate his personnel. The social and other satisfactions that may evolve from better human relations can also be considered as a proper substitute for a higher output of goods and services. Productivity is not the only or, necessarily, the most important consideration in developing a program of human relations.

INNOVATION AND ECONOMIC EFFICIENCY

Innovation is concerned with economic as well as productive efficiency; the survival of a company is ultimately related to its success in the market. The most efficient operations will lead nowhere if people will not buy the product or service. Innovation may cause declines in the demand for existing products or services and give rise to entirely new industries. The development of the automobile dealt a death blow to the carriage and livery stable industry, but it gave birth to the giant automobile industry and a cluster of related industries. Air travel has become an important substitute for travel on railroads, bus lines, and ships. Some innovations have unfavorable consequences for industries that evolved from previous innovations. Thus, television has created serious difficulties for the motion picture industry. An innovation in one industry may bring about a need for innovation in another industry. The brassiere industry, for example, was handed the problem of providing sufficient support for the plunging necklines created by Paris and New York fashion circles.

Companies should give constant consideration to the manner in which innovations may affect the demand for their products or services. A major innovation can significantly, and sometimes rapidly, reduce the revenue potential of a company. Also important are the many relatively small innovations that mark the course of the competitive game. Annual model changes in the automobile industry provide a good example. During the past decade some rather sizable shifts in competitive position have resulted from innovations in body styling. Some automobile companies greatly expanded their styling activities and organized separate styling departments to keep ahead in the race.

Advertising innovations have played an important role in many battles for competitive advantage. The major tobacco companies, for example, have been engaged in an "advertising gimmick" contest since the 1920s. Similarly, a new television idea may upset the competitive apple cart for companies in a diversity of industries. A novel installment buying idea, a new pricing system, a mechanical improvement, and the introduction of a new service represent other kinds of market-oriented innovations.

The problem of organizing production also involves economic considerations. Some innovations reduce costs without necessarily increasing physical productivity. One goal in combining such productive resources as land, labor, and capital is more efficient production. But there is also the possibility of reducing costs by substituting lower-priced resources for higher-priced ones. Thus, the substitution of capital for labor may result in short-run or long-run advantages. Companies that are more alert in this respect can charge ahead of their lagging neighbors.

INNOVATION AND UNCERTAINTY

Elaborate measures are frequently taken to prevent other companies from learning about important innovations. Nothing is more sacred in the lexicon of business than the term "trade secrets." Innovations are kept under cover until they cannot be successfully copied by competitors.

Other Environmental Considerations

Such environmental factors as culture and weather may also significantly influence business planning. Although emphasis has been given to business enterprises, the environmental problems of nonbusiness organizations are similar.

CULTURAL AND SOCIAL FACTORS

An understanding of cultural norms and social practices can be extremely important in effective planning. Attitudes toward racial segregation, the customs of different nationality groups, and religious beliefs and practices illustrate the kind of thing that may become pertinent in planning.

WEATHER CONDITIONS

The state of the weather is particularly important in such industries as agriculture, construction, and air transportation. Restaurants, amusement parks, theatres, baseball clubs, and retail establishments also find that weather conditions affect their operations. Weather was a primary factor in setting the day of the Normandy invasion during World War II. However, forecasting difficulties limit the extent to which the planner can take weather conditions into consideration. Short-term forecasts may be rather unreliable and long-term predictions are highly conjectural.

NONBUSINESS ORGANIZATIONS

Some of the environmental factors involved in planning the program of nonbusiness organizations, such as hospitals, churches, universities, and the military, are much the same as those of a business enterprise. The problem of acquiring personnel and material resources is similar in many respects. The revenues of nonbusiness organizations may be derived by making products or services available to "customers." A church offers religious satisfactions, a university retails an education, and hospitals cater to the sick and injured, in return for contributions, tuition, and fees. Many nonbusiness organizations plan their operations on the basis of "demand" forecasts. However, significant environmental differences can also be noted. The military is sometimes given a priority in the labor market by draft legislation. Churches generally cannot demand contributions from a sinner who receives religious enlightenment. Public-supported hospitals and universities have to contend with the politics of legislative bodies in obtaining revenues.

ENVIRONMENTAL AND INTERNAL PLANNING PREMISES

Planning is premised on implicit and explicit forecasts or estimates of the future. The subject matter may range from a forecast of future sales to a forecast of paper towel requirements. Some forecasts are concerned with the various environmental factors considered in this chapter. Others are concerned with factors internal to the organization, such as employee morale, research potential, and the efficiency of existing production facilities. However, a strict dichotomy between environmental and internal factors cannot be maintained in practice. A cost estimate is based on factors internal to the organization, such as productive efficiency, and on external factors, such as raw material prices and wage rates. Furthermore, consideration must always be given to the extent to which the program being planned may influence the forecast. A forecast of demand should take into account the possible effect of sales promotion and advertising plans. A cost estimate is based on certain assumptions about the production program that is being planned.

In spite of the emphasis given to the importance of a scientific attitude and method, many of the factors that influence planning are highly subjective. The health of the president, the nagging of an executive's wife, or an incident at the club may directly or indirectly affect company planning. The executive who does the planning is a human being with the psychological properties of other human beings. He may not look into crystal balls or carry a rabbit foot, but he is not immune to other manifestations of magic and sorcery.

5

THE DEVELOPMENT
OF PLANNING STRATEGIES

Executives look into the future for forces that will promote or stand in the way of organizational success. When adaptation to environmental forces becomes necessary, they will either modify the organizational objective or they may decide to push through a particular objective by modifying the forces that stand in the way. For example, the objectives of a business organization are partly determined by an analysis of consumer demand. If a decline in demand is anticipated, the organizational program may be adjusted accordingly. But another possibility is to attempt to increase demand through better product styling, technological innovation, and sales promotion. Organizational objectives may likewise be affected by such factors as inadequate plant facilities, excess capacity, poor employee morale, insufficient financial resources, a shortage of engineers or production workers, federal legislation, and the forces of nature. Not all factors can be readily overcome by organizational action. Agricultural firms can exercise little control over the weather; lobbying activities are not always successful in stopping adverse legislation; and sales promotion may have a limited effect on sales during a major recession.

Planning for Profits

STRATEGIC REVENUE AND COST FACTORS: A SYNTHESIS

Planning is given a conceptual unity by the fact that there are limited resources. The planning problem is to overcome the obstacles imposed by this condition. The problem is partly solved by successful planning at the consumer side of the business. Larger revenues enhance the ability of an organization to survive and provide a basis for growth. This aspect of planning is concerned with marketing strategies to improve the firm's revenue potential. The planning problem can also be solved with resource procurement strategies that reduce the cost of such resources as labor, raw materials, plant, and equipment. Still another approach to the problem of limited resources is to achieve higher productivity through improved methods and motivational techniques.

The manner in which planning strategies interact varies with different companies and at different times. Some companies experience periods of time when there is little possibility of increasing revenues through marketing strategies or reducing costs through more effective resource procurement. The only alternative under such circumstances is to reduce costs through improvements in operating efficiency. Changing economic conditions can alter the situation and bring about more alternatives in the areas of marketing and resource procurement.

A business firm cannot generally survive if costs are consistently greater than revenues. Management should take advantage of every possible opportunity to increase profits. Companies do not always take advantage of the alternatives available to them. The ease with which revenue can be earned during a prosperity period has resulted in a neglect of cost-reducing strategies. Far too many companies engage in highly marginal activities that do not benefit either the revenue or the cost side of the ledger. An important planning objective is to make a profit. Profits are both necessary and moral in a private enterprise society.

The planning problems of nonbusiness organizations are in many respects similar to those of business firms. Such organizations also have the problem of reducing costs through improved resource procurement and operating methods. The differences are on the "revenue" side. Legislative appropriations and charitable contributions are important sources of income for religious, political, educational, and military organizations. However, the techniques used to obtain such income do not differ in a marked degree from the marketing techniques of the business world.

The remainder of this chapter considers the three basic kinds of strategies that may be used to solve the problem of limited resources: (1) marketing strategies; (2) resource procurement strategies; and (3) efficiency strategies.

Marketing Strategies

Marketing strategy is concerned with the methods that may be used to improve a company's revenue position. It involves planned adaptation to market forces that cannot be controlled by the individual company and planning designed to overcome limitations imposed by the market.

THE COMPANY PRODUCT LINE

To survive, companies must produce something that consumers are willing to buy. If the demand for a company's products or services seems destined to dwindle to little or nothing, executives should consider the possibility of shifting to other products or services. The specialized nature of plant and equipment may make such a move difficult, if not impossible, in the short run. A company may simply have to bear the consequences of a lack of foresight or an unexpected turn of events. However, there is frequently enough flexibility to make product line adjustments. Some demand shifts can be met with gradual changes over a long period of time.

Many companies have expanded their revenue potential through product diversification. Their products compete in a number of dissimilar markets. Such a situation requires a periodic appraisal of the relative profitability of particular products, and some may have to be dropped in the interest of economic efficiency. Products are also added to obtain a more favorable competitive position, to promote organizational growth, and to maintain a given scale of operations. The search for new products may become particularly diligent when a company is faced with the problem of excess production and distribution capacity.

Many examples involving product line changes can be cited. A large farm equipment manufacturer recently decided to drop out of the fertilizer business. Continued reports that cigarettes are injurious to health have caused tobacco companies to expand their product lines in other directions. A major retailer announced that it would expand its line of merchandise and become a full-fledged department store. A small restaurant is attempting to grow by adding a bar and a floor show to its offerings; a motel plans to attract customers with a new Polynesian night club; a hotel seeks more trade through a rooftop restaurant; and a grocery store wants to add customers with a delivery service. Companies of all sizes should give constant consideration to ways in which they can improve their profit potential by adding or dropping products or services.

PRICE POLICIES

A company can sometimes enhance its revenue position by changing the price of its products or services. The revenue consequences of a price change are dependent on what economists call "elasticity of demand." The individual firm in a purely competitive industry cannot increase price above that of a competitor because its demand curve is perfectly elastic. A farmer who ships his hogs to the market in Omaha or Chicago cannot ask more than the prevailing market price if he wants to sell his product. However, the demand curves of the majority of companies are at least slightly inelastic, which makes possible some degree of price discretion. Under such circumstances a company can increase prices and not lose all of its sales to competitors. A monopolist is generally in a better position in this respect than companies that have to contend with producers in the same line of business. But even the monopolist cannot increase his price without sustaining reductions in sales. If the price of diamonds goes up too much, people will buy more rubies and emeralds.

The elasticity of demand concept means that company revenues may rise with price reductions and fall with price increases, or conversely. The reason is that *both* price and quantity sold must be taken into consideration in computing revenues. An elastic demand curve means that total revenues will rise with price reductions and fall with price increases. A reverse situation will prevail with inelastic demand curves. Thus, it cannot be assumed that an increase in price will always help a company solve a problem of insufficient revenues. A further consideration is the relationship between the quantity produced and operating costs. A company with high fixed costs and excess productive capacity can frequently gain a great deal of profit by a price reduction. The classic example is the Ford Motor Company's dynamic policy of price reductions during the Model T era. This policy was instrumental in building a mass market for the Model T, which in turn made possible a production line that turned out 10,000 automobiles per day. Ford recognized the importance of demand elasticity and the cost advantages that could be derived from large-scale production. A high price per unit policy would have stifled growth and reduced earnings. The Ford policy and experience have been duplicated by many companies both large and small.

A company's price policy may be strongly influenced by possible reprisals from competitors. This consideration is particularly important when a few companies dominate a market. A price increase may result in a loss of sales if the rest of the companies do not follow. An attempt to gain an advantage by a price cut may result in even greater price reductions by rival companies. The gasoline price war provides a good example of this aspect of price strategy. Such wars generally begin with a price cut by one gasoline company in a particular market area. This move is immediately followed by similar actions by the other dealers. There is frequently a long sequence of price reductions until the original or a new price equilibrium is achieved; the price cutter sometimes loses far more than he expected to gain originally.

Sometimes a price leader will emerge in an industry or a market area. Price leadership in various forms has existed in many industries, such as steel, cigarette, automobile, milk, and restaurant. However, it should not be assumed that uniform price changes in an industry necessarily involve collusion among the companies concerned—evidence of collusion might result in government antitrust action. Such pricing phenomena can be explained by the economic logic of profit maximization. A company may simply follow another in a price rise or price cut because it enhances revenue potential.

Many strategies and factors may be involved in a particular pricing situation. Prices may be set at a lower level than would be necessary for other reasons to keep potential competitors out of the industry. Companies sometimes attempt to increase revenues by selling the same product at different prices to different categories of customers. A price rise can be used to give dealers a larger margin with the idea that greater sales effort will cause a net increase in revenues. Uncertainly, inertia, and a fear of change are important elements in price determination. Why make a change if the present price results in a profit and causes no adverse action from government, competitors, and others? A price change might have all sorts of real and imagined consequences. Why tempt fate in the face of the unknown?

ADVERTISING

The percentage of the sales dollar used for advertising and other sales promotion techniques ranges from a fraction of a percent for some products to well over 10 percent for others. The extent to which demand can be changed by advertising varies from product to product. Such products as cigarettes, drugs, soap, cereals, beer, liquor, and cosmetics rank high in this respect. At the other end of the scale are industrial machinery and equipment, metals, and crude oil.

How does a company determine the proper amount to spend for advertising? The marginal approach of the economist provides a theoretical solution to the problem. An increase in advertising expenditures is appropriate as long as each additional dollar spent brings in more than an equivalent amount in revenues. However, uncertainty and measurement difficulties preclude the application of precise marginal analysis in a practical situation. A major problem is that the effect of advertising on revenues is difficult to determine. Advertising is only one of many factors that may cause a change in demand. An increase in sales cannot always be credited to advertising, and a decline in sales does not necessarily indicate an advertising failure. Furthermore, the long-term assets that may be created by advertising should be considered in computing the returns from a given volume of expenditures.

Another problem is to choose from among alternative advertising media and sales promotion techniques. Should a company buy newspaper advertising or should it put its money into television? Would higher expenditure for window displays or customer services offer a better alternative? The answer depends on the kind of customer the company wants to attract. Advertising in a trade publication might be better than newspaper advertising if the company sells to other companies; a television or radio program would have greater appeal to ultimate consumers. The scope of the market in which a company sells is another consideration. National television coverage would obviously not be appropriate for a company selling in a local market. The weekly newspaper is a more efficient medium for some purposes than a large metropolitan daily. A company should make adjustments in its advertising and sales promotion program until it obtains the highest possible returns from expenditures. Research, experimentation, and experience provide some basis for evaluating the alternatives, but the difficulties of measurement preclude a high degree of accuracy.

The standards used by companies to determine the size of the advertising budget are little more than "rule of the thumb" approximations. One method is the use of a fixed or variable percentage of past or anticipated sales to determine the size of the advertising budget. Another is simply to spend all that can be afforded in the light of profit expectations and liquidity considerations. Advertising expenditures are sometimes handled as a capital investment that must compete with other capital expenditures on a rate-of-return basis. A technique that came into prominence during World War II involves estimating the cost of achieving a given objective by advertising. Thus, how much money must be spent for advertising to increase sales by 5 percent? A widely used approach is to relate advertising expenditures to the amount spent by other companies in the industry. These methods generally give recognition to the idea that advertising expenditures should be judged by efficiency criteria, but they do not adequately measure the revenue consequences of particular advertising expenditures. The practical problem is that the factors that ought to be considered in planning an advertising program cannot be quantitatively measured. However, executives ought to be fully aware of the limitations of the methods that are being used. Furthermore, such methods should not become impediments to the application of better, though far from perfect, estimating techniques.

Advertising is frequently an important weapon in the competitive battle. Companies are sometimes forced to increase advertising expenditures to match the outlays of rivals. Such retaliation tends to nullify the competitive advantages sought in the first instance. Conceivably the process could continue until the combatants experience zero profits or even losses in their attempts to strike a final blow. One reason this does not occur is that there is undoubtedly some optimum point beyond which higher expenditures do not provide better results. Another is that each company recognizes the potential danger of this kind of cutthroat competition. Companies sometimes limit their advertising efforts for the same reason they do not engage in indiscriminate price cuts. But it should not be assumed that advertising never results in competitive advantages. A company may make large short-run (and possibly long-run) gains by an advertising innovation that cannot be readily duplicated.

PRODUCT AND SERVICE INNOVATIONS

New and improved products and services can play a major part in attracting customers from competitive concerns. Larger companies frequently employ hundreds of specialists in product engineering and development, design and styling, and related areas. Although such specialization offers advantages, it should not be assumed that creative thought and imagination are the exclusive property of the specialist. Smaller companies should not be taken out of the race simply because they are small. They can frequently make major contributions in this respect if sufficient time and attention are given to the problem. Some time should generally be set aside from normal operating activities for this purpose. All too frequently a possibility for successful innovation is lost because of a lack of foresight or the pressure of day-to-day operations. Managers should study the pertinent trade and technical literature, attend some of the conventions and educational meetings of their line of business, and generally keep up with current trends. The importance of product and service innovations should be emphasized throughout the company. The ideas of company personnel should be solicited through some kind of suggestion system.

Resource Procurement Strategies

The influence of resource markets on business planning was considered in the previous chapter on environmental factors. To a great extent the problem is that of successful adaptation to external market conditions. An example would be planned adaptation to an anticipated rise or fall in the price of merchandise by changes in the level of inventories. But companies also use their economic and institutional power to influence resource markets. Thus, they may attempt to lower the price for a given item by forcing active competition between two or more sellers. This section suggests the kind of strategies that may be used to gain advantages in buying such productive resources as labor, raw materials, and supplies.

LABOR COSTS, WAGE RATES, AND COLLECTIVE BARGAINING

The price of labor is an important element in the successful solution of the cost-revenue problem. The problem is to achieve a sufficient spread between the amount that a company must pay in wages and the revenues it receives for its products. One aspect of this problem is the relationship between wage rates and prices. An upward spiral in wage rates without a corresponding increase in prices may have serious consequences for a company. A failure of wages to adjust downward during a period of falling prices presents a similar problem. This discussion is concerned with the manner in which such relationships affect a particular company instead of the broader economic implications that they may have.

The extent to which a company can control the economic and institutional forces that determine wages is definitely limited. The only alternative in some instances is to attempt to overcome the problem of higher wage rates by greater operating efficiency. However, companies should give constant attention to the means that may be employed to gain a more favorable margin between product prices and wages. Effective bargaining with unions is a primary consideration in this respect for a majority of companies in the basic industries. Although market forces place limitations on the discretion of both unions and management, there is generally a bargaining range within which either party may gain some advantage.

The appropriate management strategy in bargaining with a union cannot be defined by a definite set of rules applicable to every situation. Each bargaining situation involves a complex interrelationship of many factors, such as the personalities of executives and union leaders, the history of bargaining in the company, attitudes of the workers, and economic and institutional considerations. A strategy that works well in one case may produce opposite results in another. However, the following ideas may be helpful in developing a more positive and systematic approach to the problem. Contract negotiation generally begins with union proposals for changes in the existing agreement, although some companies make the first move by offering proposals to the union. Management will normally offer a number of counterproposals at a later date. The first thing that management should recognize is that the union usually demands more than it expects to gain. The management side of the table should be careful not to give the union reason to believe that it can exceed its original expectations. This problem should be kept in mind in framing counterproposals and in statements made during negotiation.

Management should plan its bargaining strategy in advance. It should attempt to anticipate the actual expectations of the union and think through the economic and noneconomic consequences of accepting them. Particular attention should be given to the long-run implications of a union demand. How will it affect the company's competitive position? What kind of difficulties may result with a change in general economic conditions? How may the acceptance of a particular demand influence future negotiations with the union? The implications of these and other questions should be carefully thought out by the management side. Where should management draw the line? When should it be willing to force a strike to temper union demands? The military maxim "it depends on the situation" expresses the danger of giving a definite answer to these questions. On the one hand, management should not always satisfy the union's expectations. But it may also have to accept something it does not want to prevent even greater losses. The various parts of the problem should be viewed from the perspective of a total strategy. There is a time to fight and a time to refrain from fighting. A strike simply continues the bargaining in a somewhat different form. The implications of a strike should be given careful consideration. How much can be gained and how much may be lost? Strikes, like wars, should be planned ahead of time. Preparations should be made to increase the ability of the company to withstand the economic pressure that is involved. For example, companies sometimes build up inventories to mitigate the impact of a strike. Considerable thought should also be given to the strategy and tactics that may become appropriate during the course of a strike.

RECRUITMENT AND TRAINING

Companies must attract and develop good personnel if they want to survive in a competitive world. They should not simply wait for people to apply for a job, but should actively seek the best possible applicants. It takes a great deal of time and money to train people; labor turnover can be a costly process. Smaller companies in particular often fail to give adequate attention to recruitment. There is also frequently insufficient training after people are hired, which explains the reason for so much bad service in restaurants, grocery stores, garages, and department stores. A little training can improve performance by a large measure.

MATERIAL PROCUREMENT PROBLEMS

Companies can sometimes reduce costs by getting a better bargain in the markets for material resources. Such factors as price, quality, delivery schedules, the dependability of the vendor, and community relations should be taken into consideration. Companies frequently attempt to maintain more than one source of supply for some of the items they buy, a policy that mitigates the impact of such events as a fire or a strike in the vendor's establishment on company operations. A company would find itself in difficult straits if the flow of some critical part or material were suddenly stopped. Buying from more than one supplier may also increase the company's bargaining power with respect to price and other matters. Good procurement strategy involves an interrelationship of many factors. The advantages reaped in one respect may result in disadvantages with regard to other matters. A company may expect to gain a price advantage by reducing its inventories, but this action reduces the extent to which the company is protected against a shortage of supplies during the operating period. Management must balance such advantages and disadvantages in arriving at an optimum procurement strategy.

The possibility of substitution may offer important cost reduction opportunities. Many companies attempt to increase revenues by developing new consumer and industrial uses for their products. The aluminum industry is constantly adding to the more than 4000 uses of aluminum.[1] Aluminum is now being used in the production of wall and window panels, roofing, radar mast, ships and boats, railroad cars, automobiles, industrial equipment, farm machinery, paint, ladders, and a diversity of other things. The efforts of industries to expand markets can increase the substitution possibilities of companies using their products and materials in production. Companies may save considerable money by substituting aluminum for steel or copper, synthetic fibers for natural ones, and steel for lumber or aluminum. It should also be emphasized that companies may substitute machines for labor resources. Thus, a high price for labor could induce companies to increase the amount of automation in factory and office.

INVENTORY POLICIES

Inventories are a necessary feature of business operations, but they may represent unnecessary expense. How much inventory should a company main-

---

[1] *Expanding Markets for Aluminum* (New York: The Aluminum Association, 1955), p. 3.

tain? The answer depends on the nature of the company operations and economic conditions. A company must maintain enough inventory to prevent disruptions in production and distribution. Interruptions in the flow of materials from suppliers can create havoc with the production program, and a failure to stock sufficient merchandise can cause customer dissatisfaction. There would seem to be some kind of an optimum level of inventories from a purely operating point of view. However, economic factors may cause a company to increase its inventories beyond this level or reduce them to an absolute minimum. An expected increase in prices may justify a higher than normal level of inventories. On the other hand, a company may reduce its inventories during a period of declining prices even though it may interfere with efficient operations. Further considerations in determining the appropriate level of inventories are the savings that may result from volume purchases, interest and storage costs, obsolescence and deterioration, and shortages in supply.

THE PROBLEM OF LOCATION

Market proximity, nearness to raw materials, transportation facilities, adequacy of power resources, availability of labor, and community services are some of the factors that determine the proper location of distribution and production facilities. The relative advantages and disadvantages of these factors must be carefully evaluated in making a locational decision. It is generally difficult and costly to make a change after the installation has been constructed or purchased. A bad location can have a far-reaching effect on a company's profit potential. The problem should be viewed from a dynamic instead of a static perspective; the right location today is not necessarily the right location ten years from now. Technological innovation, population shifts, urbanization, and institutional and political changes can significantly influence the appropriateness of a particular location. Furthermore, management should not ignore the intangible assets that a company may possess in a particular location. A company may refrain from moving out of an area because it has developed an excellent reputation with the labor force, local suppliers, and the community. On the other hand, companies that have developed liabilities in this respect can sometimes gain by starting elsewhere with a clean slate.

Efficiency Strategies

The last two sections have emphasized the importance of product market and resource procurement strategies in solving the revenue-cost problem. Another alternative is to increase revenues or reduce costs by improvements in operating efficiency. The problem is that of technique, or how a given output of goods and services can be produced with a lower input of resources. A larger output from a given input is another way of saying the same thing. Productivity strategies are subject to the same economic logic as market and resource procurement strategies. The most efficient methods from a technological standpoint cannot always be justified from an economic perspective. When they involve expenditures for physical facilities, estimated costs must be compared with expected returns over the life of the asset. Another consideration is the cost already sunk into existing buildings and equipment; a company cannot generally afford to build a more modern plant if the existing plant is only a few years old. The possibility of eliminating activities that have doubtful revenue-producing properties can also reduce costs. Companies may overburden themselves with such activities when the horn of plenty is tipped their way and they may experience serious economic difficulties when a recession darkens the horizon.

The following sections are principally concerned with the technological aspect of productivity innovation. The work of Frederick W. Taylor at the Bethlehem Steel Company provides a good example of this aspect of the management problem. Taylor achieved a much higher output with a lower input of resources in both the shoveling and pig iron handling experiments. The introduction of automation, a complete overhaul of the material handling system, and setting up a new incentive plan exemplify some of the more drastic changes of this type. A great deal of progress may also result from a sequence of relatively small changes, such as a slight improvement in the procedure for making an employee transfer.

FACTORY AND OFFICE BUILDING DESIGN

A company with run-down and obsolete factories and office buildings operates under a serious competitive disadvantage. Such a situation may evolve from financial difficulties resulting from shifts in product demand or an economic depression. But it may also express a failure to appreciate the significance of efficient facilities or to properly plan their replacement. Expenditures for plant facilities (improvement or replacement) cannot be considered apart from alternative expenditure programs. Thus, under certain conditions, it might be more profitable to build up large cash balances or increase advertising expenditures. Companies do not have unlimited resources and, hence, cannot avoid the problem of discrimination among what sometimes seem to be equally profitable alternatives. Plant replacement and improvement should have a high priority in management's thinking. The long-term welfare of the organization should not be taxed in the interest of short-term gains. An adequate plant today may be highly inadequate in future competitive markets. The money available today may not be available at some future date. At any rate, it ought not to be frittered away on causes that have doubtful merit.

Improved plant and office facilities can reduce costs in a number of ways. There may be direct savings as the result of reduced maintenance costs, lower fire insurance rates, and more economical heating and cooling. Building design may lower costs by making possible a more efficient layout of equipment and furniture, and improvements in material handling. Also important are the contributions that improvements in design may make to better employee relations. The factories and offices of today are a far cry from the drab and sometimes dirty places that once dominated the industrial scene. Attractive colors and functional design, locker and shower rooms, cafeteria facilities, and landscaped grounds give the modern factory some of the attributes of a country club. Modern offices and furnishings also reflect the theme of pleasant surroundings and personal comfort. Office buildings often display more luxury than the mansions of our most opulent citizenry. The extent to which these improvements contribute to greater operating efficiency is difficult to determine. Some changes in the physical conditions of work are clearly related to the goal of higher productivity. Others can only be rationalized in terms of such illusive concepts as "better human relations," "better morale," and "public relations." The point is not that beauty and comfort should be eliminated from the business and industrial scene but instead that executives should give careful consideration to other possibly more productive alternatives. Thus, higher salaries and wages might give better results than carpeting in the offices or marble-lined factory rest rooms.

EQUIPMENT AND OTHER FACILITIES

Trade publications are replete with advertising copy emphasizing the cost reduction potential of factory and office equipment and machines. For example, XYZ fasteners saved one company $95,000 during the first year. Time and labor cost cut 85 percent by the use of ZIBERONES. Let the LIFTGIANT lower your material handling costs. Office efficiency can be increased 50 percent by the use of EASYTYPE electric typewriters. Executives should not go on a shopping spree every time they read an advertisement, but they should make every effort to keep up with productivity innovations in their line of business. Although the problem of sunk costs places a barrier in the road to optimum technological efficiency, innovations may increase productivity enough to justify scrapping existing equipment. Some machines and equipment are additions to industry's arsenal of productive facilities rather than improved versions of existing equipment. Equipment innovation may involve comprehensive changes in a company's mode of operations over a relatively short period of time. Automation in factory and office provides a good example of innovation in its more revolutionary form.

But such major innovations as automation should not entirely eclipse relatively less dramatic, but important, contributions to productivity. A new electric typewriter for a secretary, an improved storage rack in the supply room, more efficient ventilating equipment in the foundry, a better material handling device, and an easier-to-handle tote box are examples of small changes that add up to a great deal.

SCIENTIFIC PROCEDURES AND METHODS

The development of improved operating procedures and methods is an important element in cost reduction. As used in this section, the word *procedure* has reference to the manner in which individual factory or office activities are linked together into a process or sequence within a department or among departments. *Method* is concerned with the way in which particular activities are performed.

The first step in devising better procedures and methods is an appraisal of the way in which work is now being done. Such a study can be facilitated by the use of systematic devices developed by industrial engineers and others. One such device is the process chart, which can be used to record the sequence of actions that make up a procedure or process. A process chart shows graphically what happens to a person, part, material, or printed form as it proceeds from one selected point in the process to another. It can be used to indicate man and machine operations, transportation, inspection, delay, storage, or combinations of these categories. The time necessary to perform an operation, the distance something is moved, the department in which the work is done, and other information can also be recorded. A procedure or process is sometimes plotted on a scaled floor plan of the office or factory which may be helpful in making an improved layout of machines, work benches, desks, and files.

The analysis of a procedure begins with a series of questions. What is the purpose of an operation? Why does it need to be done? Can it be eliminated in whole or in part? Who does the work? Can someone else do it better? Is the work duplicated elsewhere in the department or in some other department? Can the operation be assigned to someone with less skill? Can the activity be delegated to a lower level in the management hierarchy? Will a change in the location at which something is done reduce the amount of transportation? Can the procedure be improved by changing the time sequence of operations? Should two or more operations be combined into one? These and other questions may lead to significant savings in space, time, and effort.

Procedure analysis is concerned with improvements that can be made in an overall factory or office process. The elimination of unnecessary operations and inspections, reductions in travel distance, improved factory and office layout, and reduced material or paper handling are some of the results that may be obtained from this kind of analysis. An intensive analysis of particular activities or operations in a procedure may also bring about cost-saving improvements. Although procedure analysis generally precedes operation analysis, a detailed study of operations frequently brings to light improvements in procedure. Thus, procedure and operation analysis should be viewed as mutually dependent instead of as independent activities.

Operation analysis is concerned with the activities assigned to an individual factory or office worker. The point at which one operation begins and another ends in a procedure may vary from one plant or office to another and at different times. Operations may involve only human activity or a combination of human and machine activities. The analysis begins with a study of the present method for doing the work. An operation chart may be used to detail elemental right- and left-hand motions and the layout of fixtures, equipment, tools, and materials. Such a chart can be analyzed to determine a better set of motions to achieve a particular purpose. A more precise and complex technique for operation analysis is micromotion study, which involves the use of a motion picture camera. A frame-by-frame projection of the film permits a study of motion details that cannot be differentiated by simple observation. The speed of the camera or a special timing device indicates the time used to perform various types of motion.

Procedure and methods analysis frequently results in large increases in productivity at relatively little cost. A ten-dollar fixture may save as much as $2000 a year. It can cost as much or more to develop an inefficient procedure or method than an efficient one. Many improvements are made by people who are not specialists in methods and procedure analysis and without specialized devices and techniques. Factory and office supervisors and employees should not be neglected in the quest for work simplification. Many companies report that their employees come up with more good suggestions than do the specialists. The problem is generally not a lack of ideas but of motivating people to contribute their ideas. A further problem is that workers sometimes refuse to give their full cooperation and resort to tactics that reduce the gains that can be made from work simplification. Yet, improved procedures and methods undoubtedly result in some increased office and factory productivity even when serious cooperation difficulties are present.

STANDARDIZATION AND SIMPLIFICATION

Standardization and simplification may significantly increase operating efficiency and reduce costs. Product line simplification by the development of standard models and designs and the use of standard interchangeable parts reduces the number of separate components and increases the size of production runs. Quantity production makes possible a higher degree of labor specialization and the utilization of relatively less skilled and costly labor. Much greater use can be made of specialized machines, equipment, and tools because the cost can be spread over more units of output. The turnover of raw materials and parts inventories is increased, volume purchases lead to lower unit costs, and savings may arise from lower supervisory, clerical, and selling costs.

Other benefits can be derived from the development of technical standards. Such standards promote uniformity in quality throughout a company. They tend to increase quality by imposing minimum requirements and to reduce costs by inhibiting the use of higher than necessary quality standards. Closer tolerances may be good from a purely technical point of view, but they cannot always be justified from an economic perspective. The problem is to find an appropriate balance between the gains from higher quality and the increases in cost that may be involved. Uniform standards facilitate coordination by reducing conflicts among different functional interests on quality and other matters. For example, manufacturing and sales executives sometimes disagree with product designers and engineers on tolerances that should be maintained. Better coordination may result from the uniformity of information made available to different departments, such as engineering, manufacturing, purchasing, and sales. Each department is given a frame of reference for the performance of the responsibilities assigned to it.

PLANT CAPACITY AND UTILIZATION

Average per unit cost of output can be greatly affected by the degree to which a company utilizes its fixed resources. This problem is partly a technological problem, that is, certain combinations of plant, equipment, labor, and other resources produce relatively more physical output per unit of input than others. Another consideration is that per unit fixed cost is lower with a higher output. A major difficulty is that companies cannot perfectly predict the future market for their products or services. As a result, they frequently overestimate or underestimate their fixed resource requirements. Short-term economic fluctuations also prevent perfect adjustment even though longer run market expectations are about right.

What can a company do to achieve a better relationship between demand and fixed resource capacity? The problem of excess capacity can be partly solved by more accurate market forecasting. Although long-range forecasts may be highly unreliable, some companies might gain by taking greater advantage of systematic forecasting techniques. Business executives sometimes become overoptimistic in planning plant expansion, particularly during a relatively long period of economic prosperity. However, their critics should remember that hindsight does not always reflect prior wisdom. Production to inventory and product diversification are sometimes helpful in solving excess capacity difficulties. However, the accumulation of inventories to prevent excessive variations in the volume of production may involve a great deal of cost and risk. This alternative is generally feasible only if demand can be estimated with a high degree of accuracy and then only for very short periods of time. Additions to the product line are possible only if fixed resources are not highly specialized.

THE PROBLEM OF MOTIVATION

The motivation problem is an important element in achieving productivity. One aspect of this problem is the distribution of monetary rewards (wages, rent, interest, and profit) to resource contributors, such as workers, stockholders, and executives. But equally important is the creation and distribution of nonmonetary incentives, such as social satisfaction and status. These and related problems will be considered in Part IV of this book.

6

THE PLANNING PROCESS

This chapter considers the planning process from a number of perspectives. The importance of profits, the impact of cost on planning, and the time dimensions of planning are discussed in the first section. Attention is then directed to various scientific and subjective planning techniques. In the final section, the planning process is viewed from the standpoint of a particular company.

Preliminary Perspectives on Planning

TO PLAN OR NOT TO PLAN

Planning enhances the ability of the organization to adapt to future eventualities. To paraphrase Professor Newman, the executive should not always sit back and wait for lightning to strike.[1] Planning is frequently essential even though the eventuality for which plans are prepared is not likely to occur. Much military planning could be eliminated if the time and locale of the next war were certain, but it would be foolhardy to stop military planning simply because the planner must operate under conditions of uncertainty. The prospect of defeat by a ruthless enemy is appalling enough to override even the arguments of the most avid economy-minded politician. A failure to plan may also have serious consequences for a business organization. One result may be a loss of important opportunities. For example, the time gained by forward planning may be sufficient to reap a large harvest of sales made possible by a sudden increase in demand. Planning may also be important in combating adversity. A planned contraction of operations is less costly and disruptive than

---

[1]William H. Newman, *Administrative Action*, 2nd ed. (Englewood Cliffs, N.J.: Prentice-Hall, Inc., 1963), p. 66.

make-shift contraction. Such emergencies as fires and floods have also empha-sized the importance of planning.

If the future could be accurately predicted, executives could plan ahead without fear that their effort had gone for nought. Uncertainty always places limitations on the practicability of forward planning. Furthermore, since the distant future is generally more uncertain than the immediate future, long-range planning may be extremely hazardous. The executive must constantly balance the benefits that may be derived from planning with the possibility that the time and effort so spent may have been in vain. There is little purpose in planning for the sake of planning. But planning for an eventuality that can be anticipated with reasonable accuracy may be highly desirable. However, the executive cannot always restrict the planning period because his crystal ball is hazy. He is frequently forced into long-range planning whether he likes it or not. The reason is that some decisions commit the organization for a long period of time. For example, the construction of a specialized plant involves an explicit or implicit projection of sales far into the future. Uncertainty makes such projections highly conjectural, to say the least. Yet such decisions cannot be avoided if the organization is to prosper and survive.

Some degree of stability is necessary in all organized endeavor. Effective coordination cannot be achieved without a common objective and a sense of direction. For this reason executives frequently undertake long-range planning in spite of the hazards that may be imposed by uncertainty. As one executive has said: "Accurate planning beyond one year is difficult at best, and long-range plans are very apt to be changed before completion. Nevertheless, they serve a definite purpose in setting up an orderly approach to the problems of long-range growth of the company."[2] Subjective considerations may also influ-ence the executive in this respect. Long-range planning presents a challenge to organizational participants. It gives them a purpose beyond the ordinary and sometimes tedious tasks of today.

PLANNING FOR PROFITS

The achievement of a favorable balance between revenues and costs is gen-erally the primary goal of planning in a business concern. A profit, particu-larly over a long period of time, is usually accepted as evidence that planning is in good hands. However, the fact that uncertainty about the future is always present sometimes means that a good plan will result in losses and a bad plan in profits. Another consideration is that planning cannot always be differenti-ated from other managerial activities such as communication and leadership. A mediocre plan that is well executed can provide better results than a good plan that is badly executed. Also important are assets and liabilities from the

2"Industry Plans for the Future," *The Conference Board Business Record*, Vol. 9, No. 8, August 1952, p. 324.

past. Planning mistakes in the past can set the stage for ultimate disaster even though present planning is efficient. On the other hand, the success of the past can, for a time at least, counterbalance the inefficient planning of today.

Planning is concerned with the future potential of the organization. Some companies are more aggressive than others in taking advantage of opportunities for profits and expansion. Some managers either fail to see opportunities or lack the inclination to take appropriate action. It takes courage to cut through a web of inertial forces that impede change. It takes courage to plan into the future with all of the uncertainty that is involved. However, companies have also faced problems from too much enthusiasm and too little intelligent planning.

Profits result from organizational activity and will normally result only if that activity is well planned. Planning involves adaptation to product and resource markets, governmental policies, and cultural and social factors. Equally important are the strategies devised by the organization to control and to modify its environment, such as product line changes, price policies, advertising and sales promotion, product and service innovations, resource procurement strategies, and improvements in operating and motivational techniques.

The Past is Prologue

The planning process begins with an existing organization having certain human, material, and financial resources. As in a game of chess that is half over, future moves are restricted and influenced by the action that has gone before. Once an organization is committed to a particular objective, a major change in objective is difficult and sometimes impossible. An automobile manufacturing plant cannot be readily adapted to produce steel ingots. The tools and equipment in such a plant cannot be used to make pajamas or chicken pot pies. An educational institution would experience difficulties in shifting to the manufacture of bar stools or fly swatters. A religious organization cannot make major changes in its doctrinal position from day to day without serious consequences. A student cannot easily change his academic program during the last semester of the senior year.

THE COST OF CHANGE

A major restriction to change is imposed by the length of time necessary to depreciate specialized resources. The cost of plant and equipment, for example, cannot usually be absorbed in the short run under normal economic conditions. The specialization of executive, technical, and operating personnel also inhibits change because such personnel cannot be readily reassigned to radically different activities. Although personnel can be replaced from the outside, the real and hidden cost is generally high. Much of the money spent in the past for training and morale-building programs will have to be written off as a loss. Furthermore, the development of inexperienced personnel into competent employees is expensive and time consuming. The cost of past advertising and other sales promotion effort may also go down the drain with a major change in objectives.

The disruptive impact of change on formal and informal organizational relationships is another consideration. People generally do not relish the uncertainty that accompanies status changes. Morale and productivity are sometimes seriously affected by such disturbing forces. The possible adverse consequences of change cannot always be measured in objective terms. Some costs are purely subjective and can only be expressed by such terms as apprehension, worry, and anxiety. They are sometimes sufficient to counterbalance more objective considerations.

THE FUTURITY OF PLANNING

To the extent that the consequences of past planning are irrevocable, they reduce the capacity of the organization to adapt to environmental changes. The obstacles placed in the path of change may have both beneficial and destructive properties. Some degree of stability is necessary in the conduct of all human affairs. People seem to have a limited capacity to absorb changes in their physical and social milieu. But an inability to adapt to external changes may destroy the organization. Thus, a reduced product demand may bankrupt a company because it cannot shift to the production of another product.

However, the past is important only to the extent that it gives a better understanding of the limitations placed upon future action. Planning is concerned with the problems of the future; the question is not, what has been done, but, what shall be done? The planner should view each problem in terms of what is now pertinent. The errors of the past should not be perpetuated into the future. As an outstanding executive has written:

"We ask not only what a thing is *now* worth but what it *did* cost, often a fact interesting for deplorable reasons but utterly irrelevant to the present decision that the merchant must make—to sell it for what it is now worth or not sell it at all, whether he shall make a past error of decision the basis for a new error of decision or deal with present circumstances."[3]

Some corrective action will always be necessary in an environment of uncertainty. The mistakes of the past are rarely fatal if executives act promptly and decisively.

PLANNING HORIZONS

According to a survey conducted by the National Conference Board, three to five years seems to be a common measure for long-range planning, al-

[3]Chester I. Barnard, *The Functions of the Executive* (Cambridge: Harvard University Press, 1951), p. 208.

though some companies think in terms of decades.[4] Many companies plan all activities for the same length of time. A target date is set and all planning is conducted with that date in mind. The planning period may vary with different kinds of activities, such as capital expenditures, research, and sales promotion.

Capital expenditures are more subject to long-range planning than any other planning area. Such plans frequently form the basis for all other planning. As one executive remarked: "We attempt to set our sights ahead as far as possible as to capital expenditures, and then each move that we make in other fields is in the direction of that plan."[5]

Working capital requirements, dividend policy, tax payments, marketing programs, research projects, raw material procurement, production allocation, and personnel development are frequently planned far in advance. One company plans its contributions to philanthropic organizations on a long-run basis.

The basic operating program is generally planned for a year. The plans for the first month or quarter are more definite and detailed than plans for the succeeding months or quarters. Appropriate changes are made in the overall plan whenever necessary and possible. An unexpected increase in demand may lead to an upward revision of production and marketing schedules; a sudden shortage of raw materials would have an opposite effect.

Some companies contend that they do not plan at all. However, such a state of affairs evolves from semantics rather than reality. All executives and organizations engage in some kind of planning. To say otherwise is to repudiate the very essence of the executive function. Planning may be conducted in a haphazard way, or it may involve highly systematized procedures. Some of it may represent little more than reflective thinking by executives. The appropriate amount of planning cannot be determined without a careful appraisal of particular situations. Uncertainty sometimes makes any kind of long-range planning a marginal pursuit. Some companies undoubtedly plan too little, but still others plan too much.

Planning Instruments and Techniques

LIMITED RESOURCES AND COMPANY STRATEGIES

The planner should give careful consideration to the limitations imposed by internal and external factors. Thus, sales objectives cannot exceed the capacity of company production and marketing facilities. An expanded research program cannot be launched if competent personnel is not available. Additional production facilities cannot be constructed or purchased with inadequate financial resources. Although the planning problem always involves limitations in resources, the planner should take into account the alternative strategies

---

[4]Industry Plans for the Future," *The Conference Board Business Record*, pp. 324–328.
[5]Ibid., p. 324.

that can be used to overcome such limitations. Some of the strategies that may be employed to increase revenues and reduce costs were indicated in Chapter 5. The revenue potential of product line changes, price increases or reductions, advertising and other sales promotion techniques, and product and service innovations should be evaluated. Careful consideration should also be given to strategies that reduce the cost of procuring such resources as money, plant and equipment, personnel, raw materials, merchandise, and supplies. The development of higher productivity through improved factory and office building design, better machines and equipment, more efficient procedures and methods, standardization and simplification, and more complete utilization of facilities represents another aspect of planning strategy.

STRATEGIC OR LIMITING FACTORS

Effective planning is directed toward what have been called limiting or strategic factors.[6] A strategic factor is the missing link in whatever system of integrated conditions or actions is necessary to achieve a given objective. Such a factor "is the one whose control, in the right form, at the right place and time, will set the complementary factors at work to bring about the results intended."[7] In the following oft-quoted saying, an insignificant little nail significantly influenced the course of events.

> For want of a nail the shoe was lost,
> For want of a shoe the horse was lost,
> For want of a horse the rider was lost,
> For want of a rider the battle was lost,
> For want of a battle the kingdom was lost—
> And all for want of a horseshoe nail.[8]

Although few kingdoms have been lost for want of a nail, the importance of this idea is illustrated by the bombing of German transportation facilities, ball bearing plants, and oil refineries during World War II. The destruction of any one of these vital resources, the planners reasoned, would seriously impede the German war effort.

This experience from World War II illustrates the importance of directing attention to strategic factors. Thus, the bombing of German corset factories or breweries would have contributed far less to Allied victory. The strategic factor (or factors) constantly changes during the planning process. At one period of time, the strategic factor may be a shortage of a mineral resource, at another an inadequate organizational structure, at still another employee morale,

---

[6]John R. Commons, *Institutional Economics* (New York: The Macmillan Company, 1934), pp. 627–633; Barnard, *The Functions of the Executive*, pp. 202–205.

[7]Commons, *Institutional Economics*, p. 628.

[8]Benjamin Franklin, *Poor Richard's Almanack* (1758).

and so on. For example, the General Electric Company, which launched a major expansion program in 1945, gave initial emphasis to such matters as organizational structure and production facilities. But, as the planning and execution of the program progressed, other factors became relatively more important. This point was emphasized by a statement attributed to GE's Ralph Cordiner: "Not customers, not products, not money, but managers may be the limit on General Electric's growth."[9] The strategic factor may change as a result of changes in the environment and within the organization. Customers would be a more strategic factor during a serious recession than during a peak prosperity period. Furthermore, the planning process itself generates a sequence of strategic factors. For example, a short supply of iron ore may be solved by importing ore from a foreign nation. The strategic factor may then become that of transporting the ore or changing the location of the steel mill.

ANALOGUE MODELS: THE GANTT CHART AND PERT

A highly useful planning technique is to build an analogue model of the activities that will be necessary to achieve an objective. This kind of model can be used to develop and improve plans before and during actual operations and can perform important control functions. The famous Gantt Chart plots activities and time along a horizontal scale. Planned activities can be compared with actual performance as the work progresses. Recently developed planning instruments utilize networks to show sequences of activities and the time that will probably be required to achieve planned objectives. A good example is the Program Evaluation and Review Technique (PERT) which was developed in 1958 to plan the Polaris Weapons System. PERT and related planning instruments have played an important part in United States military and space programs. Comprehensive consideration will be given to the Gantt Chart and PERT in Chapter 16.

OPERATIONS RESEARCH

In addition to the techniques of scientific management developed by Frederick W. Taylor and his lieutenants, a large number of organizations utilize operations research to help solve planning problems. Many of the factors and relationships involved in planning are quantitative in nature and can be expressed by the mathematical formulations of operations research. It should be noted in this respect that only large companies can afford a full-fledged operations research department. However, small and medium-sized companies can often profitably take advantage of the techniques involved through consulting arrangements. Some of the following kinds of problems are particularly susceptible to operations research:

[9]Edward C. Bursk and Dan H. Fenn, Jr. (editors), *Planning the Future Strategy of Your Business* (New York: McGraw-Hill Book Company, Inc., 1956), p. 46.

Inventory Problems

Such problems are concerned with balancing the costs involved in holding inventories against the costs that may result from insufficient inventories. Loss of customers, delays in production from material shortages, relative costs of different-sized production runs, and the advantages of quantity purchasing are some of the variables that make up this problem. Inventory models can be helpful in determining how much and when inventory should be purchased or produced to achieve a minimum cost situation.

Allocation Problems

A company can frequently use productive resources in different ways and for a variety of purposes. Thus, there are alternative combinations of processes that can be used to produce a particular product, or different combinations of products can be produced with the resources at hand. Allocation models can be used to determine the least cost combination of processes and the most profitable product line. Such restrictions as limited machine capacities, limitations in storage space, raw material shortages, and a lack of skilled personnel are taken into account in solving this kind of problem. Similar models can be used to determine the most economical transportation routes for the shipment of company products. This problem becomes particularly difficult when routes must be planned for shipments between a number of plants and warehouses and to customers in various locations. The problem of selecting from alternative ways to meet a given set or sets of product specifications can also be categorized as an allocation problem. For example, gasoline used in automobiles or aircraft can generally be blended in various ways without hindering performance. The nutritional requirements of commercial feeds can usually be met by alternative combinations of ingredients.

Waiting-Time Problems

One aspect of such problems are queues or lines of trucks at loading docks, busses at terminals, patients at doctors' offices, or customers at store counters awaiting service. Another view is that loading dock personnel, employees at bus terminals, doctors, and sales personnel are sometimes idle awaiting the arrival of trucks, busses, patients, and customers. Waiting-time or queuing models can be helpful in reducing the costs involved in the two kinds of waiting time. One approach is to improve the schedules of the things or persons requiring services and the other is to provide additional service facilities. For example, a department store might use advertising techniques to increase the flow of customers during slack periods of the day and add sales personnel during rush periods to reduce customer waiting time. Trucks can often be dispatched and routed in a way that reduces the time drivers must wait at loading docks and, at the same time, reduces idleness on the part of loading dock personnel. Models can also be helpful in determining the proper order in which various kinds of work should be done. For example, if jobs X, Y, and Z are waiting for a drill press operation, what kind of sequencing will reduce time or cost?

Replacement Problems

Equipment becomes less efficient over time as the result of operation or innovation. A 10-year-old lathe is generally less efficient than a new one and even more so if major improvements have been made in subsequent design. An unused Model T Ford is better than one that has been driven 100,000 miles, but a new 1972 Ford is better than a new Model T. How often and when should a company replace such equipment as lathes, drill presses, typewriters, and trucks? Replacement models attempt to balance the cost involved in purchasing new equipment with the costs of lower efficiency and maintenance. Another kind of problem is to determine the replacement pattern for things subject to complete failure, such as light bulbs and electronic tubes. For example, how frequently should light bulbs in a large sign be replaced to minimize the cost involved in intermittent bulb failures and replacements?

COMPUTERIZED PLANNING SYSTEMS

Significant improvements in planning can occur through the use of comprehensive computerized models of the economic system or an industry. Some of the larger and more progressive companies make extensive use of econometric models for sales and other forecasting. Progress has also been made through models that simulate particular environmental and organizational realities. Alternative planning strategies can be tested to determine the manner in which they may influence profits and other planning variables.

Once organizational objectives (the sales forecast) have been determined, computerized planning systems can be most helpful in translating organizational objectives into subsidiary objectives. Much of the production planning and control problem, inventory and purchasing programs, budgetary process, and cost analysis and control can be effectively programmed for computer operations.

The electronic computer and all of the techniques that relate to it (such as operations research) will play an increasingly important part in planning the means necessary to achieve organizational objectives. Executives will be less concerned with means and will find themselves more directly burdened with the problems of uncertainty and values. Electronic computers will make many of the objective decisions, leaving for executives the decisions that can only be made through subjective techniques.

Emphasis should be given to the idea that small and medium-sized companies can effectively utilize computers for planning and other purposes through shared-time systems. A sizable number of banks have already made such services available to smaller business concerns, and there is every likelihood that this sort of thing will expand in the future.

SUBJECTIVE DECISIONAL TECHNIQUES

Objective decisional techniques involve attempts to solve problems by the use of methods and measurements that have an existence apart from the mind of the decision maker. The conclusions that result can be verified by other persons using the same methods and measurements. But objective techniques are never completely devoid of subjective elements. Subjectively derived imagination and ideas are an integral part of the objective problem-solving process.

There are physicians, physicists, chemists, mathematicians, psychologists, economists, and executives who have skills they cannot explain in objective terms. The president of a large metal-producing company had this to say on the subject: "I don't think businessmen know how they make decisions. I know I don't."[10] A top executive from the steel industry came to a similar conclusion: "You don't know how you do it; you just do it." Another executive commented: "If a vice president asks me how I was able to choose the right course, I have to say, 'I'm damned if I know!'" A possible reason is provided by the president of a large manufacturing company: "It is like asking a pro baseball player to define the swing that has always come natural to him."

The extent to which subjective elements enter the decisional process is partly determined by the nature of the problem under consideration. For example, the executive is frequently forced to form an essentially subjective conception of what the future might hold. Previous experience cannot provide data that can be measured by the techniques of probability theory. The only alternative is to fill the void with subjectively derived solutions. However, subjective techniques may be appropriate even when the decisional problem can be solved by an objective approach. Many decisions become routine or habit for the experienced executive with resulting economies in time and cost. Executive decision also involves creativeness and innovation, which are at least partly a product of subjective processes. Although objective techniques are important in solving decisional problems, subjective techniques also play a significant role.

AN OPTIMUM COMBINATION OF STRATEGIES

The problem of the planner in determining the organization objective is to plan the best possible combination of strategies. Some strategies are complementary in the sense that organizational action in one area requires actions in other areas. A market strategy designed to increase sales by a large percentage

---

[10]The statements that follow are reproduced from John McDonald, "How Businessmen Make Decisions," *Fortune*, Vol. 52, No. 2, August 1955, p. 85.

is obviously futile if no provision is made for necessary expansion of plant and office facilities or a larger volume of raw material flow. Other strategies are competing in the sense that attempts to achieve a greater advantage in one respect leads to disadvantages in other respects. Strategies that successfully promote market dominance sometimes compete with strategies that reduce the risk of government antitrust action. Thus, a company may deliberately plan a market strategy that gives it lower sales and revenues than another strategy because it fears a zealous government lawyer who wants to justify his salary.

Some of the variables in the planning problem can be synthesized by mathematical techniques—simple arithmetic computation is frequently all that is required. Sales forecast information can be used to determine production schedules which in turn may be used to plan the purchasing program. Alternative strategies can be evaluated in terms of revenue forecasts and cost estimates. However, the planner should remember that much of the quantitative data used in planning evolves from highly subjective forecasts and estimates. Some values are translated into quantitative terms even though they are essentially subjective judgments. For example, how will a styling innovation or a television program influence future sales? The planner must assess the impact of not only his own plans in this respect but also the unknown plans of his competitors. The logic of mathematics does not offer any final solution to problems of this kind; it is frequently more economical to simply "juggle things around." The only thing that is gained by mathematical techniques in some instances is a more precise wrong answer. Thus, although a quantitative and computational approach is useful, a more fundamental problem is to make judgments about the expectations that are being quantified. The final outcome under the best possible circumstances will contain some degree of error. Fortunately, many of the planning errors made today can be corrected at some future date.

THE ORGANIZED PLANNING PROCESS

Planning in companies beyond a certain size is an organized process involving the cooperation of many executives and specialists. The process can be analytically divided into two phases. The first phase is concerned with the formulation of organization and departmental objectives. It generally involves much formal and informal interaction among executives at different levels of the management hierarchy.

The second phase of the planning process occurs after the organization objective has been given final approval. Although the top executive (an individual or a group) may solicit advice and information from subordinates and specialists from various parts of the organization, the final decision as to the nature of objectives to be pursued is his responsibility. Planning during the second phase follows hierarchical lines more rigidly than during the first phase.

It involves a further refinement of objectives into more particular objectives as the process moves from the top to the bottom of the hierarchy.

Objectives, Plans, and Policies

ORGANIZATIONAL OBJECTIVES AND THE PLANNING PROCESS

Organizational objectives and the plans that are developed to achieve them are mutually dependent concepts. Objectives determine the nature of the activities that will be necessary, but at the same time the activities that are planned operationally define the objective. A given objective at the beginning of the planning process may be given different operational definitions if two or more plans are possible. Whenever the planner selects one alternative plan instead of another, he is in effect making a decision about objectives. The determination of objectives is an implicit or explicit problem throughout the planning process.

THE SALES FORECAST

Organizations frequently define their objectives in the form of a sales forecast. Such a forecast may be defined as a quantitative projection of objectives over some period of time. It is generally expressed in both product unit and dollar value to meet the needs of overall sales, production, and financial planning. The data may be differentiated by time period (month, quarter, year), geographical area (state, district, foreign), type of customer (industrial, ultimate consumer), or mode of distribution (wholesale, retail). Separate sales forecasts are sometimes prepared for major operating units, such as product divisions, manufacturing plants, and sales territories.

Sales forecasting and planning should be viewed as mutually dependent functions. On the one hand, the sales forecast is an important basis for planning the company program, and, at the same time, the plans being developed have a bearing on sales potential. A sales forecast involves far more than an appraisal of conditions in the product markets. It also reflects the manner in which other environmental factors, such as resource markets and governmental policies, may influence sales objectives and reflects the limitations that evolve from the productive capabilities of the organization. The problem is to make a sales forecast that yields some optimum relative to opportunities and restrictions imposed by the environment and the organization. The solution involves a consideration of many interrelated alternatives. One executive has described the procedure used in his company to determine the sales forecast.

"We look at the first estimates to see if the predicted results are what we want. If they're O.K., fine; we let them go through. But maybe the estimates show that we won't have the necessary funds available, or that the forecaster has figured to sell more of a certain item than we can get the material to produce.

Too, the projected profit may be unsatisfactory. In such cases, we go to work to juggle things around, as best we can, to get a set of estimates that we want. Sometimes we can decide to put on a new promotion, which would raise the forecasts, but other times nothing we can do would seem to improve the situation, and we have to let them go through."[11]

SUBSIDIARY OBJECTIVES: INTERNAL FORECASTS AND ESTIMATES

A distinction is generally made in the literature between external and internal forecasts. External forecasts are concerned with economic, political, social, and other environmental conditions that must be taken into consideration in planning the company program. Such external conditions as product demand, the supply of labor, and raw material prices may significantly influence planning. Internal forecasts are more directly concerned with conditions within an organization. Some internal forecasts, such as the sales forecast, involve a blending of many external and internal factors. Internal conditions, such as the capacity of plant and office facilities and the productivity of personnel, are as important in projecting sales as external economic and market conditions.

The sales forecast is both the most widely used and the most important internal forecast. It becomes the "official" objective of the organization after approval by duly constituted authority and becomes a basis for other internal forecasts and estimates from which subsidiary objectives may be derived. For example, production schedules can frequently be directly developed from the approved sales forecast.[12] Production schedules can in turn be used to make inventory and purchasing plans, to estimate personnel requirements, to plan additional facilities, and to determine financial requirements. Internal forecasts and estimates are generally prepared by functional specialists in production planning, engineering, industrial relations, accounting and finance, market research, and purchasing. They become the "official" objective of the departmental unit after they are approved by the department head. The approved forecasts at higher hierarchical levels provide information and limitations for the forecasts and estimates made at lower levels. For example, the production department must plan its program in terms of explicit and implicit conditions set forth in the "official" company sales forecast.

BUDGETARY PLANNING SYSTEMS

Budgets express organizational and departmental objectives in financial and nonfinancial quantities. They anticipate operating results over some future

---

[11]Interviewed and quoted by C. M. Crawford, *Sales Forecasting Methods of Selected Firms* (Urbana, Ill.: Bureau of Economic and Business Research, College of Commerce and Business Administration, University of Illinois, 1955), pp. 38–39.

[12]Companies that do not produce standardized products generally build up production schedules as customers' orders are received.

period or periods of time and provide a basis for measuring performance as plans are translated into accomplishments. A diversity of budgeting practices is found in different companies. Some companies have a comprehensive budgeting system that incorporates every aspect of operations and finance into budgets. Other companies limit budgeting to certain phases of their activities, such as sales and production. Still others do not prepare formal budgets but have developed informal procedures that vaguely approach a budget system. It is not possible to plan a company program without some consideration of quantitative factors. The production department does not plan its program without some idea about the plans of the sales department. Purchasing does not go on a buying spree without at least some knowledge of production schedules. The difference between informal and formal budgeting is the degree to which budgetary procedures are systematized and integrated into the planning process.

Although budgeting is not necessarily the *sine qua non* of good planning, a budgeting program may facilitate planning and other aspects of decision making in a number of ways. Budgeting gives emphasis to the importance of planning and frequently leads to a more systematic approach to planning problems. It tends to promote the use of scientific methods in solving forecasting and other measurement problems. It forces executives to establish clear-cut objectives and to coordinate their objectives with those of other departments. It increases participation in the planning process and expedites the flow of information within the management hierarchy. It sets forth objective standards that can be used to evaluate the efficiency of managerial and operating personnel. However, budgeting should be viewed as a facilitating technique instead of a substitute for good planning. It is generally a consequence rather than a prerequisite for effective managerial action. An effective budgetary program is not possible without a sound organizational structure with clearly defined responsibilities, a systematic approach to the solution of planning problems, adequate external forecasts of product and resource market conditions, internal cost records that can be used for estimating future costs, and a cooperative attitude on the part of managerial and other personnel.

MECHANICAL DRAWINGS AS PLANNING DEVICES

Organizational and departmental objectives are often indicated by mechanical drawings of products and their component parts. An assembly drawing shows the complete product with all its parts in proper relationship. Subassembly drawings are concerned with particular groups of parts that make up the product. Detail drawings show each part individually and indicate dimensions, material specifications, and other information. Much of the planning in manufacturing companies is based on the specifications provided by mechanical drawings. Departmental responsibilities are generally assigned on the basis of assembly, subassembly, and parts drawings. These drawings, together with data about the quantities to be produced, provide the basic information required for planning the production process. Nonmanufacturing departments may also formulate plans from mechanical drawings. The tooling department uses them to plan the tooling that will be required in manufacturing. The purchasing department can obtain information about the raw materials and parts that will have to be purchased from the "bill of materials" shown in the drawings. Mechanical and design specifications can also be used to plan aspects of the marketing program.

PROCEDURES AND METHODS

Managerial and operating personnel are sometimes assigned objectives with discretion as to the manner in which they will be achieved. On the other hand, objectives may carry with them explicit instructions about the procedures and methods to be followed. Procedures outline the manner in which managerial or operating activities are linked together into an integrated system of activities; methods are concerned with the way in which particular operations are to be performed. Executives at top levels of the management hierarchy are mainly concerned with objectives and only vaguely concerned with the problem of means. More and more attention is given to procedures and methods as planning proceeds from higher to lower levels. The ultimate consequence of the planning process is an elaborate network of procedures or interrelationships of operations. Some procedures involve only the operations that are necessary to achieve the objectives of particular departmental units. Others cut across departmental lines and relate the activities of one department to that of other departments. The whole system of procedures forms chains of human activity which are directly and indirectly concerned with the achievement of departmental and organizational objectives.

STANDARDS OR NORMS

Plans set forth standards or norms to guide the behavior of managerial and nonmanagerial personnel. The profit norm is the basic planning criterion in business and industrial organizations. The planning process translates the profit norm into a variety of subsidiary standards. Some standards, such as profit and cost standards, are highly abstract with many implicit assumptions about appropriate behavior. Other standards, such as purchase specifications, quality standards, procedures and methods, and wage incentive standards, are more explicit behavioral directives. An important problem is to develop standards that are effective from a communication point of view. They should provide sufficient information and accurately communicate the intentions of the planner.

POLICIES AND THE PLANNING PROCESS

The planning process sets forth new behavioral norms and standards that result in some change of company policies. The degree of change depends on the extent to which the norms set forth in the new program differ from those that now exist. Many policies remain in effect over a long period of time despite periodic planned changes. The specific changes that occur from one year to the next may not be noticed except by an alert observer. On the other hand, environmental or organizational forces can cause a major shift in some company policies. A new chief executive may radically depart from his predecessor's way of doing things; a court decision on "fair trade legislation" may prompt a major change in company price policies; a serious inflation or deflation may have an important impact on inventory and purchase policies.

PART III

Organizing

7

THE ORGANIZATIONAL STRUCTURE

Most organized endeavor is managed by a group ranging in size from a few persons to several thousands. Such groups are generally structured in the form of a hierarchy as the result of formal planning or informal processes.

The Nature of Hierarchical Organization

The management hierarchy ranks and relates positions and persons in the manner indicated in Figure 7-1. It simultaneously represents a decentralization and centralization of decision making. Decisional responsibilities are decentralized in the sense that they are dispersed among whatever number of executives are necessary to do the job. Proceeding from the bottom to the top

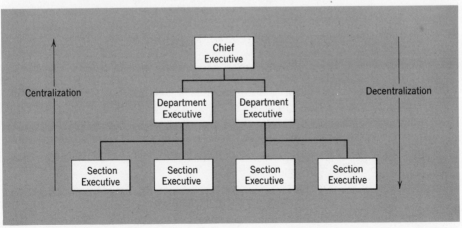

FIGURE 7-1. A simplified management hierarchy.

of the hierarchy, they are centralized in fewer and fewer numbers of executives until the apex is reached. All persons in the organization, managerial and nonmanagerial, are required to respond to decisions from that point.

COOPERATIVE EXECUTIVE ACTION

The hierarchy sets the stage for cooperative executive action. Each executive is assigned some part of the total decisional burden. Executives at lower levels function within an area of discretion determined by executives at higher levels. They make decisions on their own initiative, but they are also required to respond to decisions from superiors. The decisional responsibilities at the various levels are differentiated by a process called "departmentation." The executives who occupy the basic positions in the hierarchy are generally assisted by staff and service personnel. Committees may also be used to perform decisional responsibilities and serve other purposes.

HIERARCHICAL SPANS AND LEVELS

The limited capacity of the executive makes hierarchical organization essential. An executive can reduce his work load by the delegation of work to the next lower level, but delegation simultaneously increases the work load by the amount of supervision that must be given to subordinate executives. The reduction in work load by delegation is usually greater than the resulting increase in supervisory responsibilities. Another level in the hierarchy may become necessary when the amount of supervision begins to exceed the executive's capacity. The number of subordinates under an executive, which is often referred to as "the span of management," is related to the number of levels in a hierarchy. A larger span generally means fewer levels, and conversely.

THE SPAN OF MANAGEMENT

How many subordinates can be effectively managed by an executive? Is there an ideal number or a minimax solution to the problem?

A Biblical Account

An early reference to the span of management concept is found in the Biblical account of the Exodus.[1] Moses, who had led the Israelites out of Egypt, was kept busy from morning until evening counseling the people, who had to wait for long periods of time. His father-in-law, Jethro, suggested that Moses appoint rulers of thousands, rulers of hundreds, rulers of tens and give attention only to the really important problems.

A CONCLUSION FROM MILITARY HISTORY

Sir Ian Hamilton, a British general, concluded from the history of military organization that spans should range from three to six. He wrote that three

---

[1]Exodus 18:17–22.

would keep an officer fairly busy while six would probably require a ten-hour day. Hamilton thought that "the nearer we approach the supreme head of the whole organisation, the more we ought to work towards groups of three; the closer we get to the foot of the whole organisation (the Infantry of the Line) the more we work towards groups of six."[2]

FAYOL'S HYPOTHETICAL HIERARCHY

Henri Fayol, the French industrialist, uses these data in constructing a hypothetical hierarchy.

"Each fresh group of ten, twenty, thirty workers brings in a fresh foreman; two, three or four foremen make necessary a superintendent, two or three superintendents give rise to a departmental manager, and the number of links of the scalar chain continues to increase in this way up to the ultimate superior, each new superior having usually no more than four or five immediate subordinates."[3]

Actual spans in government and industry indicate that there is no one best solution that can be universally applied. For example, a survey of 141 well-managed companies by the American Management Association showed that the number of subordinates reporting to the president ranged from 1 to 24 with a median of between 8 and 9 for large companies and 6 and 7 for median-sized concerns.[4] These and other data on actual spans warn against any dogmatic conclusions as to numbers.[5] There is no general rule that can be used to determine the proper span for particular situations. Spans should probably be smaller at higher levels than at the first-line supervisory level.

[2]Sir Ian Hamilton, *The Soul and Body of an Army* (New York: George H. Doran Company, 1921), p. 230.

[3]Henri Fayol (Constance Storrs, translator), *General and Industrial Management* (London. Sir Isaac Pitman & Sons, Ltd., 1949), p. 55.

[4]The results of this survey are reported in Ernest Dale, *Planning and Developing the Company Organization Structure*, Research Report, No. 20 (New York: American Management Association, 1952), pp. 56–60.

[5]The span of management concept has generated a great deal of controversy in recent years. One rather unrestrained exchange on the subject began with an article by Waino W. Suojanen which concluded that the span of management (control) is not a valid concept to the extent that coordination can be achieved through formal and informal group activity. "The Span of Control—Fact or Fable?" *Advanced Management*, Vol. 20, No. 11, November 1955, pp. 5–13. Suojanen's article brought about a lengthy response from Lt. Col. Lyndall F. Urwick, the British management expert, who contended among other things that Suojanen was wrong and that the span of management (control) concept is still a most important precept in the array of management principles. "The Span of Control—Some Facts about the Fables," *Advanced Management*, Vol. 21, No. 11, November 1956, pp. 5–15. See also: Herbert A. Simon, "The Span of Control: A Reply," *Advanced Management*, Vol. 22, No. 4, April 1957, pp. 14, 29; Waino W. Suojanen, "Leadership, Authority, and the Span of Control," *Advanced Management*, Vol. 22, No. 9, September 1957, pp. 17–22; Lyndall F. Urwick, "The Manager's Span of Control," *Harvard Business Review*, Vol. 34, No. 3, May–June 1956, pp. 39–47.

There would also seem to be an upper limit to the number of subordinates a superior can effectively supervise; 100 subordinates are too many under almost any circumstances, but whether the number should be 5 or 25 cannot be given a definite answer. An executive with 10 subordinates may have a lighter work load than one with only 3 or 4. The reason is that the amount of work involved in different superior-subordinate relationships may vary a great deal. Some subordinates require frequent and extensive supervision; others can work out their problems with little attention from above.

FACTORS THAT AFFECT SPANS

A variety of factors influence the span of management. Some of them have general applicability and others help explain the wide divergence of spans in different organizations.

Physical and psychological fatigue obviously place an outer limit on the capacity of a manager. The range of knowledge necessary to conduct the affairs of an organization is another consideration. For example, accounting and engineering are often given separate status even though the number of people involved does not require it. Also important is the personality of the manager; an "empire builder" may have a larger span than a submissive individual.

A theory developed by V. A. Graicunas, a French management consultant, gives recognition to the idea that supervising others is both an individual and social problem.[6] Management must deal not only with a variety of individual personalities but also with different combinations of individuals or group "personalities." Social interaction, group norms and sentiments, and informal leadership are important in understanding subordinate behavior. A hostile clique or conflict among subordinates presents problems that do not exist with a spirit of teamwork.

In addition to subordinate relationships, there are interactions with managers at the same and higher levels as well as contacts with customers, union officials, suppliers, the public, and government. The nature of organizational activities can significantly affect the span. The pace and pattern of work may vary in different kinds of organizations (such as business, educational, or military), different departments (such as production or finance), and different situations (such as winter or summer seasons). The size of the span can also be affected by geographical dispersion. Although the problem of distance has been partly solved by rapid communication and transportation, such factors as the need for important on-the-spot decisions and more elaborate control techniques make for larger spans.

[6]V. A. Graicunas, "Relationship in Organization," *Papers on the Science of Administration* (New York: Institute of Public Administration, Columbia University, 1937), pp. 183–187; an analysis of managerial relationships is also found in: Fayol, *General and Industrial Management*, p. 55.

FLAT VERSUS TALL STRUCTURES

Some organizations have developed "flat" or "horizontal" structures by increasing the span of management and reducing the number of levels. Others have developed "tall" or "vertical" structures through shorter spans and more levels. An argument for a flat structure is that the "administrative distance" between top and bottom levels is reduced. This fact often facilitates communication and cooperation through closer personal relationships between executives at different levels. Also important is that longer spans make close supervision impossible, thereby forcing subordinates to assume responsibility. Executives who lack self-confidence and competence are weeded out and superiors tend to take more care in selecting subordinates. Another argument is that less supervision often results in higher productivity.

A tall structure places less burden on crosscommunication among subordinates situated at the same level. Communication among equals can create problems that are as difficult as communication between persons at different hierarchical levels. Indeed, authority can be helpful in getting a message across. Also significant is that tall structures tend to reinforce the authority relationship through the emphasis given to status.

The Departmentation Process

Departmentation divides the work of the organization into semiautonomous units or departments. The consequence of departmentation is a delineation of executive responsibilities and a grouping of operating activities. Every level in the hierarchy below the apex is departmentalized, and each succeeding lower level involves further departmental differentiation.

TYPES OF DEPARTMENTATION

The activities necessary to achieve the organizational objective are a basic consideration in organizing. The nature of such activities may differ significantly with such diverse objectives as making steel, waging war, selling insurance, and educating students. However, the types of departmentation have general applicability and can be applied in many different situations. The types most commonly used are the following: (1) functional, (2) product, (3) service, (4) territorial, (5) time, (6) equipment, and (7) alphanumerical.

TERMINOLOGICAL VARIATIONS

The terms used to denote the "departments" that result from departmentation vary a great deal. Business organizations use such terms as division, department, and section; the military uses regiment, battalion, group, and company; governmental units are called branch, department, bureau, and section. Terminology may vary in different fields of endeavor (Table 7-1) and from

TABLE 7-1.   Typical Patterns of First-Order Functional Departmentation in Various Fields

---

Bank (large)
  Comptroller
  Economics and business research
  Legal
  Maintenance
  Operations (generally divided by type of service, such as pension, personal and corporate trust, banking)
  Personnel
  Public relations
Department Store
  Controller
  Merchandising
  Personnel
  Sales promotion (publicity, advertising)
  Store superintendent (a group of service functions, such as maintenance, traffic, delivery)
Insurance
  Accounting
  Actuarial
  Advertising
  Agency
  Claim Adjustment
  Investment
  Medical
  Personnel
  Underwriting
Manufacturing
  Engineering
  Finance (comptroller)
  Industrial relations (labor relations, personnel)
  Marketing (sales)
  Production (manufacturing)
  Purchasing
  Research and Development
Public Utility (Electric)
  Accounting
  Construction
  Controller
  Engineering
  Operations
  Personnel (industrial relations, employee relations)
  Purchasing
  Sales

---

company to company. The principal operating units may be called departments in one company and divisions in another. Similar variations appear in the descriptions of functional departments. Production departments are sometimes called manufacturing and operations departments, and the terms employee relations, industrial relations, and personnel may be used synonymously. The types of departmentation are also subject to problems of nomenclature. Territorial departmentation is often called geographical or location departmentation, and commodity departmentation is substituted for the term product departmentation.

Functional Departmentation

Departmentation based on such primary functions as production, sales, finance, engineering, and personnel is common. Some kind of functional departmentation is present in nearly every organization. Functional departmentation may begin at different levels of the management hierarchy. Some organizations make almost exclusive use of this kind of departmentation; others interlace functional, product, customer, and territorial departmentation. See Figures 7-2, 7-3, and 7-4.

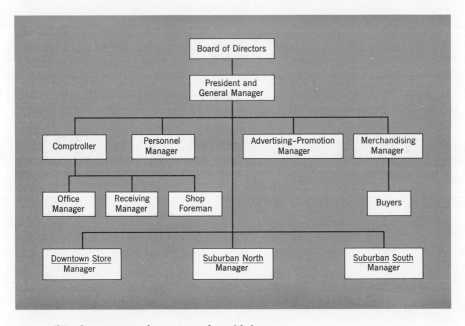

FIGURE 7-2. Organization chart: A retail establishment.

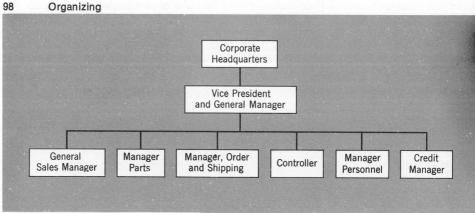

FIGURE 7-3. Sales branch organization: A farm equipment company.

PRIMARY FUNCTIONS

Some functions that seem to be basic in the operation of business and industrial organizations are almost universally given important departmental status. These functions have been called "organic functions" because their performance is vital and essential to the survival of the organization and the values

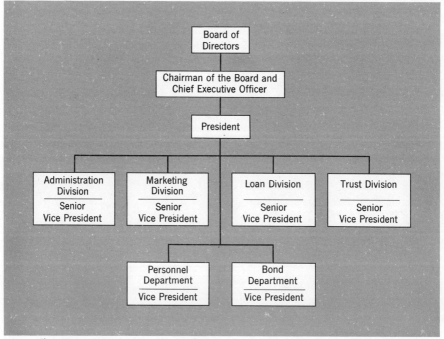

FIGURE 7-4. Basic organization of a bank.

they create are indispensable.[7] Although there are some differences of opinion on the subject, the functions that are generally so classified are production, sales, and finance.[8]

Although some functions occupy an important hierarchical position in almost every organization, a wide diversity can be found in the status accorded particular functions. In some companies the quality control executive reports directly to the executive vice-president or president, and in others this department is a subdivision of the production department. Public relations is sometimes a top echelon function, but it may also be a sub-department in the sales department. Engineering and purchasing may be found in the production department, or they may appear at the same level as production.

The answer given to the problem of functional departmentation by a particular organization depends on a variety of intraorganizational and environmental factors. A company engaged in the production of defense material for the government may establish a contract administration or a government relations department. A desire to improve public and community relations may prompt the creation of a public relations department. One company set up a consumer service department, independent of sales and production, because the sales department complained that production caused consumer dissatisfaction by not meeting production schedules. The avalanche of taxes with which industry has been endowed during the last two decades has brought about specialized tax departments in many organizations. A company faced with serious customer credit problems may attempt to correct the situation with a credit department. A highly competitive market may bring about a sales promotion or an advertising department, and greater emphasis may be given to the research and development function.

SECONDARY FUNCTIONS

The process of functional differentiation may continue through several successive levels in the hierarchy. The organization or a subdivision thereof (such as a territorial or product division) may first be divided into sales, production, finance, personnel, and purchasing departments. If further differentiation is necessary, functional subdepartments may be created and such units may in turn be departmentalized. Table 7-2 shows this process through three succes-

---

[7]Ralph C. Davis, *The Fundamentals of Top Management* (New York: Harper & Brothers Publishers, 1951), pp. 205–213.

[8]Davis, ibid., p. 207; Henri Fayol divides all the operations of a business organization into six basic functions: (1) the technical functions (production), (2) commercial functions (sales, purchasing), (3) financial functions, (4) security functions (protection of property and persons), (5) accounting functions, (6) management functions. Only the first five are horizontal functional differentiations. *General and Industrial Management* (London: Sir Isaac Pitman & Sons, Ltd., 1949), p. 3.

sive levels. However, functionalization can continue only as long as there exists a sound basis for further differentiation. Another type of departmentation may be employed when functional departmentation has been utilized to the fullest extent. For example, large accounts receivable departments are often subdivided on an alpha-numerical basis, purchasing departments frequently use product as a basis for further departmentation, and sales departments may turn to territorial units.

THE LOWER LEVELS

Departmentation at higher levels follows a similar pattern in many organizations, but there may be a marked dissimilarity in the departmentation that occurs at lower levels. The lowest level in an automobile body manufacturing plant includes the following departmental units: wet sand, wheel polish, trim line, hang doors and lids, and spot weld quarters. Similar departments in basic steel are melting, combustion, and dolomite; in an automatic washer plant such departments as porcelain finishing, sheet metal, and paint finishing are common.

FUNCTIONAL CENTRALIZATION AND DECENTRALIZATION

Should the purchasing function be centralized in a purchasing department, or should it be decentralized in production, sales, and other departments? Should each department provide its own stenographic service, or would a central stenographic department be more efficient? What are the advantages

TABLE 7-2.   Levels of Functional Departmentation in a Manufacturing Company

FIRST LEVEL FUNCTIONAL DEPARTMENTATION
  Finance
  Industrial relations
  Marketing
  Production
  Research and development
SECOND LEVEL FUNCTIONAL DEPARTMENTATION
  Production
    Engineering
    Manufacturing
    Production control
    Purchasing
    Quality control
THIRD LEVEL FUNCTIONAL DEPARTMENTATION
  Purchasing
    Buying (usually divided by product or type of supplier)
    Expediting
    Receiving and storage

of a centralized plant maintenance department? Should there be a personnel department, or should each department do its own personnel work? Under what circumstances should an organization department be established? Some of the factors that relate to these questions are considered in this section.

Size and Specialization

Size is an important determinant of the extent to which functional centralization is feasible. Departmental status cannot be given to an otherwise separable function if the volume of work does not justify it. For this reason such departments as purchasing, quality control, public relations, and personnel are not generally found in small organizations. These functions are performed by the existing departments. Such a situation may be illustrated by a manufacturing establishment with a sales, production, and finance department. The various executives handle their own personnel problems, purchase whatever is required, and carry out public relations functions, such as sending material to a college professor or giving a speech at the Lions Club. The quality control function is handled as an integral part of production work. Foremen inspect the quality of the work in addition to their other duties. When a serious quality problem arises, the head of production may give it his personal attention and confer with his foremen, workers, the sales manager, and the chief executive.

Company growth often leads to some higher degree of functional specialization. A particular function may be assigned to one or several persons on a full-time or part-time basis. The purchasing function, for example, may gradually become the primary responsibility of someone in the production department, possibly a foreman who shows interest and capacity in this work. A full-fledged purchasing department may eventually emerge as the company grows and prospers. A similar evolutionary process applies to personnel, quality control, research and development, and other functional areas.

An argument for functional centralization is the greater efficiency that may result from a reduction in the diversity of functions in a department. The time and talent of a production specialist, for example, may be better utilized by limiting his responsibility to purely production matters. Furthermore, executives in such primary functions as sales and production may not give adequate attention to peripheral functions. They may neglect what to them is a less important functional responsibility. Centralizing such functions as purchasing, personnel, research and development, and public relations tends to give them higher status in the total picture. It also makes possible the employment of specialized personnel and the use of specialized machines and equipment.

Control and Coordination

Functional centralization is sometimes used to promote control and coordination. A need for greater uniformity in wage and salary schedules can often be facilitated by a centralization of the personnel function. An organization department can be helpful in coordinating organizational planning and development. The channeling of outgoing information through a public relations department may become necessary to prevent a release of contradictory statements and information detrimental to the interests of the organization. Control over the flow of paperwork can often be improved by a centralized procedures department. This kind of departmentation frequently results in better coordination and control with respect to the functions being centralized, but the resulting increase in the number of functional departments can have consequences in an opposite direction.

Revenues and Costs

An important factor in determining the relative merits of functional centralization or decentralization is monetary return in the form of lower costs or additional revenue. Centralization may reduce costs through greater managerial and operating efficiency, but such gains must compensate for any additional expenditure for personnel and physical facilities. The determination of costs before and after centralization presents many difficulties. However, functional centralization sometimes promotes improved cost control by bringing hidden cost into the open.

Functional centralization should pay its way on the revenue side of the ledger. A statistics department may develop quality control techniques that result in increased customer satisfaction and sales. A public relations department may increase revenues through improved customer relations. However, such consequences are often indirect and, as in the case of cost evaluation, difficult to measure in objective terms.

Functional Empires

Although a reason for centralization is to give greater emphasis to a necessary function, the result is sometimes an expansion beyond the needs of the organization. Functional executives are not immune to "empire building," which can overemphasize the importance of a function in the total scheme of things. They may engage in projects that cannot be economically justified. For example, an executive in one organization asked the research department to provide information about the influence of temperature on product behavior.[9] He wanted an approximate answer, which he thought would cost about $100. He was amazed a few months later to receive a research report that had cost the company $10,000. Some functional departments find themselves pushed into overexpansion by other departments. This problem seems to be most prevalent in cases that involve an intraorganizational service, such

[9]P. E. Holden, L. S. Fish, and H. L. Smith, *Top-Management Organization and Control* (New York: McGraw-Hill Book Company, Inc., 1951), p. 175.

as engineering, research, statistics, and personnel. As Holden, Fish, and Smith point out, these departments are expected to give speedy and adequate service and as a consequence frequently feel compelled to maintain larger than necessary facilities to prevent criticism from other departments.[10] This situation in turn invites more work from other departments and requires even more resources. The result is too much use of service personnel for work they should not be doing. For example, research engineers may be engaged in functions that can be more economically performed by production engineers.

THE PROBLEM OF JURISDICTIONAL DELINEATION

The responsibilities of functional departments cannot always be clearly differentiated, which is illustrated by the centralization of human relations functions in personnel departments. As an executive has written:

"By centralizing the personnel function in a personnel department, too many people have assumed that you can centralize human relations. That was perhaps the error in the thinking of the production people and general managers who felt that it would be very helpful if we could just put all our personnel headaches into one hat and let somebody else worry about them for all of us. And it did bring some measure of relief to many production people. But I am not sure that the process helped human relations. The personnel function is by no means a one-man function or a one-department function."[11]

The centralization of the purchasing function presents similar difficulties. The purchasing department is usually in a better position to evaluate the alternative ways for meeting a requirement than are the departments that use the materials. But, as one purchasing executive has said, it "should not necessarily have the authority to over-rule the experience and judgment of those who use materials."[12] Where should the line be drawn? Under what circumstances should the purchasing department be permitted to modify or change specifications designated by the using departments? Who should have the final word on the determination of the quality of the items requested on a requisition? The final verdict on specifications and quality generally comes from production and other user departments, with purchasing having the right to question specifications, but the nature of this relationship differs from company to company. Similar peripheral problems are present in many other areas. Credit departments sometimes experience jurisdictional difficulties with sales departments; manufacturing and production control departments have disagreements

[10]Ibid.

[11]Glenn Gardiner, "The Operating Executive and the Personnel Department," *Personnel Functions and the Line Organization*, Personnel Series No. 121 (New York: American Management Association, 1948), pp. 3–4.

[12]R. C. Moffitt, *Purchasing*, Technical Paper No. 138 (New York: United States Steel Corporation), p. 8.

over their respective responsibilities for production scheduling; and public relations, advertising, and sales promotion departments experience similar difficulties.

INTERDEPARTMENTAL COORDINATION

The problem of achieving coordination among functional departments has been a recurring subject of discussion in management circles.[13] Much of the work of the organization flows across functionally differentiated departmental lines with each department contributing some portion of the total activity necessary to achieve the organizational objective. Implicit in these ideas are two potentially conflicting forces. On the one hand, the responsibility of a departmental executive is the successful accomplishment of a functional objective. By pursuing his departmental interests, the executive serves the interests of the organization, but the two interests are not always compatible. Under such circumstances, a subordination of departmental interests to organizational interests becomes necessary. However, the balance should not be tipped too far in this direction as Urwick has so aptly noted.

"Many people argue that the departmental manager should subordinate his departmental point of view to the good of the whole. That is nonsense. Either his department has no excuse for existence or its point of view is *needed in the whole*. It must be reconciled with all the other points of view involved, but it must not be abandoned. Men should never be encouraged to de-departmentalise themselves. They should be taught to inter-departmentalise themselves."[14]

Interest Conflicts

Conflicts of interests among functional departments are not uncommon. Sales executives are inclined to promise delivery dates that cannot be met by production or to approve customer-initiated design changes that cause production difficulties. Production executives sometimes fail to appreciate that customer demands cannot be ignored if the company is to survive. Sales personnel may make sales even when they involve considerable credit risk. The credit executive, on the other hand, is generally more interested in keeping down bad debt losses than in an additional customer. The safety engineering department's effort to reduce hazards is often considered to be unreasonable by production executives.

[13]For example: Henry H. Farquhar, "The Anomaly of Functional Authority at the Top," *Advanced Management*, Vol. 7, No. 2, April–June 1942, pp. 51–54, 83; *Personnel Functions and the Line Organization*, Personnel Series No. 121, pp. 3–12; *Coordination between Engineering, Production and Sales*, Production Series No. 193 (New York: American Management Association, 1950), pp. 10–20; L. Urwick, *The Load on Top Management—Can It Be Reduced?* (London: Urwick, Orr & Partners Ltd., 1954), pp. 26–32.

[14]L. Urwick, *The Elements of Administration* (New York: Harper & Brothers Publishers, 1943), p. 115. (Italics in the original.)

Interest conflicts are frequently founded in differences about how best to achieve the organizational objective. Urwick has emphasized that different functions always involve different points of view.[15] Nothing much would be accomplished if there were no difference of opinion. An absence of internal conflict is not necessarily a good sign, but the line between constructive disagreement and destructive dissension is sometimes difficult to draw.

Personal Conflicts

When executives are primarily motivated by self-interest, interdepartmental differences can become a serious obstacle to effective action. A sales executive who seeks only to make a good impression upon the chief executive, irrespective of the difficulties he creates for other departments, is generally a detriment. His desire to break sales records may cause him to accept orders that cannot be fitted into the production schedule and then blame the production executive for failures to meet delivery schedules. Although some such propensities are the property of humans generally, they cannot dominate the scene without doing serious damage. Functional departmentation is probably more susceptible to this kind of problem than other types of departmentation. The difficulty of defining jurisdiction and pinpointing responsibility makes a fertile field for personal conflict. A further aggravating factor is the narrow perspective of some functional specialists.

FUNCTIONALIZATION VERSUS UNITY OF COMMAND

Frederick W. Taylor introduced functional foremanship at the Midvale Steel Company in the early 1880s. This experience convinced him that functional foremanship should be considered an important principle in management. His views on the matter were presented in *Shop Management*, which was originally published in 1903.

"Throughout the whole field of management the military type of organization should be abandoned, and what may be called the "functional type" substituted in its place. . . . If practicable the work of each man in the management should be confined to the performance of a single leading function."[16]

Under the Taylor plan, workers were subject to the dictates of as many as five foremen on different functional matters. Such a differentiation of managerial responsibility may not cause serious difficulties if coordination occurs at a level not too far removed from the foreman level. Taylor assumed that this would take place, but he envisioned a more complete functionalization of management. Only a few years after Taylor announced his plan, Henri Fayol wrote that it is "dangerous to allow the idea to gain ground that unity of com-

---

[15]Urwick, *Top Management*, pp. 26–30.
[16]Frederick W. Taylor, *Shop Management* (New York: Harper & Brothers, 1911), p. 99.

mand is unimportant and can be violated with impunity."[17] More recent critics have lamented the extent of functionalization, particularly at the upper levels of the hierarchy.[18] Urwick has this to say on the subject:

"When the principle is applied at higher levels where the sense of unity is less, where personal contact is not so close and real differences of outlook and emphasis inevitable and desirable, the chief executive is apt to be overwhelmed with problems of co-ordination."[19]

A number of solutions have been given to the unity of command problem. An oft-used arrangement is a line-staff system that retains many of the advantages of functional specialization without violating unity of command. Under such a system, functional departments and executives perform activities in a staff relationship to the operating departments. Some companies have product or territorial operating departments and facilitating functional staff and service departments. Formal committees are also used to improve coordination and develop interfunctional communication. The sections that follow give comprehensive consideration to these organizational techniques.

PRODUCT DEPARTMENTATION

Products can be used for departmentation purposes in many companies. Some product departments are multifunctional in the sense that they encompass the major functions, such as production, marketing, sales, personnel, and purchasing. In other cases, a company may have a product structure with the exception of one or more functional areas, such as finance or sales. Product may also be used to further departmentalize sales, purchasing, production, and other functional departments. Some organizations are exclusively in the business of producing services, and in others, services represent an aspect of product producing and selling activities. Different kinds of services can become the basis for departmentation in the manner of product departmentation.

PRODUCT-FUNCTIONAL COMBINATIONS

Some departments involve a fusion of product and functional departmentation. The basic operating units of a department store, for example, result from a product differentation of the merchandising function. Each of these departments handles a particular line of merchandise, such as home furnishings, shoes, apparel, and linens. Department managers, usually called buyers, are responsible for both the buying and selling functions. Production departments frequently manufacture different products, subassemblies, and parts in separate plants. The purchase of such items as steel, glass, and specialized equip-

---

[17]Fayol, *General and Industrial Management*, pp. 69–70.
[18]For example: Farquhar, op. cit.; Urwick, *Top Management*, pp. 26–32.
[19]Urwick, ibid., p. 28.

ment is often departmentalized in large purchasing departments. Industrial, consumer, and other product categories are used in the departmentation of the sales function. Research and development activities are often conducted on a product-project basis.

COORDINATION ADVANTAGES

Some people contend that product departmentation at higher levels can reduce the coordination problems of functional departmentation. A functional perspective is assumed to be more disruptive to a unity of purpose than a product perspective.[20] Also important is that product departmentation provides interfunctional coordination centers at lower levels of the hierarchy. This idea is illustrated in Figure 7-5, which shows alternative structures for a firm producing two products. In the functional structure the chief executive is faced with the problem of coordinating sales and production for both products A and B. In the product structure these functions are coordinated by the executives who head the product departments. However, these alternatives are not available to every company. Some companies are not large enough for functional specialization in more than one structure. The lack of a diversified

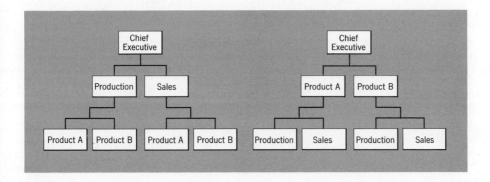

FIGURE 7-5. Alternative structures for a company with two products.

20Urwick, *Top Management*, p. 32.

product line or a product that can be divided into distinct subassemblies and parts is another limiting factor. But as Urwick has emphasized, a company does not have to be as large as General Motors to organize on a product basis.[21]

CONTROL ADVANTAGES

Product departmentation may facilitate the measurement and evaluation of managerial and operating performance. Revenues and costs can generally be more readily differentiated and assigned in a product than a functional structure. Market and profit criteria can be directly applied in product departments that incorporate the major functions of an independent company. Another advantage of product departmentation is that an unprofitable department can be dropped with less disruption to the rest of the organization. Product differentiation within functional departments may also help pinpoint responsibility for particular difficulties.

EXECUTIVE DEVELOPMENT

A product department provides an excellent training and proving ground for executive personnel. The problems of many multifunctional product departments are much like those of a complete company. The top executives of such departments gain a diversity of functional experience, which seems to be generally more important than a diversity of product experience. Functional executives are sometimes too inclined toward the perspective of their specialization after they become chief executives. However, such an orientation may be appropriate under certain circumstances. A cigarette company, for example, may prefer a president who thinks like an advertising executive.

TERRITORIAL DEPARTMENTATION

Territorial departmentation is frequently used when the activities of an organization are dispersed over a wide area. However, the fact that an organization is dispersed territorially does not mean that departmentation is territorial. All types of departments occupy different physical locations, which does not make all departmentation territorial. Departmentation is territorial only when location is the primary consideration in defining and differentiating executive responsibility.

THE NATURE OF TERRITORIAL DEPARTMENTS

As in product departmentation, territorial departmentation can be used to divide larger organizations into relatively self-sufficient units. Grocery, drug, and department chain stores, local telephone exchanges, and branch banks exemplify such departmentation. Territorial differentiations may also be used

[21]Ibid., p. 31.

to further subdivide functional and product departments. Different spatial spheres of managerial responsibility are often appropriate for different functions. A manufacturing company may organize territorial departments that include the functions of manufacturing, engineering, personnel, and accounting but develop a sales organization with different boundaries. In other instances, a number of functions, such as purchasing, sales, and production, may use different territorial delineations. A similar situation frequently prevails within a particular functional field. The sales manager in a metropolitan location may have a small territory compared to the manager in the wide open spaces of the western plains.

TERRITORIAL SPECIALIZATION

Little emphasis has been given in the management literature to territorial specialization. As Chester I. Barnard points out, "the 'same kind' of work is always different when the location is different."[22] Knowledge of the local environment is an important element in effective managerial action.

Operations can be greatly affected by climatic conditions in different geographical regions. The problems faced on a construction project in Minnesota during the winter differ from those of a similar project in Alabama. Operating a bus line in an area with heavy snowfall presents problems not encountered in a warm climate. The impact of climate on military operations is illustrated by the Russian campaigns of Napoleon and Hitler; the planning and command problems in the deserts of North Africa or the jungles of Viet Nam are significantly different. The problems of operating a railroad or a trucking line in a mountainous area are not the same as those in a plains area.

Variations in the culture of different areas make for differences in managerial problems. Chain department stores are faced with dissimilarities in consumer preferences in various areas. Bikini bathing suits may sell like hotcakes in a "sophisticated" metropolitan community but not in the domain of the "bible belt." Specialty foods, such as rattlesnake meat, generally have a good market in areas infested with gourmets, but few sales are made in a "meat and potato" region. Business practices are also affected by similar factors. Businessmen have reported, for example, that sending out monthly statements is not well received by customers in some areas.

DEPARTMENTATION BASED ON TIME

Departmentation can result from the fact that work is performed during different periods of time. When a company operates on a three-shift basis, a "department" is not one but three departments, although they all may be alike in terms of objectives and activities. It should be noted in this respect that

---

[22]Chester I. Barnard, *The Functions of the Executive* (Cambridge: Harvard University Press, 1951), p. 129.

people often "specialize" on the basis of time. Someone who has always worked during the day shift will experience difficulties in adjusting to night work. Similar adaptations are necessary in traveling by jet aircraft through several time zones; the term jet-lag is used to denote this phenomenon.

EQUIPMENT DEPARTMENTATION

A heat-treat furnace or an electronic computer can give rise to a separate department, particularly when the equipment is required by a number of departments and cannot be duplicated for economic reasons. Such departmentation may also result because the equipment cannot be placed in the physical area occupied by the user department. Heavy equipment cannot always be installed on the second or third floor of a factory or office building. The difficulties of supervising personnel from a distance may justify an additional departmental unit. The specialized skill required to operate some equipment is another contributing factor.

ALPHA-NUMERICAL DEPARTMENTATION

This method is frequently used at lower levels of the hierarchy. Telephone companies divide work by a series of telephone numbers, personnel records departments use alphabetical differentiations, and accounts receivable sections allocate responsibilities by number or alphabet. Alpha-numerical departmentation is not as simple as it sounds and can present difficult problems under certain circumstances. An alphabetical system, for example, does not always result in even workloads when the number of persons so classified increase or decrease because sampling techniques do not always provide the right distributions. Although numbers offer greater flexibility than the alphabet, changes that may occur in the problems of people so categorized can lead to unequal workloads. For example, the amount of work represented by the early numbers in a series used to identify customers may change because long-time customers often have different problems and attitudes than newcomers.

FUNCTIONAL, PRODUCT, TERRITORIAL, AND OTHER COMBINATIONS

The responsibilities of executives may involve several types of departmentation. An executive may be responsible for the *production* of a particular *product* within a given *territory*. Actual departments cannot generally be neatly divided into the categories found in this chapter. The nature of the contents placed into a filing case does not always correspond to the system that has been planned. There does not seem to be one best pattern of departmentation even in similar situations; companies have solved the problem in a variety of ways with what are probably equally good results.

8

LINE-STAFF-FUNCTIONAL AND OTHER STRUCTURAL RELATIONSHIPS

This chapter is initially concerned with the nature of line, staff, and functional relationships and the manner in which they relate to the management process. The analysis then turns to centralization and decentralization and their importance in performing managerial functions. In the final sections, the contributions that can be made by committee organization are evaluated and the managerial functions of boards of directors are explored.

Line-Staff-Functional Relationships

Staff assistants are often employed to help executives with their work; staff departments perform facilitating functions for operating departments. The difference between line and staff relationships is that line executives have command prerogatives and staff personnel does not. However, as will be shown later in this chapter, staff may do everything except command and may exert a large amount of influence. The staff concept makes possible the utilization of functional specialists without violating unity of command. To quote one writer on the subject: "Specialists are necessary, but 'they should be on tap—not on top.'"[1] The military has always recognized the importance of maintaining unity of command in combat units. Staff personnel is attached to each position to assist the commander in the exercise of his responsibilities.

[1]Henry H. Farquhar, "The Anomaly of Functional Authority at the Top," *Advanced Management*, Vol. 7, No. 2, April–June 1942, p. 51.

FUNCTIONS OF THE MILITARY STAFF

The staff officers of a military unit assist the commander in the performance of his command responsibilities. Paraphrasing Urwick, ostensibly the staff officer provides only information, yet he makes all the arrangements that enable the fighting forces to perform their duties with the maximum of unity and the minimum of friction.[2] The staff officer commands no one, yet he assists the commander to command everyone. More specifically, military staffs

". . . perform the basic functions of procuring information for the commander, preparing details of his plans, translating his decisions and plans into orders and then causing the orders to be transmitted to the troops. It is also . . . the duty of the staff to bring to the commander's attention any matters which require his action, or about which he should be informed, and make a continuous study of the existing situation and prepare tentative plans for possible future action. Another important function of the staff officer is to supervise the execution of plans and orders and to carry out the commander's intentions."[3]

The commander and his staff should be viewed as a single entity relative to other commands in the military hierarchy. Each command acts as a coordinated unit in the name of the commander and the command headquarters.

The military staff function is a unified and coordinated function. The commander is not surrounded by autonomous staff advisors whose activities and counsel he must constantly evaluate and supervise. Such a staff might well be a hindrance instead of a help. All staff activities are channeled through section chiefs who coordinate the staff work within their respective functional areas. The chief of staff coordinates, directs, and supervises the activities of the entire staff and assigns the staff responsibilities necessary to implement the orders of the commander.

COMPLETED STAFF ACTION

The function of the staff is to provide the commander with answers, not to plague him with questions. Staff activities are organized in the manner of an assembly line; the product is *completed staff action*, which is presented to the commander for approval or disapproval.

STAFF SUPERVISION

A frequent misconception about the staff function is that it is restricted to informational, planning, and advisory activities. As was pointed out above,

[2]L. Urwick, "Organization as a Technical Problem," *Papers on the Science of Administration* (New York: Institute of Public Administration, 1937), p. 63.

[3]J. D. Hittle (Lt. Col.), *The Military Staff* (Harrisburg, Pa.: The Military Service Publishing Company [now The Stackpole Company], 1949), pp. 2–3.

the military staff provides the commander with completed staff action. Every detail required to implement a given course of action is worked out by the staff. But the process does not end with the completion of operational orders. The staff also supervises the execution of the orders issued in the name of the commander. The staff sees to it that the intent of the commander is carried out by subordinate and related commands and makes recommedations for modifications and elaborations when needed to cope with unforeseen and unusual circumstances. Supervision should be placed high on the list of basic staff responsibilities. A badly executed plan is tantamount to having no plan at all. The plans of mice and men go most often astray because the doing that is planned is not done.

LINE AND STAFF RELATIONSHIPS

Many half-truths about the line and staff relationship have been perpetuated by nonoperational definitions. The idea that the line officer commands and the staff officer does not command affords little enlightenment about the relationship. Although a line commander is formally required to respond only to commands from a superior line commander, he obviously cannot ignore the superior's staff officers. Suggestions from higher echelon staff officers are rarely taken lightly. Every line commander knows that he is subject to the commands of the staff officer's headquarters and that a staff officer's suggestion can be followed by a formal order in the name of the superior commander. Even a staff officer of low rank may have considerable actual "authority" if he comes from high headquarters.

The line commander subjects himself to possible reversal when he refuses to deal reasonably with the superior's staff officers. But the staff officer faces a similar consequence if he fails to conduct himself properly. The staff officer does not have to respond to the orders of a subordinate line commander, but he may be reversed by his commander. The relationship tends to promote cooperation because a lack of cooperation can have undesirable consequences for both the line and staff officer. In actual practice the superior line commander is rarely forced to resolve differences between his staff and a subordinate commander. When such difficulties do arise, they are generally settled informally.

STAFF FUNCTIONALISM

Staff organization found at different command levels is dissimilar in many respects, but the basic staff functions are found in some form at all command levels. The functional pattern found in lower command staffs follows that of higher staffs. Such staff functions as supply (logistics), intelligence, and operations are found at all levels in the hierarchy. At lower levels staff functions are frequently performed on a part-time basis by regular line officers, who may have a number of different staff responsibilities.

Although the formal rules governing line and staff relationships are generally observed, a great deal of interaction along functional lines occurs between staff specialists at different levels in the command hierarchy. Formal and informal contacts are made through staff visits, inspections, and conferences. Much of the written communication between different headquarters is channeled along functional lines. Reports from a subordinate to a higher headquarters are usually sent directly to the appropriate staff officer by the message control center.

Line, Staff, and Functional Relationships in Business Organizations

Military staff organization provides interfunctional coordination at every decision-making center in the hierarchy. It preserves unity of command without sacrificing the advantages of functional specialization. Many business organizations, faced with jurisdictional and coordination problems among functional executives, have turned to prototypes of the military staff system.

STAFF ASSISTANTS

Part of the burden of an executive position can be reduced by clerical, technical, and administrative assistants. An important facilitating position is that of the private secretary, who generally assumes responsibility for planning and supervising the routine clerical work of an executive office. Many executives report that their secretaries keep track of business engagements and appointments, answer routine letters in their names, and decide who is going to talk to them over the telephone.[4] Some secretaries buy the boss' shirts, theater and football tickets, and write checks for his personal bills. A similar type of assistance is given by clerical and stenographic personnel. An efficient filing clerk assures the availability of important letters and reports when needed by the executive. A receptionist helps maintain control over the executive's personal contacts. An efficient office force familiar with the routine work of the executive position may frequently mark the difference between efficient and inefficient executive performance.

Many other types of staff assistance can be noted. A ghost writer may be extremely helpful to an executive who has to give many speeches; an attorney may be retained to advise on legal matters; a budget expert may be hired to assume responsibility for budgetary planning and control; an economist may be added to help appraise immediate and long-term economic prospects. Sometimes an executive delegates a variety of duties to general administrative assistants. The addition of staff assistants does not increase the number of decision-making positions in the management hierarchy. However, it does in-

[4]*Fortune*, Vol. 34, No. 4, October 1946, p. 14.

crease the number of individuals who perform the major and minor tasks that make up executive work.

THE PURE LINE-STAFF RELATIONSHIP

The line-staff relationship in business organizations is not always maintained with the formality of the military system. Business staff assistants are frequently permitted to give instructions and recommendations in their own names to subordinate line executives. Their responsibilities and relationships are usually not as rigidly defined as those of the military staff. Such departures from the formal doctrine do not alter the situation as long as line and staff executives understand the line-staff relationship and act accordingly.

A MODIFIED LINE-STAFF ORGANIZATION

Some confusion exists in making distinctions between line and staff in business organizations. Personnel managers, purchasing agents, budget directors, and comptrollers are sometimes called staff personnel when they are in fact line executives.[5] The functional nature of their decision-making responsibilities does not necessarily make them staff. Functional executives may be staff, line, or a combination of the two. They are staff when they act as a representative of a superior in dealing with subordinate executives. They may have a line status with respect to the affairs of their own departments and, at the same time, serve in a staff capacity in relation to other departments. They may also have some functional decision-making prerogatives that cut across departmental lines.

FUNCTIONAL LINE-STAFF RELATIONSHIPS

A functional structure gives each executive decision-making responsibilities over a functional area, such as sales, production, personnel, purchasing, and finance. Under such an arrangement subordinate personnel is frequently subject to the decisions of several executives. The first step toward a line-staff organization is taken when functional executives are given exclusive decision-making prerogatives over activities and personnel in their departments. Such a change restricts the decision-making jurisdiction of functional executives and creates a dual line and staff role. Each executive has line prerogatives within his own department; he functions in a staff capacity in dealing with personnel in other departments.

The major operating departments, such as production and sales, are often formally designated as line departments, and executives in charge of these departments as line executives. A staff designation is frequently given to per-

[5]Luther Gulick, "Notes on the Theory of Organization," *Papers on the Science of Administration* (New York: Institute of Public Administration, Columbia University, 1937), p. 31.

sonnel, accounting, organization, and budgetary control departments and executives. Such formal descriptions do not change the basic functional line-staff relationships defined in the previous paragraph. Staff departments are frequently so designated because most of their activities involve personnel in the operating or line departments toward whom they function in a staff capacity. For example, personnel executives spend most of their time with people in other departments; production and sales executives are chiefly involved with people in their own departments, a line relationship. It should be noted that executives from line departments function in a staff capacity when they deal with subordinates in a staff department.

Operating executives generally assert the need for full decision-making prerogatives over the activities and personnel of their departments. There is a danger, however, in placing these executives in too dominant a position. If the counsel of staff executives is constantly ignored, the advantages of functional specialization may be lost. The staff executive must have an effective communication channel to the superior line executive and an opportunity to gain line support for his program. The proper execution of such a relationship inhibits line myopia to staff suggestions without eliminating unity of command.

FUNCTIONAL DECISION MAKING BY STAFF EXECUTIVES

Functional executives, who occupy an essentially staff status, may retain some decision-making prerogatives over the affairs of operating departments. For example, college-trained technical personnel are frequently hired on a company-wide basis by a centralized personnel department. Such a delegation of decision-making prerogatives to staff executives may present some of the coordination and control difficulties discussed in Chapter 7. The problem is to maintain a proper balance between the advantages of functional decision making and the need to preserve unity of command in operating departments.

Business executives have not always appreciated the possibilities inherent in a military-type line-staff organization. The staff relationship, when properly executed, does not preclude the delegation of almost all the responsibilities of an executive position. The superior executive need only give a formal stamp of approval to the arrangements worked out by the staff. The personal intervention of the superior is needed only when staff and line executives cannot resolve their differences.

How does the delegation of functional decision-making prerogatives change the basic staff relationship? The pure staff system gives line executives direct access to the superior executive on all problems that arise between them and the superior's staff. Subordinate line executives do not have such access on those matters over which the staff executives are given decision-making prerogatives. Any direct communication with the superior is equivalent to skipping a level in the hierarchy. In other words, staff executives become duly constituted superiors over some functional activities. Although the line executive may theoretically appeal to a higher level, such action is not as feasible from a practical point of view. Ignoring a superior and "skipping levels" is not usually considered the best way to please the superior executive who did the delegating in the first instance. The delegation of functional decision-making prerogatives may provide greater release from certain responsibilities. The superior may feel that an exclusively staff basis obligates him to give some personal attention to the arrangements made by staff executives. But if carried to an extreme, functional decision making can destroy the unity of command present in the pure line-staff system.

PRODUCT, TERRITORIAL, AND FUNCTIONAL LINE-STAFF RELATIONSHIPS

The managerial structures of many business organizations incorporate the advantages of two or more types of departmentation. The basic operating departments or divisions are generally organized on a product or a territorial basis with operating executives reporting directly to an executive vice-president or the chief executive. A second group of major executives is composed of functional specialists in production, engineering, personnel, public relations, research, and other functions. These executives, frequently called general staff executives, report to the chief executive or to an executive who serves as the chief of staff. Such a managerial structure offers the coordination and control advantages of product or territorial departmentation in the operating part of the organization. At the same time, the knowledge of the functional specialist is made available to top management and the operating executives.

Managerial Relationships in Perspective

An important organizational problem is to strike a proper balance between the unity of command principle and the equally important need for managerial specialization. The military has generally given priority to the unity of command principle. The need for specialized advice and services has been met through a highly efficient staff system. Business organizations have been more inclined to give decision-making prerogatives to functional specialists. However, the problems of overlapping spheres of responsibility, jurisdictional controversy, and coordination difficulties have caused many business organizations to adopt some kind of a line and staff management structure. The result has generally been a modified line and staff structure that retains some of the features of a functionally differentiated managerial structure, but at the same time assures a significant degree of unity of command in the operating units.

STAFF MUST BE USED

A line and staff organization cannot effectively serve the need for specialized knowledge if operating executives ignore the counsel of staff executives. An important reason for the success of the Prussian staff system was the requirement that the commander give full consideration to the recommendations of the staff. The following quotation from an RCA publication on managerial relationships also gives explicit attention to the problem: "It is the duty of every line executive to use staff services to best advantage in planning, directing, controlling and improving his operations."[6] The staff cannot become an effective instrument of management action without the cooperation and support of the line.

FUNCTIONAL DECISION MAKING AND UNITY OF COMMAND

A modification of the pure line and staff relationship by giving functional decision-making prerogatives to staff executives gives recognition to certain functional activities. It assumes that the functional specialist should play a primary role with respect to these matters, even though the unity of command principle is violated in some degree. How much functional decision making is too much? The theory of organization does not offer a precise answer to this question. Organizational practice indicates that a significant amount of functional decision making can occur without seriously disrupting unity of command. The use of coordination centers at each level of the management hierarchy seems to provide an important safeguard against the difficulties that sometimes accompany functionally differentiated decision making. See Figure 8-1. A clear definition of functions and relationships also serves a useful purpose in this respect.

THE PROBLEM OF ATTITUDE

Operating executives are prone to regard the activities of staff executives with aversion. They sometimes feel that staff executives are barriers between them and their superior. Such an attitude may be reinforced if the superior appears overzealous in his support of staff recommendations. Another frequently expressed view is that staff executives are "ivory-tower" planners who do not understand the problems of operating departments. The fact that such attitudes are often a product of the imagination does not make the problem less difficult.

The staff should not constantly seek the support of the superior line executive to overcome resistance from operating executives. The function of the staff is to make the arrangements and solicit the cooperation of subordinate executives. Constant appeal to the superior increases his work load and re-

[6]*The RCA Organizational Realignment* (New York: Radio Corporation of America, 1954), p. 10.

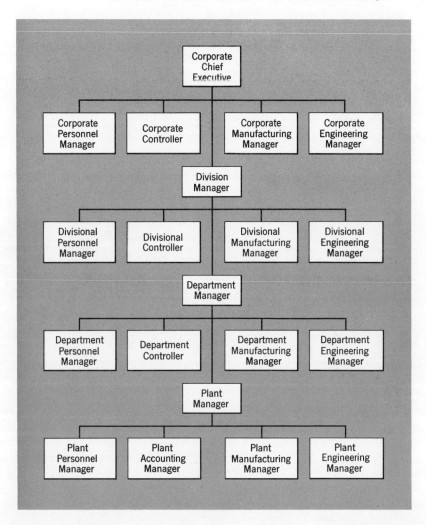

FIGURE 8-1. A simplified functional structure with coordination at each hierarchical level.

pudiates the role that the staff should play. Many barriers to line and staff cooperation can be overcome by good human relations on the part of the staff. The staff executive cannot approach the operating executive like a bull in the china shop and expect to get anywhere. He should not assume that opposition to his ideas always results from a closed mind. Skepticism is not a synonym of of stupidity. The staff executive must be willing to sell his ideas and show the operating executives how he can solve their problems; he must also sell himself as a person. He must convince operating executives that he is interested in *their* welfare. He must frequently subordinate his normal desire for recognition by giving credit for success to the operating executives.

The superior also has a responsibility for the development of good line and staff relationships. He should not hesitate to support or to restrain his staff or operating executives whenever constructive differences of opinion begin to deteriorate into internecine warfare. He should not be content to sit back and let them fight it out. A policy of "let them read my mind" may be a good sport, but it hardly helps mold constructive organizational behavior. Frequent intervention is generally not necessary, but when it does occur it should be positive and clearly understood by all parties concerned.

SERVICE AND AUXILIARY FUNCTIONS

The establishment of staff relationships generally results in a grouping of activities. Staff executives are not isolated individuals who assist in the performance of the management function; they frequently manage personnel who provide a service to the basic operating departments. For example, the intelligence officer of the army general staff conducts intelligence operations, and the styling section of the General Motors Corporation is actively engaged in styling activities for the operating divisions.

A distinction is generally made between the departments engaged in primary operating activities and auxiliary or service departments. This kind of classification reflects the different values assigned to the various activities performed in the organization. Such functions as production and marketing are generally accorded higher status than personnel, research and development, purchasing, and budgeting. Although the success of the organization is closely related to the efficiency of the primary operating departments, the auxiliary departments also play a vital role. The activities of the personnel department often mark the difference between good and bad labor relations. A long strike can cost millions of dollars in sales and significantly affect the ability of the organization to survive in a competitive market. The failure to keep up with styling trends or to advance in the field of research and engineering may have equally fatal consequences. The appearance of functional decision making within the framework of a line and staff organization is partly explained by the importance of some activities to the organization. The result is both a centralization of decision making and a grouping of particular functional activities.

Centralization and Decentralization

Centralization and decentralization describe the manner in which decision-making responsibilities are divided among managers at different levels of the managerial hierarchy. They are concerned with the extent to which higher managers delegate important responsibilities to lower levels. The problem of decentralization is essentially the problem of delegation.

THE PROCESS OF DELEGATION: PROBLEMS AND LIMITATIONS

Delegation becomes necessary when the work load of an executive position exceeds the physical and psychological capacity of the executive. The delegation process reduces the executive work load, but it also adds to the work load by increasing the number of subordinates or span of management. This process can continue until the work load that evolves from an increasing span of management exceeds the executive's capacity to carry the burden. Additional levels of management become necessary when this limit is reached.

The superior's responsibility is not absolved by the act of delegation. Delegation involves taking a risk on the capability of subordinates. This risk cannot be entirely avoided, but it can be mitigated by exercising some degree of supervision over the activities of the subordinate. Decentralization is greater or less to the extent that executives are willing to delegate important decision-making responsibilities and exercise a minimum of supervision and control.

An important argument for greater decentralization is the need to develop initiative and self-reliance among subordinates. Many executives believe that the subordinate should be constantly challenged by greater responsibility. Sears, Roebuck and Company has deliberately followed a policy of creating long spans of management, which forces greater delegation and restricts the amount of supervision. Such a policy gives the executive more freedom of action and throws him on his own resources. It tends to weed out those who do not have the necessary potential and promotes the development of experienced and dynamic executives.

The extent to which a policy of decentralization can be carried out may be limited by the personality of the executive. The psychological makeup of some executives inhibits their willingness to delegate decision-making prerogatives. Henry Ford, Sr., for example, felt that he had to fit every piece into the puzzle. Having built a "billion dollar" corporation from a very humble beginning, he disliked giving anyone else a part of what he considered to be a "one-man show." He delegated decision-making responsibilities in the most haphazard fashion and frequently reversed subordinates without consulting them.

A refusal to delegate may also be prompted by the degree of risk involved. As Ernest Dale has written, "hard times and increased competition may foster centralization."[7] The organization's ability to absorb a mistake by a subordinate may be greatly reduced under such circumstances. As a consequence, the top executives may exercise more decision-making prerogatives than would otherwise be necessary and increase the extent to which subordinates are supervised.

The lack of competent executives frequently explains a reluctance to delegate. Although decentralization often enhances the development of executive

[7] Ernest Dale, "Centralization Versus Decentralization," *Advanced Management,* Vol. 20, No. 6, June 1955, p. 13.

talent, it is not always possible to make a silk purse out of a sow's ear. A policy of decentralization, even under the most favorable circumstances, cannot be implemented overnight. Some executives do not have the ability to assume additional responsibility and have to be gradually removed through the retirement system or induced resignation. Younger executives generally require extensive supervision by experienced superiors before they can be given more responsibility.

COORDINATION AND CONTROL

As was pointed out earlier in this chapter, decentralization always involves some degree of centralized planning and control. Every level of management below the chief executive is subject to decisions made at a higher level. Such an arrangement is necessary to coordinate activities and to achieve an organizational unity of purpose. The freedom of action given to executives through decentralization is always restricted. The executive is on his own, but never completely. His situation is similar to that of the driver of an automobile on a public highway, who may drive as he pleases within the limits set by traffic regulations. Decentralization diminishes the amount of direct supervision exercised by a superior over the activities of a subordinate, but this reduction in personal supervision is replaced by other forms of control, such as budgetary, profit, and cost controls. Such controls are an essential feature of decentralization; without them there would be far less inclination to delegate important decision-making prerogatives.

EXECUTIVE DEVELOPMENT

Industrial and business leaders have often lamented the dearth of executive material, yet a part of the responsibility for this situation must be placed on their doorsteps. Too many executives have failed to see that a puppet can never become a puppeteer. The experience of recent wars indicates the existence of a large reservoir of potential leadership material. A large part of military leadership below the division level came from men who were barely out of their teens. Many of these youthful company, battalion, and regimental commanders were eminently successful in the discharge of great responsibility. To be sure, considerable risk was involved in such an extensive delegation of decision-making prerogatives to an inexperienced officer corps, and some officers did not have the capacity for the responsibility imposed upon them. Failures as well as successes must be placed on the scoreboard, but the overall results probably exceeded expectations.

The experience of industrial establishments with a history of decentralization has been similar to that of the military. Although formal training is an important factor in executive development, experience molds the final product and gives a subordinate a chance to prove that he can make the grade. A willingness to risk delegation to lower levels reduces the hazards of promotion and helps provide a reservoir of qualified executives. It also helps indicate which executives do not have the capacity to assume greater responsibility.

MANAGERIAL SPECIALIZATION

Centralization is sometimes favored because it permits a higher degree of managerial specialization. This argument undoubtedly has validity in the case of small enterprise. The advantages of specialization are generally greater than the disadvantages that may evolve from a higher degree of centralization. However, the net advantages that may be derived from specialization diminish rather rapidly as the size of the firm is increased. The coordination, control, and communication difficulties that tend to accompany centralized decision making by functional specialists are important elements in reversing the process. Large organizations have generally turned to product and territorial departmentation and decentralization to solve the problems of overspecialization. Many medium-sized and some small firms, as Urwick has suggested, can benefit from greater decentralization along similar lines.[8] An integral part of such a decentralization program has been the development of functional staff and service departments to advise and assist those who make the decisions. However, it should not be assumed that all centralized decision making by functional specialists has been eliminated. The most avid practitioners of decentralization on a product or territorial basis have retained important functional decision-making prerogatives at the top management level. A reason is that some forms of specialization become possible only in large organizations. Also, the point of decreasing returns from specialization is not reached at the same time in all areas of managerial decision making.

Committee Organization

A committee may be defined as a group of people engaged in the performance of some aspect of the executive function. Committees may be used for informational and advisory purposes, to promote coordination, and to facilitate communication and cooperation. Some committees, which are often referred to as plural executives, exercise decision-making responsibilities.

A survey of executive attitudes on the subject of committee organization might well lead to the frustrating conclusion that committees must be the worst and the best means to achieve a goal. One side of the argument is illustrated by such comments as: the best committee is a three-man committee with two men absent; minutes are taken, but hours are wasted. In spite of such

[8]L. Urwick, *The Load on Top Management—Can It Be Reduced?* (London: Urwick, Orr & Partners, Ltd., 1954), pp. 30–31.

criticism, committees are found in many organizations and, when properly used, are important instruments of managerial action.

The Nature of Committees

Organizational practices indicate a variety of committee types and purposes. Some committees are a formally constituted part of the managerial structure with duly designated functions, procedures, and membership. Other committees are little more than informal gatherings of executives to discuss whatever subjects seem appropriate at the time. Committees cannot always be readily distinguished from the informal interactions that occur among executives; many organizations have the equivalent of a committee system through informal meetings.

INFORMAL "COMMITTEE" ACTION

An informal gathering of executives rarely occurs without some reference to company business. Many organizational problems are solved during coffee breaks, luncheon engagements, golf games, or a round of cocktails. The organizational consequences of such informal meetings and committee meetings may be similar. The difference between the two types of group activities is that the formally designated purpose of a committee is to consider an organizational problem whereas informal meetings evolve from nonorganizational purposes. This distinction frequently involves some fine hairsplitting. A luncheon engagement is a committee meeting if its primary purpose is to discuss company business; it is an informal meeting if its primary purpose is to eat lunch. However, personal and organizational purposes are generally merged and cannot be readily differentiated. Although this section is primarily concerned with formally constituted committees, it recognizes that informal meetings frequently serve an equivalent function.

PERMANENT AND TEMPORARY COMMITTEES

Some committees are permanent; others have a relatively short life-span. Committees may be created for a special purpose and dissolved when their mission has been accomplished. Permanent or standing committees generally perform a continuing and vital managerial function. The life-span of committees is also influenced by the inclinations of their creators. Executives may delay the dissolution of temporary committees by giving them additional assignments. On the other hand, permanent committees can be dissolved and replaced by another organizational device. Committees sometimes have a propensity to perpetuate their own existence, particularly when membership has high status value to the participants.

COMMITTEES AND HIERARCHICAL LEVELS

Committees are used at all levels of the management hierarchy. At the apex of the hierarchy is the board of directors, which is the legally constituted governing body of a corporation. Some boards perform their managerial functions during regular board meetings; others delegate specific prerogatives to special and permanent committees of the board. Committees at the top-management level may also be established by the president and other top-level executives to assist them in the performance of their managerial functions. The extent to which committees are used in the major operating divisions or departments may vary a great deal. Some executives appoint committees at the drop of a hat; others take a negative attitude toward committees. When company policy dictates that committees be used, executives frequently place the imprint of their own personality upon this policy. A few may simply go through the motions and let the committees wither on the vine. At the plant level, joint employee-management and union-management committees are common.

MEETING PLACES AND COMMITTEE PROCEDURES

Committee meetings are held in a variety of physical settings, such as conference rooms, offices, the executive dining room, and the employee cafeteria. Organizations sometimes hold top-level conferences at resort hotels in distant places. A similar diversity can be found in committee procedures and methods of operation. Although most committees have a chairman, the role of the chairman differs a great deal. Some chairmen have only one vote; others have the right to veto committee action; and still others make the final decision after hearing the deliberations of the committee. Committee procedure ranges from strict "Robert's rules of order" methods to a highly informal "talk when you can or have an idea" approach. Some committees require members to submit formal reports on the subject matter under consideration, and others merely require a presence of person and mind. Committees may have a definite membership roll, or they may vary participation with changes in the nature of the problems being considered.

ADVANTAGES AND DISADVANTAGES OF COMMITTEES

An important advantage of committee organization is that it makes possible integrated group judgment. People from different specializations, such as engineering, production, and sales, from different geographical regions, and from different hierarchical levels can be combined to consider a problem. Highly important in this respect is that committees can help bridge departmental lines on matters that involve more than one department. The committee process can also help bring about better management teamwork through the formal and informal interactions to which it gives rise. Subordinate participation can be fostered through committee involvement with possible improvements in morale and performance. The cooperation of such interest groups as creditors, customers, suppliers, labor unions, and stockholders can frequently be facilitated by representation on committees. Still another possible advantage is that younger executives can learn from older experienced executives and gain important insights through committee participation.

The above advantages should be viewed in the light of possible disadvantages. The monetary cost of committees in the form of salaries of the participants and such expenses as travel and lodging should be given careful consideration. The cost of committee deliberations prohibit their use for trivial and routine matters. Too much compromise and indecision, one-man or minority domination of the proceedings, and the problem of making a group accountable are other possible obstacles to effective committee action.

Fundamentals of Effective Committee Operation

The means by which more effective committee action can be achieved are considered in this section.

PLANNING FOR COMMITTEE ACTION

The part that a committee will play in the managerial process should be planned. Committee responsibilities and relationships should be understood by everyone who is directly or indirectly involved. A detailed job description is frequently useful for this purpose. The effectiveness of committees may also be enhanced by the following procedures.

1. A membership list should be maintained together with other pertinent data, such as the dates and conditions of appointment. Each member should be formally notified and informed about his responsibilities.

2. Whenever possible, a schedule of meetings should be planned with the dates, length, time, and place of meeting. The schedule should take into consideration other responsibilities of the participants and the amount of preparation required for a meeting.

3. A carefully prepared agenda can be an exceedingly helpful device. If possible, the agenda and other material, such as reports, recommendations, and proposals, should be made available to committee members well in advance of the meeting. This procedure makes possible a study and appraisal of the matters to be considered. Some members may wish to obtain the opinion and counsel of others before the meeting.

4. The duties of the chairman and committee staff personnel, such as secretaries, should be carefully defined.

5. Provision should be made for maintaining and distributing a record of committee proceedings, recommendations, and decisions.

6. A formal control mechanism should be devised to evaluate the effectiveness of committees. A periodic summary report from the committee chairman on the number of meetings, attendance, man-hours expended, committee progress and accomplishments and other such matters may be useful in this respect.

TYPE OF COMMITTEE MEMBERSHIP

The question of who should be included in the committee membership is closely related to the nature of the committee purpose. A committee that is primarily concerned with informational, advisory, or problem-solving functions should include individuals who have the required knowledge and skills. Thus, if engineering or accounting talent is needed, one or several engineers or accountants should be included. Functional proficiency may not be the primary consideration in selecting membership for a committee designed to promote better coordination or cooperation. A coordinating committee, for example, should include executives from the departments concerned. When the purpose is to promote cooperation, the sociological structure of the organization is an important consideration. An attempt should be made to include informal leaders and provide representation for formal and informal interest groups. The ability of individuals to effectively participate in group activities also warrants attention in making up a committee roster.

THE SIZE OF COMMITTEES

Is there an optimum committee size? How many members are too many or too few? These questions have received a variety of answers, but, as Robert F. Bales of the Harvard Laboratory of Social Relations has pointed out, "so far they seem to come mostly from numerology rather than from scientific research."[9] The question of size is related to such factors as the purpose of the committee and the personalities and participational skills of the members. The optimum size differs under different conditions.

Individuals are never identical; the structure of group interaction may be significantly changed by one individual. Adding individual X may make the group seem large and unwieldy, which might not result if Y and Z, rather than X, were included. In spite of such difficulties, the concept of size should be given consideration. A large committee is not suited for certain types of group action, such as the achievement of a genuine group consensus. But a committee of 50 may not be too large if the primary purpose is to give information to the participants. At the other extreme, a committee can be too small for effective action. For example, a 3-man committee is often unsuitable because "the tendency of two to form a combination against the third seems

[9]Robert F. Bales, "In Conference," *Harvard Business Review*, Vol. 32, No. 2, March–April 1954, p. 48.

fairly strong."[10] The result is frequently a lack of a "healthy" amount of dis-agreement.

EFFECTIVE COMMITTEE PROCEDURES

Why are some committees effective and others not? One approach to this problem is to observe successful committees in action. The experiments conducted by the Laboratory of Social Relations at Harvard University indicate that most successful groups go through three stages in the solution of a problem.[11] First, they attempt to acquire the largest pool of common information about the facts of the situation. During the second stage they make inferences and evaluations and try to form common opinions in a general way. Finally, after an extensive groundwork has been laid, they get around to more specific suggestions and solutions to the problem.

It should not be assumed that an agreement on facts is always easy to achieve. Facts evolve from sensory perceptions, which make them vulnerable to the vagaries of individual interpretation, and they are often clouded by emotional reactions and hearsay. Yet, the accumulation of scientific knowledge assures us that proper methods and attitudes make possible agreement on many matters.

After agreement has been achieved on the essential facts of the situation, every participant should be given adequate opportunity to express his views. Individuals will frequently depart from the facts and express nonlogical sentiments and attitudes. They will express antagonism and harmony, agreement and disagreement, altruism and egotism. Such reactions should be viewed as an integral part of the committee process. They tend to become a deleterious force only if either extreme is permitted to completely dominate the scene. Too much agreement may be as bad as too little agreement, and conversely.[12]

A critical stage in the process occurs when the committee begins to consider specific solutions to the problem. However, the danger of stalemate or stagnation is mitigated if the facts are permitted to cast some light throughout the deliberations. In the words of Robert F. Bales:

"In an environment barren of consensus, only a fact can survive; and, where there is hostility, even facts find a slim foothold. But a rich background of common facts lays the groundwork for the development of common inferences and sentiments, and out of these common decisions can grow. No decision rests on facts alone, but there is no better starting point. To start the decision-making process at any other point is to multiply the risk of a vicious circle of disagreement—and at no saving of time in the long run."[13]

[10]Ibid., pp. 48–49.
[11]Ibid., p. 47.
[12]Ibid., p. 46.
[13]Ibid., p. 47.

THE ROLE OF THE CHAIRMAN

The chairman may play an important facilitating role in the committee process. He can help initiate the proceedings by a carefully worded statement of objectives and promote participation by directing questions to specific committee members. He can frequently lead the group away from digressions that take a great deal of time and go nowhere. A periodic summary by the chairman can help the group crystallize its thinking.

As was pointed out earlier, the chairman should not dominate the group. It is his duty to be impartial and assist the group in achieving a consensus, even though the final outcome differs with his own views. He should respect the opinions of every man on the committee and give each an opportunity to freely express his opinion. He should not put the committee into a "strait jacket" by too many formal procedural requirements. On the other hand, he cannot permit the proceedings to flounder in circumlocution. Effective chairmanship demands a high degree of social manipulative skills. The chairman must lead and yet not seem to be leading. He must be resolute, but never intolerant. He must solicit views with which he may disagree violently. He is frequently forced to intercede when antagonism begins to dominate the scene, but he must be careful not to antagonize the antagonists.

The Board of Directors

A corporation is a legal instrument through which large numbers of people engage in cooperative endeavor. It is a creature of the law with many of the legal rights and privileges of persons, but of course it has no intrinsic human qualities. It is a legal entity apart from the property and persons necessary to bring it into existence. The board of directors provides an important link between the corporation as an inert legal concept and the reality of the corporation as a dynamic phenomenon of human cooperation.

THE BOARD OF DIRECTORS AND THE MANAGERIAL FUNCTION

In spite of the important powers and duties conferred by the law, the boards of directors of some corporations are plural executives in name only. They exist because the law requires it. Actual control is in the hands of the board chairman, a few directors, large minority stockholders, or the operating management. Under such circumstances, the board is little more than a rubber stamp for the controlling interests and has little real voice in the affairs of the enterprise.

The extent to which boards of directors are powerless puppets in managerial affairs cannot be determined with any degree of accuracy. However, the past few years have brought a significant amount of speculation and introspection about the functions of boards of directors. There is evidence that boards are less inclined to be "backseat drivers," particularly in the larger corporation. As John C. Baker concluded in his study of directors and their functions:

"Directors are awakening today to their responsibilities. There is a widespread concern among them to know their functions and a desire to perform them properly. Corporation directors are making exceedingly important contributions to business development, irrespective of the criticisms leveled against them and misunderstandings which have existed."[14]

The question of the role that directors should assume is subject to a diversity of opinion. Some executives and directors feel that the board should do little more than formally fulfill the requirements of the law; at the other extreme are those who believe the directors should actively participate in operating matters. Executives, particularly in larger corporations, seem more inclined to accept the board as an integral part of top management. Increasing recognition is being given to the idea that the individual and group judgments of well-qualified directors can make a significant contribution to the welfare of the corporate enterprise.

The managerial functions performed by a large number of boards of directors studied by the Harvard Graduate School of Business Administration differed from company to company.[15] But, as one of the Harvard studies concluded, "taken as a whole, they covered practically the entire range of top management functions."[16] The basic functions performed by boards of directors can be divided into three major categories: (1) selection of executives, (2) policy formulation, and (3) appraising company and executive performance.

The procedures used by boards to carry out their functions involve the making of decisions, confirming decisions made by the executives, counseling of executives on possible courses of action, and reviewing results and reports. A considerable amount of action by the directors is performed on an informal basis. Formal board meetings and minutes are important, but a failure to recognize informal means leaves out an important part of the picture. The size of boards varies a great deal. There appears to be a considerable range within which boards can function effectively. A number of surveys indicate as few

---

[14]John C. Baker, *Directors and Their Functions* (Boston: Division of Research, Graduate School of Business Administration, Harvard University, 1945), p. 133.

[15]Melvin T. Copeland and Andrew R. Towl, *The Board of Directors and Business Management* (1947); Myles L. Mace, *The Board of Directors in Small Corporations* (1948); and Baker, *Directors and Their Functions.* Published by the Division of Research, Graduate School of Business Administration, Harvard University.

[16]Baker, *Directors and Their Functions*, p. 12.

as 3 to as many as 36 members with a median size of 10 to 13.[17] The composition of boards is also subject to considerable variation. Some boards are inside boards in that they are controlled by company executives; others are at least partly subject to a diversity of outside interests, such as customers, educators, stockholders, suppliers, and creditors. The amount paid directors is sometimes exceedingly small if they are paid at all, but there appears to be a trend toward higher compensation. The frequency of board meetings cannot be readily placed into a formula; some boards meet once or twice a year, others are on a quarterly schedule, and still others meet once a month or more often. Many boards delegate important responsibilities to such board committees as the executive committee and the finance committee.

THE BOARDS OF SMALL CORPORATIONS

The management literature has given relatively little attention to the boards of directors in small corporations. A noted exception is a study by Professor M. L. Mace of the Harvard Graduate School of Business Administration.[18] The chief executive of a small corporation usually cannot confine his activities to the overall direction of the enterprise. He must frequently devote a great deal of time and effort to such specialized functions as production, sales, finance, advertising, and personnel. Too often, he is a jack-of-all-trades and a master of none.

It also became apparent to Mace in his study that the typical board of the small corporation exists simply to meet the formal requirements of the law. He found that directors are often appointed by the owner-manager and that they take no active part in management. In order to determine the possible contributions that could be made by boards of directors, a number of situations in which boards assumed a more active role were given scrutiny.[19] Mace concluded that a board composed of active and able directors makes for a more balanced judgment on many matters. They can broaden the manager's perspective and help him make better decisions by suggesting alternative solutions to particular problems. They can act as a sounding board for new ideas and give him counsel, encouragement, and moral support.

---

[17]Jeremy Bacon, *Corporate Directorship Practices*, Business Policy Study No. 125 (New York: National Industrial Conference Board, Inc., 1967), p. 2; P. E. Holden, L. S. Fish, and H. L. Smith, *Top-Management Organization and Control* (New York: McGraw-Hill Book Company, Inc., 1951), p. 221; Robert A. Gordon, *Business Leadership in the Large Corporation* (Washington, D.C.: The Brookings Institute, 1945), p. 117.

[18]Mace, *The Board of Directors in Small Corporations.*

[19]The cases studied were those in which the management owned 51 percent or more of the voting stock; no consideration was given in this respect to the less typical situation in which the managers did not have full legal control.

In some respects a board of directors is more useful in a small corporation than in a large one. The management of a small enterprise is not surrounded by an array of technical, professional, and executive talent. The possibility of obtaining the services of such personnel on a consulting basis is often precluded by limited financial means. The board of directors provides a possible source of much-needed advice and counsel. Considerations other than monetary provided the necessary incentives in many cases studied by Mace. Although a director should not be elected simply to obtain "free advice," many university professors, attorneys, bankers, accountants, and executives seem willing to give a great deal of time and effort to the affairs of a small enterprise. As Mace pointed out: "Many business and professional men served as board members for the business education they gained thereby; others served as contributions to the welfare of their communities."[20]

Owner-managers are sometimes so concerned with operating problems and their own stake in the business that they fail to recognize a broader framework of responsibility to minority stockholders, the community, employees, customers, and other interest and participating groups. A competent and active board can frequently help create an awareness of such responsibilities and their significance to the long-term welfare of the organization.

It should not be assumed that a more effective use of boards of directors is a panacea for all the ills of small corporate enterprises. The best physicians in the world cannot cure a patient who has been hacked to death by a quack. However, a competent group of directors and a willingness on the part of managers to heed their counsel provide a frequently neglected and important ingredient for better management in many small corporations.

TOWARD MORE EFFECTIVE BOARDS

A prime requisite for more effective boards would seem to be competent directors. The selection process should be given careful scrutiny so that the best possible choices are made for the purpose at hand. The effectiveness of boards, like committees generally, can be increased by capable leadership. The board chairman, whether he be the chief executive or a separate officer, can greatly enhance the effectiveness of a board. The chairman can direct the attention of the board to important policy questions and matters that involve the concept of trusteeship. He can help maintain a good relationship between the board and the corporate executives. Planning the agenda, presiding at meetings, and developing effective procedures are other ways in which a board chairman can improve board operations.

Good organizational practices should not be neglected. Some corporations specify board functions in the organization manual; others do not even in-

[20]Mace, *The Board of Directors in Small Corporations*, p. 89.

clude the board in the structure of management positions displayed in the organization chart. Although the powers and duties of the board are broadly defined in the bylaws of the corporation, a clear and concise differentiation of functions assigned to the board and corporate executives would seem to be desirable.

9

STRUCTURAL CHANGES
IN ORGANIZATION

The development of a sound organizational structure generally has a high priority in management thinking. A major difficulty is that the structure is constantly being "organized" and "reorganized" by informal and formal means. Actual behavior may depart significantly from the structure of positions and responsibilities planned by management. Many organizational changes are relatively minor and are barely noticeable from the perspective of the short run. Such changes are often prompted by expediency and the exigencies of the moment and do not take into account the needs of the total system. Other structural changes are systematically planned to make radical modifications in managerial positions, responsibilities, and relationships. Reorganization can also result from changes in managerial personnel through recruitment, promotion, and retirement. This aspect of organizational dynamics will be given consideration in the chapter that follows.

Functional Structure and Organizational Behavior

An organizational structure tends to develop even when no prior planning has taken place. A good example is provided by a street corner gang studied by sociologist William Foote Whyte.[1] Doc was the top man in the Norton gang. Danny, who was Doc's best friend, and Mike occupied the second rung in the Norton organization. Friendship with the three top leaders gave Long John a somewhat superior standing in the gang. Nine other members occupied

[1]William Foote Whyte, *Street Corner Society*, 2nd ed. (Chicago: The University of Chicago Press, 1955), pp. 3–51.

subordinate positions and responded to directions from above. See Figure 9-1. Large and complex organizational structures do not simply evolve as a by-product of the social process. They are systematically planned for the achievement of predetermined organizational purposes.

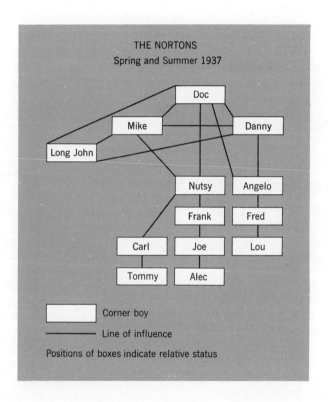

FIGURE 9-1. Informal hierarchical structure. (Reproduced with permission from William Foote Whyte, *Street Corner Society*, 2nd ed. Chicago: The University of Chicago Press, 1955, p. 13.)

FUNCTIONAL DESIGN THEORY

The theory of functional design is impersonal in its approach and is an attempt to construct an "ideal" organizational structure. The approach is human only to the extent that the planned responsibilities cannot exceed the capabilities of personnel available to the organization. It is evident that an organizer cannot plan positions that can be filled only by people with the intelligence of an Einstein or the physical stamina of a Tarzan. The motif of a functional design is how best to achieve the organizational objective. The organizer disregards the impact of personality and social behavior; his goal is the best possible functional plan.

The argument of the functional purist is that, although a good functional design will not necessarily assure efficient cooperation, a bad one will make it even more difficult. As the industrialist Henry S. Dennison has pointed out:

"The importance of right structure of organization is sometimes undervalued, because with the right men almost any kind of organization can run well. This is true, but is by no means the whole truth. With the finest of personnel, an illogical organization structure makes waste through internal friction and lost motion; it fails to retain and develop good men and to invite into its membership new men of high quality."[2]

Some people have suggested that a purely functional design is inadequate. They contend that personality should be given consideration in planning the organizational structure.

FUNCTIONAL DESIGN: THE PERSONALITY PROBLEM

The functional theorist does not ignore the impact of personality after the plan is put into effect. His argument is that personality should play a minimum part, if any, in planning the organization. A contrary view is held by Charles R. Hook, Jr., an experienced executive, who contends that:

"An organization is people—not a collection of functions. Too much of the thinking devoted to organization planning has been done as though we were embarking upon the structuring and staffing of a brand-new but as yet non-existent organization. If this were the case, our problems would be simple indeed! Under such a situation, it is not only possible but almost imperative that our planning should be carried on without regard to any particular human being. Aren't most of us, however, concerned with the improvement of an *already existing* organization, a *living*, breathing organism? . . . *Oftentimes the most important outcome of an organization plan is to give a really good man a chance to go to work.*"[3]

Lyndall Urwick, on the other hand, laments the lack of attention given a functional approach to organizational structure.

"Emphasis has been laid on this question of thinking consciously and technically about organisation, of laying out structure first and not thinking about

[2]Henry S. Dennison, *Organization Engineering* (New York: McGraw-Hill Book Company, Inc., 1931), pp. 5–6.

[3]Charles R. Hook, Jr., "Organization Planning—Its Challenges and Limitations," *Organization Planning and Management Development*, Personnel Series, No. 141 (New York: American Management Association, 1951), p. 21. (Italics in the original.)

individuals till structure has been determined, because it is still rare to find any general acceptance of this principle. The number of human institutions which do put correct structure first and politics second is very limited. The majority of social groups being left to grow like Topsy find, sooner rather than later, that Topsy has married Turvy."[4]

Although there appears to be some difference of opinion between Hook and Urwick, the area of disagreement is more apparent than real. Urwick is pointing to the danger of letting organizational politics play a dominant part in shaping and reshaping the organizational structure. Hook gives emphasis to the idea that professional and personal differences cannot be ignored or eliminated in organization planning. The relative weight that should be given to function and personality cannot be answered with any degree of certainty. It would obviously be a mistake to let either dominate the scene completely. The organizational structure should not become a strait jacket that restrains personal adaptation and initiative. Executives rarely achieve results in exactly the same way. One executive may organize a particular department differently than another with no loss in productivity. There does not seem to be one best way to achieve an objective.

Executive personality may significantly affect the apportionment of managerial responsibilities. An aggressive "empire builder" will absorb available responsibilities; a submissive individual may give up important functions. An authoritarian leader will delegate responsibilities differently than a democratic leader. An executive who is heavily endowed with social skills will not have the same approach to managerial problems as one who lacks this quality.

FUNCTIONAL DESIGN: INFORMAL ORGANIZATION

An organizer cannot possibly plan the totality of activities and interactions that make up organizational behavior. The people in organization amplify and modify the formal or planned organization and create more comprehensive and complex behavioral patterns. The difference between the formal organization and the behavior that actually prevails can be categorized as the informal organization. The formal organization is the behavior that is planned by superiors. The informal organization is the behavior that subordinates themselves have "planned" to contend with organizational and personal problems. It can become a disruptive force that impedes progress toward an organizational objective. But it can also play a constructive part in achieving goals and provide a means for more effective organization.

Informal organization can compensate for inadequacies in the planned structure. If the organization plan fails to provide adequate communication channels, the informal system frequently corrects the difficulty. Much of the com-

[4]L. Urwick, *The Elements of Administration* (New York: Harper & Brothers Publishers, 1943), p. 39.

munication across departmental lines is informal; the formal communication chain is often short-circuited to facilitate information flow. Many organizations have an effective "committee system" even though none has been planned. Coordination in one large industrial company is achieved almost exclusively through informal means. A considerable amount of leadership comes from people who have not been charged with such responsibilities. Subordinates sometimes make up for failures on the part of superiors. They may even assume personal risks involving their careers to serve the organization. Such informal instrumentalities are often important ingredients of organizational efficiency. Organizers should take care not to disrupt them without providing equally effective alternatives. Zealous organizers who seek a functional ideal not infrequently destroy more than they create.

Formal Structural Modifications

Informal adaptations in the organizational structure are generally accompanied by planned or formal changes in managerial authorities and responsibilities. Executives should generally be given considerable discretion to reshape the structure to meet professional and personal needs. Too much autonomy and too little planning, however, can lead to problems over a period of time. There must be organizational planning if the parts are to properly relate to the whole.

A CONTINUOUS SEQUENCE OF PLANNED CHANGES

Organizing is a continuous process in a going concern. New departments are formed to take advantage of specialization and to contend with such matters as public and labor relations difficulties. Additional activities are assigned to existing departments and transferred from one department to another. Coordination problems lead to the establishment of committees, and too many committees result in their elimination or a committee to investigate committees. Staff assistants are added to reduce the burden of executives and to contend with special matters. The scope of organizing activities may range from changes in one or a few positions to comprehensive changes in the whole hierarchy. The term "reorganization" is often used to describe major structural and personnel adjustments.

THE DEVELOPMENT OF AN ORGANIZATION PLAN

An important step in organization planning is to survey and review the present structure. A good starting point is to assemble existing organization charts and manuals, job descriptions, salary schedules, written procedures, and executive orders. Questionnaire and interview techniques can be used to obtain information from executives. The questionnaire approach is less expensive and time consuming than interviews, but it generally provides little information about informal aspects of executive action. The more costly interview technique can be used to supplement results obtained from questionnaires. The benefits that can be derived from additional information must be balanced with the cost of that information. Another limiting factor is that many executives have an aversion to giving information about their activities. Subordinates tend to be cautious about anything that may directly or indirectly affect their status, and superiors are not inclined to want subordinates to know too much about activities in the "executive suite."

The information obtained from an organization survey should be carefully scrutinized and evaluated, and used to prepare organizational and departmental charts, written descriptions of responsibilities and relationships, procedures, and other pertinent instruments. The existing structure may be accepted as the point of departure for future planning with or without minor modifications. On the other hand, information about the present state of affairs can be used to develop a more adequate plan. The organizer should search for evidence of unsound structure and inefficient performance. Overlapping and duplicating functions, jurisdictional conflict, communication and control inadequacies, executive work-load difficulties, friction between line and staff, and delays in decision and execution represent some of the more common problem areas. Attention should also be given to the manner in which such environmental factors as secular economic development, changes in product demand, cyclical fluctuations, and technological innovation may influence the situation.

IMPLEMENTING THE ORGANIZATION PLAN

Phase charts and plans are sometimes used to indicate the time sequence of reorganization. Organizational changes can be put into effect immediately or over a period of time with or without the participation of subordinates. Many reorganizations are spread over a six-month to three-year period and, in most cases, executives and other personnel are consulted for opinions and suggestions. In other instances, reorganization involves gradual changes over a relatively long span of time. The idea is to create as little disruption as possible and to assure continued cooperation.

THE ADMINISTRATION OF THE PLAN

Organizing can be regarded as a part of the totality of planning that occurs in a company. The organized hierarchical process by which planned changes are made in the production or marketing program is also used to make changes in the organization. The extent to which executives at various levels can institute changes without approval from higher levels differs from company to company. Some companies have centralized organization planning and maintain an elaborate system of control to enforce conformity to an overall plan. Organizing in other companies is more decentralized with less emphasis on uniformity in the pattern of organization.

Organization Departments

Some companies have established organization departments to assist top executives in planning and controlling the organization. Such departments may employ from one to a dozen persons and are usually headed by a manager who reports to the president. Companies without a full-fledged organization department often assign organizing activities to the personnel or industrial engineering department. But it should not be assumed that executives can wash their hands of organizing responsibilities by centralizing them in a departmental unit. The organizing function, like the human relations function, is not a one-man or a one-department function.

Organization Charts

An organization chart portrays managerial positions and relationships in a company or a departmental unit. Most companies use a pyramid-type chart with rectangular boxes[5] containing such information as position, title, name and rank (as vice-president) of the person holding the position, and, sometimes, a brief description of responsibilities and duties. The boxes are generally linked together with solid lines to show line relationships and broken lines for functional and staff relationships. Lines of different colors may also be used to relate positions and indicate relationships. Some companies use horizontal-line charts that list positions in columns with indentations for different hierarchical levels.[6] A series of diverging circles may also be used to indicate reporting and communication lines. However, the important consideration is not form per se, but the clarity and correctness with which a chart presents information. Organization charts are useful for the dissemination of information, but their limitations should also be noted. They picture only a small part of the totality of executive activities and interactions. Another limitation is that a chart is a static picture of a dynamic organism and needs consant revision if it is not to give wrong information about the actual situation. A chart can be manipulated apart from the thing it is supposed to represent

[5]Circular rather than rectangular "boxes" may be used.

[6]The National Industrial Conference Board has compiled organization charts of sixty-two companies, most of which are pyramid–rectangular box charts. Horizontal-line charts were used by two participating companies. Harold Stieglitz, *Corporate Organization Structures*, Studies in Personnel Policy, No. 183 (New York: National Industrial Conference Board, 1961). This report also contains information about good organizing practices and charting techniques.

and, if improperly constructed, can give a highly distorted representation of reality. People may also infer something that was not intended. For example, the fact that positions are shown on the same level does not necessarily mean that they have the same status.

Organization Manuals

Manuals can help promote an understanding of responsibilities and relationships, facilitate the training of managerial personnel, and provide a basis for the study of organization problems. They may contain comprehensive information about the entire organization, or their contents may be limited to particular divisions, departments, plants, and functions. Although organization manuals differ in format, the following kinds of material are commonly included.

Job Descriptions. Many manuals present detailed descriptions of the responsibilities and relationships of executive positions. The number of descriptions may be limited by various criteria, such as scalar rank, nature of the function, salary level, and official corporate status. The material that may be included in a job description is indicated by Table 9-1.

TABLE 9-1.   General Manager, Manufacturing Division

I. FUNCTION

Conducts the manufacturing, packaging, plant facilities and equipment operation, engineering, maintenance, plant and process design, technical service, and plant and warehouse construction activities of the company, and warehousing.

II. RESPONSIBILITIES AND AUTHORITY

The responsibilities and authority stated below are subject to established policies.
A. Operations and Activities.
   1. Formulates, or receives and recommends for approval, proposals for policies on manufacturing, packaging, plant facilities and equipment operation, engineering, maintenance, plant and process design, technical service, and plant and warehouse construction activities; administers such policies when approved; and conducts such activities for the company.
   2. Establishes and administers procedures pertaining to manufacturing, packaging, plant facilities and equipment operation, engineering, maintenance, plant and process design, technical service, and plant and warehouse construction.
   3. Recommends new or altered products and the discontinuance of products.
   4. Operates such warehouses as are necessary to the accomplishment of his function.

5. Conducts necessary buying activities, calling upon the services of the Supply and Transportation Department as necessary.

B. Organization of His Division
   1. Recommends changes in the basic structure and complement of his Division.
   2. Recommends placement of positions not subject to the provisions of the Fair Labor Standards Act in the salary structure.
   3. Arranges for preparation of new and revised Management Guides and position and job descriptions.

C. Personnel of His Division
   1. Having ascertained the availability of qualified talent from within the company, hires personnel for, or appoints employees to, positions other than in management within the limits of his approved basic organization.
   2. Approves salary changes for personnel not subject to the provisions of the Fair Labor Standards Act who receive not over $ .... per month, and recommends salary changes for such personnel receiving in excess of that amount.
   3. Approves wage changes for personnel subject to the provisions of the Fair Labor Standards Act.
   4. Recommends promotion, demotion, and release of personnel not subject to the provisions of the Fair Labor Standards Act.
   5. Approves promotion, demotion, and release of personnel subject to the provisions of the Fair Labor Standards Act.
   6. Approves vacations and personal leaves, except his own.
   7. Prepares necessary job and position descriptions.

D. Finances of His Division
   1. Prepares the annual budget.
   2. Administers funds allotted under the approved annual budget, or any approved extraordinary or capital expenditure program, or any appropriation.
   3. Approves payment from allotted funds of operating expenses and capital expenditures not in excess of $ ...., which are not covered by the approved budget, any approved expenditure program, or an appropriation.
   4. Recommends extraordinary or capital expenditures.
   5. Administers fiscal procedures.
   6. Receives for review and recommendation the items of the annual budgets of the staff departments and the field divisions coming within his province.

III. RELATIONSHIPS

A. President
   Reports to the President.

B. General Manager, Marketing Division
   Coordinates his activities and cooperates with the General Manager of the Marketing Division on matters of mutual concern.

C. Department Managers
   Coordinates his efforts and cooperates with the Department Managers and seeks and accepts functional guidance from them on matters within their respective provinces.

D. Government, Labor and Vendors
   Conducts such relationships with representatives of government and labor and with vendors as are necessary to the accomplishment of his function.
E. Others
   Establishes and maintains those contacts necessary to the fulfillment of his function.

Source. Franklin E. Drew and George L. Hall (editors), *The Management Guide,* 2nd ed. (San Francisco: Standard Oil Company of California, 1956), p. 55.

Organization Objectives. Objectives can be expressed in such subjective terms as "being a good citizen of the community" and "preservation of the American way." They are also defined operationally, that is, the objective is the same as the function necessary to achieve it. Overall objectives are broken down into such subsidiary objectives as production, sales, finance, purchasing, and personnel.

Organization and Management Principles. Some manuals highlight good management practices: how to develop and train a suitable successor; line executives should take full advantage of staff and service facilities; it is the duty of the subordinate to keep his superior informed about certain kinds of contacts (the conditions are usually stipulated); and subordinates should not be praised or blamed before their equals or subordinates. Principles related to organizing might include such statements as every function necessary to achieve an objective should be assigned to an existing or a newly created department; hierarchical levels should be kept to a minimum; and responsibilities should be delegated to the lowest possible level.

Terminology. Organization manuals sometimes devote space to a clarification of such terminology as "function," "responsibilities," and "accountability." They may also contain an organization creed, which expresses the philosophy of management on a variety of subjects, such as social responsibility, human relations, and economic values. A statement of the qualifications necessary to fill various positions is sometimes included, and a few manuals consider particular company organization problems.

Manuals and Charts Are Facilitating Instruments

Effective organizing involves more than drawing organization charts and writing manuals. Some executives, who feel that such devices create more difficulties than they cure, cite the danger of misinterpretation and rigidity, and the failure to adequately record complex and changing relationships. Although these problems cannot be completely overcome, they can be mitigated by good construction and composition, frequent revisions, and training in the use of the manual. The preparation and maintenance of manuals is costly and time consuming; however, most companies can afford and many can advantageously use some kind of written presentation on organizational matters. Some hard thinking and a little elbow grease plus a typist and a mimeograph machine can accomplish much along these lines.

Organizational Problems and Policies

Formal organizations are formed to achieve predetermined objectives as efficiently as possible. In a business organization the basic problem is to make a profit. Efficiency is partly a matter of good functional design. People are brought into the organization for particular purposes. They cannot obviously behave in any manner that pleases them. But at the same time the nature of man and the power accorded him in a private enterprise system precludes any kind of perfect adaptation to the needs of an organization. The discussion that follows pinpoints some common organizational problems and indicates policies that can help overcome them.

FORMAL ORGANIZING AND INFORMAL "REORGANIZING"

A sound functional structure is a good point of departure for most organizational purposes. Particular personal qualities and social situations should be considered during the planning phase of organizational development only when there are substantial reasons. But a modification of a planned structure cannot be avoided, except in Aldous Huxley's *Brave New World* or George Orwell's *1984*. Human beings cannot be forced into a rigid functional structure without being reduced to the level of social insects.

Bureaucracy in a Gypsum Plant

The extent to which human behavior can be molded into a particular pattern varies with conditions. A good example is provided in Alvin W. Gouldner's study of bureaucratization of a gypsum plant.[7] The plant employed about 225 people in two basic operating divisions, a subsurface mine and a surface factory. There was much socializing among all levels in both the plant and the community. The management was informal in approach and lenient in attitude. Then the old manager died; a new manager, given the pseudonym of Vincent Peele, was brought in to put things in order. The highly informal approach of the past was drastically disturbed. New rules and regulations were formulated and old ones were enforced. A discharge and a demotion indicated to all concerned that Peele meant business. Many of the past informal arrangements and alliances were broken and gradually replaced by new attitudes and groupings. However, Peele's attempt to reduce the amount of informal action and replace it with more formal approaches was not univer-

[7]Alvin W. Gouldner, *Patterns of Industrial Bureaucracy* (Glencoe, Ill.: The Free Press, 1954).

sally accepted. The workers in the surface factory were far more willing to respond favorably than the subsurface miners. The miners refused to submit to close bureaucratic control. An important barrier to bureaucracy was the miners' belief system. For example, the miners believed and strongly supported the idea that "down here we are our own bosses." The hazards of working in the mine helped reinforce the miners' resistance to control. The miner felt that he had the right to oppose orders that might endanger his life. A refusal to abide by work rules and authoritarian demands was often justified on the basis of dangerous working conditions. The miner was thought to be entitled to an occasional release, such as getting drunk and not showing up for work the next morning. The danger also helped keep down the number of people willing to work in the mine, thereby reducing the power of management to replace an uncooperative miner. Informal solidarity among the miners increased the effectiveness of their resistance to management's attempts to impose rules and regulations.

The Importance of Informal Organizing

The organizational structure should generally be defined broadly enough to permit a significant amount of informal organizing. Some discretion is essential if people are not to be put into a strait jacket which stifles initiative and self-reliance. An attempt to place too many restraints on human behavior will create control problems and costs that repudiate any reasonable concept of efficiency. It would make necessary an elaborate policing system that could be far more costly than any revenues that might be derived from improved behavioral responses. Another important consideration is that people do not like to be treated as though they were normally incompetent and irresponsible. As Professor Douglas McGregor has noted: "Man will exercise self-direction and self-control in the service of objectives to which he is committed."[8] The notion that most human beings attempt to avoid responsibilities and have to be subjected to many rules and close supervision is not always a valid assumption. Organizations should be viewed as *means* rather than ends. There are generally a number of equally good ways to achieve an objective. Informal techniques that get the job done are better than formal techniques that fail.

FORMAL REORGANIZATION

Formal reorganization, as used in this section, is assumed to involve major planned changes in an organizational structure. Such changes can produce higher profits, but they can also produce difficult problems. This discussion deals with strategic factors that relate to reorganization.

---

[8]Douglas McGregor, *The Human Side of Enterprise* (New York: McGraw-Hill Book Company, Inc., 1960), p. 47. Professor McGregor compares the traditional concepts with the theories that have evolved from behavioral research.

Should There Be Reorganization?

The existing organizational structure is not always as bad as it may seem. Management should consider the possibility that the problem is not the structure, but the personnel. A relatively small number of ineffective people can seriously disrupt an otherwise sound structure. On the other hand, people can make a bad structure perform well. Another consideration is that behavior may only appear to be efficient or inefficient. A smart "military look" does not always mean that an individual or unit will perform well in combat. A businesslike atmosphere does not always denote productivity. Efficiency also has stereotypes. Results instead of appearance should be scrutinized in evaluating an organization.

Reorganizations are often launched for the purpose of improving the profit situation. Such a goal is eminently proper. The difficulty is that a failure to make adequate profits can have many causes. Increased competition, high labor costs, ineffective advertising, changing consumer tastes, inadequate equipment, and many other factors can paint a bad profit picture. Some organizations have undoubtedly gone through the throes of reorganization only to find that the diagnosis was wrong. A situation that seems to require a major reorganization can sometimes be corrected by minor adjustments. A problem in one part of the organization can cause a chain reaction of problems in many other parts. In one organization the removal of a vice-president through early retirement solved a whole series of problems. In another the overhauling of a small department was all that was needed to correct a number of major production difficulties.

THE RESULTS OF REORGANIZATION

Reorganization frequently occurs only after productivity has begun to decline in a marked degree. Organizations often do not take action until they are pushed by a possibility of complete disaster. Too many people are like the grasshopper of Aesop's fables who starved to death because he failed to store sufficient food for the winter. However, the real culprit is sometimes a lack of knowledge rather than a lack of foresight. The efficiency of an organizational structure is difficult to measure. The factors that contribute to productivity or a lack of it cannot be readily isolated. However, a long period of success under a diversity of economic conditions may indicate that a particular kind of structure is more efficient than another. The relative profit picture may also be important in this respect.

Reorganization should generally be viewed as a long-run phenomenon. The money and human costs cannot normally be recouped in less than something like three to five years. The fact that reorganization frequently occurs when performance is down may further complicate matters. An improved structure may not become effective in time to prevent disaster. A reorganization should not normally be launched in the midst of other major problems. For example, a company engaged in a comprehensive plant modernization program might experience difficulty if it also made unrelated radical organizational changes.

THE PROCESS OF ORGANIZATIONAL CHANGE

This section is concerned with sociopsychological problems that relate to changes in the organizational structure. Functional requirements can create havoc with human relationships, and conversely.

The Social System

Organizing and reorganizing involves far more than formally defined authorities and responsibilities. Indeed, formal organizing actually disorganizes in that it disrupts and in some instances destroys an informally organized social system. Such a system plays an important part in the process through which people cooperate in pursuing common purposes. The organizer should recognize this fact and retain as much social continuity as possible.

Informal groups can cause serious cooperative problems by supporting personal goals that are contrary to organizational needs. In such situations an organizer may deliberately attempt to break up the informal social pattern. Some structural changes may be made specifically for this purpose. Another approach is to change the leadership and membership of informal groups by personnel transfers and forced resignations. This technique represents an attempt to create favorable changes in attitude through different combinations of personalities. The organizer should give consideration to the *ultimate* consequences of changes in the formal structure. What will an enthusiastic "empire builder" do with it? Will it benefit those who are more concerned with personal aggrandizement than with organizational welfare? How can a particular change be used for purposes other than those intended? Will people be forced to unduly circumvent the formally constituted organization to get the work done? These and similar questions should be carefully scrutinized in making structural modifications. It should be remembered that there are many devious and ingenious ways to serve selfish interests. However, such ways are sometimes necessary to promote organizational purposes.

Developing Cooperation

The effectiveness of organizational planning is highly dependent on the cooperation of managerial and other personnel. People are usually reluctant to accept changes that might adversely affect their status. They may appear to approve the new organization and then use every available means to make sure it will not be successful. The social mechanisms that were used to help achieve the organizational objective and, not infrequently, to make an unsound structure function are now used to impede the cooperative process. This kind of redirection of effort explains why the "bad" structure of the past performed better than the "good" structure that followed.

A systematic training program can be helpful in overcoming resistance to change. Such a program should give recognition to the fact that reorganization creates sociopsychological problems that frequently require as much attention as functional matters. Some companies invite the active participation of subordinates through periodic conferences and meetings that provide information about organizational changes and help dispel conditions that create status anxiety. The burden of adverse changes in position can sometimes be eased by the manipulation of status instruments. A person who feels that his position is being lowered may be given a more impressive title, a higher salary, a larger office, and other compensating inducements. Such status instruments may also become important for face-saving purposes. Although organizational changes should be made as palatable as possible, management should not attempt to hide the obvious. Early retirement, demotions in position, and outright dismissal are necessary under some circumstances. An organization can be compromised to death by a lack of executive courage and resoluteness.

Pruning Deadwood

Reorganization may accomplish the transfer of incompetent executives from important positions and from the organization. Productive personnel during earlier years may no longer be effective. Some deadwood is a normal product of the difficulty of forecasting human capacities. Technological innovation can complicate a situation by causing radical changes in personnel requirements. Changes in the organizational structure, some of which may be superficial, can provide a good means for bringing about necessary personnel adjustments. However, an organization should not cut off its nose to spite its face. A little deadwood, even in high places, is better than a dead tree.

10

STAFFING: MANAGEMENT DEVELOPMENT

The need for management development should be evident to anyone familiar with the affairs of organizational and human life. Yet competent executives have shown reluctance in recognizing the importance of this problem[1] Human beings do not always relish the idea that the bells may someday toll for them.[2] Many executives do not like the thought that the organization may survive without their unique contributions. The difficulty of measuring the revenue and cost implications of executive development also explains failures to take action. Executive development can frequently be delayed for a long period, but it can rapidly become a strategic factor as time makes inroads into the work-span of key executive personnel. The future can become better than the present only if the leaders of today help create the leaders required for tomorrow.

Position Responsibilities and Personnel Qualities

Descriptions of the responsibilities of present or planned managerial positions are useful in the development of recruitment, promotion, and training programs.

[1]L. Urwick, *The Elements of Administration* (New York: Harper & Brothers Publishers, 1943), pp. 23–24; Myles L. Mace, *The Growth and Development of Executives* (Boston: Division of Research, Graduate School of Business Administration, Harvard University, 1950), p. 5.

[2]This attitude has caused life insurance companies to avoid such terms as "death insurance." It is also reflected in the fact that many people do not have wills or own cemetery plots.

POSITION DESCRIPTIONS

There are no definite rules on the amount of information that should be included in position or job descriptions. The descriptions should generally indicate the basic kinds of activities that make up the position. The detail that is necessary depends on the information requirements of the user. An interviewer in the personnel department may need more specific information about a production planning position than someone from the production department. Position responsibilities should be expressed in operational terms whenever possible. For example, communication requirements might be described as giving speeches to large audiences of customers, preparing standard sales presentations, writing sales letters, and conducting classes for salesmen.

The nature of the duties performed by present occupants provides a basis for position descriptions. However, the fact that positions may be modified by sociopsychological factors should be taken into account. A different description might be appropriate for another person. As one executive put the problem: "When we evaluate the position of Mr. Executive Brown we evaluate the position as it *is done* by Mr. Brown. Mr. Smith, doubtless would perform it differently. Thus, we would in all probability have a different position if Mr. Smith were the incumbent."[3] Positions should not be so rigidly defined that they keep down a good man or keep out qualified persons who do not fit the exact pattern. As was emphasized, a balance should be maintained between functional requirements and personal differences.

EXECUTIVE QUALITIES

The appropriate qualities for a position can be inferred from position responsibilities. For example, the position of production manager requires knowledge about production processes and the position of research engineer demands an engineering background. Qualities can be categorized in various ways. Some common classifications are education, knowledge, skills, personal traits, responsibility, and physical characteristics. They may be more specifically defined by such requirements as university degree, years of college, high school diploma, kinds of education (business administration, engineering, or sociology), type and length of experience (three years' production planning experience), skill factors (communication or leadership), and particular personal traits (loyalty or self-confidence).

The manner in which qualities are related to a position is illustrated by the following statement of qualifications for a subsidiary manager in one company, Table 10-1.

[3]R. H. Hoge, "Evaluating Executives' Jobs," *Personnel Journal*, October 1955, p. 167.

TABLE 10-1.   Qualifications

Minimum Qualifications	
Education	College graduate with major in business administration or the equivalent in practical business experience.
Experience	Five years' successful experience including Merchandise Manager, Operating Manager, or Controller.
Knowledge	Must have an appreciation of good merchandise and good customer service. Must have a good working knowledge of all phases of subsidiary activities. Should be thoroughly conversant with company policies and must understand and accept company objectives and standards.
Ability and skill	Ability to plan and organize work, supervise and direct people, delegate responsibility and authority wisely, and secure performance. Must be able to interpret company policies intelligently, and use good judgment in making decisions. Must be able to apply himself to details while directing a large organization.
Personal characteristics	Forceful leadership qualities. Analytical, thorough, cooperative, and aggressive. Must have good expression orally and in writing. A pleasing personality which inspires confidence, loyalty, and enthusiasm. High personal standards.
Physical requirements	Good health and businesslike appearance.

Source. Myles L. Mace, *The Growth and Development of Executives* (Boston: Division of Research, Graduate School of Business Administration, Harvard University, 1950), pp. 42–43.

These specifications involve inferences about the nature of and the relationship between various factors. For example, the "college graduate" requirement assumes something about the qualities that result from four years of higher education. The experience requirement is based on the premise that future performance can be predicted with a degree of accuracy from past experience. The subjective content of some of the terminology is another source of difficulty. Such terms as "pleasing personality," "businesslike appearance," and "forceful leadership qualities" may be given significantly different meanings by different persons. A businesslike appearance might mean a Brooks Brothers suit to one person and not to another. But scientific endeavor has provided few good definitions of what constitutes appropriate behavior for various purposes. The diversity of conditions found in particular situations also complicates the matter.

FORECASTING FUTURE NEEDS

A forecast of executive requirements is an important prerequisite for executive development planning. The forecast should take into account dynamic economic and technological factors. A company may need to double or triple its executive force during a relatively short period of time. Innovations such as electronic data-processing make for changes in the number and kinds of personnel required. Also important are planned modifications in the structure of the management hierarchy.

The accumulation of data about dates of retirement and estimates of preretirement disabilities and deaths has caused many companies to view executive development in a different light. The shocking revelation that most of the major executives will be gone in a few years is sometimes the straw that breaks the back of complacency.

The capacities of people at subordinate levels should also be given consideration in appraising executive requirements. The situation is often better or worse at one level of the hierarchy than another; there may be a large potential supply at lower levels but a dearth of persons fitted for top positions. Differences may also appear with respect to functional and other types of management specialization. They can result from the fact that executives in some departments gave more attention to executive development than those in other departments. The market supply of executive personnel can also contribute to this situation.

DEVELOPMENT PROGRAMS

Companies seem to obtain good results from executive development programs that differ in marked respects. A number of factors make for variations in such programs. The extent to which executive development activities can be specialized is limited by the size of the company. A rapid rate of growth sometimes forces a company to avail itself of every possible means of meeting executive needs, and shortages in market supply may necessitate drastic increases in recruiting and training activities. The economics of revenues and costs can influence the situation in various ways. Companies with high profits can support and justify programs that might be marginal for companies with low or no profits. Some companies have to take chances with inexperienced personnel because they cannot afford to compete for top-notch people.

Companies should learn from the experience of others, but they should recognize that some or many aspects of established executive development programs may not fit their needs. They should not follow the Joneses into deep water if they cannot swim. The important consideration is to recognize the problem and develop an approach to its solution. Partial failures that result from planning are better than absolute failures resulting from inaction.

The Recruitment of University and College Graduates

The college graduate is the basic raw material for internal executive development programs. A company's supply of executive talent can be significantly enhanced by recruitment planning. Although this section is primarily concerned with college recruitment, many of the techniques apply as well to the recruitment of experienced personnel.

THE QUALITY OF EDUCATION

Recruitment planning should take into consideration the kind and quality of education in different institutions of higher learning. The relative emphasis given to liberal arts, science, and applied areas may be an important factor for some purposes. Institutions may have excellent faculties and facilities in engineering but not in the humanities or history, and conversely. The quality of graduates in terms of academic achievement may vary; a "B" grade average in one institution may be equivalent to a "C" average in another. However, some graduates from a substandard college or university have as much or more academic competence than the best from a highly rated institution. Companies should give explicit recognition to such factors in planning university recruitment programs and make appropriate adjustments. For example, they may hire more engineering or business administration graduates from one institution than another.

RECRUITING TECHNIQUES

A variety of techniques are used in recruiting for potential executive capacities. One technique is to recruit specialists in such areas as engineering, chemistry, marketing, and purchasing with the idea that a sufficient number of them probably have executive capacities. Another is to recruit some persons who have adequate preparation in specialized areas but who also have qualities that make for success in executive work. Still another is to give primary emphasis to executive capacities with little regard for preparation in a specialized area. Such techniques can be combined with a variety of educational and training programs. For example, graduates may be recruited for executive work and spend the first year or two in a program planned for this purpose. They may also be hired for particular positions in production, accounting, purchasing, market research, product engineering, or design, and be selected for an executive development program later in their career.

IMMEDIATE AND FUTURE NEEDS

Companies are often faced with the problem of compromising immediate needs with the requirements of the future. A specialized education may be appropriate for the positions that are presently available but it may not give a company the personnel capable of promotion to higher functional or scalar positions. Explicit attention should be given to this problem in planning the recruitment program. It may be necessary in some instances to tax the present in order to better serve the needs of the future.

INFERRING QUALITIES

A major problem in recruiting for executive development is to determine present and potential capacities from inferences that have varying degrees of reliability. The criteria that should be used for this purpose depend on the qualities required for executive work and also on the availability of information about a prospective graduate's personal qualities and past performance. The following kinds of information are frequently used as a basis for evaluating potential executive capacity.

Academic Performance

There is a diversity of opinion on the relationship between academic achievement and progress in management. Some contend that above average grades are not necessary for future success in a managerial career. Others have an opposite point of view on this subject. Recent research by the Bell Telephone System has provided important insights.[4] This research related rank in college graduating class with salary progress for some 10,000 men at various managerial levels. The main criterion in the study was annual salary earned by a man as compared to that earned by others with the same length of service in the company. Adjustments were made for differences in salary levels in different parts of the United States and between different departments. The salary distributions for each length of service were divided into thirds and compared with rankings in college graduating classes. The results are indicated in Table 10-2.

TABLE 10-2.   Rank in College Graduating Class as Related to Salary Progress (In Percentages)

	Top Salary Third	Middle Salary Third	Bottom Salary Third	
Top tenth of class	51	32	17	100
Top third of class	45	34	21	100
Middle third of class	32	36	32	100
Bottom third of class	26	34	40	100

Source. American Telephone and Telegraph Company, New York, N.Y.

[4]Data obtained from the American Telephone and Telegraph Company, New York, N.Y.

The data indicate a significant relationship between academic ranking and progress in the Bell System. Fifty-one percent of the men who graduated in the top tenth of their class and 45 percent of those in the top third were in the top salary third. On the other hand, 26 percent of those in the lowest third of their graduating class had attained this salary level. Only 17 percent of the top graduating tenth and 21 percent of the top third were found in the lowest salary third, compared with 40 percent for those who were in the lowest rank of their college classes. These results are similar to those obtained in an earlier Bell System study made in 1928.

The quality of the college from which the manager graduated made some difference in the results. The middle third graduate from above average colleges was in the top salary third 38 percent of the time, as compared with 28 percent for the same category from average colleges. Extracurricular achievement was found to be somewhat compensatory for lower rank in the graduating class. The extent to which the graduate earned his own college expenses had no appreciable effect on salary progress. The major field of study (arts, sciences, business, and engineering) did not appear to have any relationship to managerial rank.

The Bell System warns against applying the above results in a mechanical way. Although academic achievement appears to be highly important in management progress, this conclusion does not close the door to all who stand upon the lowest rung of the grade point ladder. At the same time, the study indicates that some ideas on the importance of grades are based on tenuous assumptions. An oft-heard statement is that "C" students have "better" personalities for the practical affairs of business than "A" or "B" students. The truth of the matter undoubtedly points to the other direction. A "C" student may be more intelligent than some "A" or "B" students, but why did he fail to give forth the necessary effort to earn higher grades? Companies should be wary of intelligent graduates who have a lackadaisical attitude toward the matter of grades. It might be better to hire a "C" student with less intelligence but with enough ambition to achieve an important objective.

Formal university curricula do not generally afford much opportunity for the development and practice of social and leadership skills. Some extracurricular activities contribute more in this respect than the educational program. Active participation as members or officers in student government, fraternal and other clubs, debating societies, and such organizations as the Society for the Advancement of Management would seem to indicate important qualities for executive work. However, the lack of such experiences does not necessarily mean a lack of social and other skills. Some students deliberately ignore extracurricular activities to gain time for academic pursuits or part-time jobs with which to pay their college expenses. Part-time jobs provide opportunities for the development of skills important in executive work. This consideration does not mean a student should work if he does not need the money; the time can frequently be better used in the library or laboratory. The matter of part-time employment and extracurricular activities should be viewed in terms of the total situation. The important question is whether the applicant used good discretion in balancing the alternatives. For example, a potential "A" student who became a "B" student in order to engage in extracurricular activities did not necessarily make a bad choice. A similar statement cannot be made about a low "C" student who worked a part-time job to maintain a sports car and participated in numerous clubs to become a "Big Man on Campus." But, a low "C" student who was forced by circumstances to work forty hours a week might be a better prospect than some "B" or "A" students.

Psychological Testing

Useful inferences about potential executive capacities can be made from testing information.[5] The tests mentioned below are often used in executive recruitment and for related purposes.

Intelligence Tests. These tests attempt to measure learning capacity and the ability to adapt to situations. There is some question about the nature of intelligence and the extent to which it can be isolated from other qualities that may be involved in the test results. The "innate" potential a person may possess is subject to modification by the learning that has already taken place. Acquired knowledge and skills play a part in the results obtained in intelligence tests; the factors measured tend to be similar to the factors involved in achievement testing.

Aptitude Tests. These tests differ from intelligence (general aptitude) tests in that they are concerned with specific aptitudes, such as the ability to perceive spatial relationships, memory capacities, and manipulative skills. They attempt to measure potential rather than prior learning through a simulation of the basic elements involved in a pursuit. For example, a person who can readily solve an abstract puzzle with certain spatial properties is assumed to have the capacity to perform tasks that have similar properties. In other words, the test is an abstract model of selected aspects of the realities of the work situation.

Achievement or Proficiency Tests. These tests are designed to measure the knowledge and skill acquired from systematic educational and training programs. The examinations given in university courses illustrate this kind of testing.

Vocational and Other Interest Tests. These tests seek to determine the na-

---

[5]The results of a study of executive attitudes toward testing and company experiences with various tests are reported in: Mace, *The Growth and Development of Executives*, pp. 83–91.

ture of a subject's interests by the choices he makes from among alternative activities. For example, a person might be asked which he prefers to do most (or least): play football or watch a football game, compose music or play a musical instrument, read a book or watch a television show, hunt elephants or visit a zoo, and so on. The basic assumption is that particular patterns of interests have a relationship to the qualities and motives required for particular pursuits. Thus, if most executives or physicians prefer mountain climbing over book reading, a person with a similar interest has "something" that may make for success in these professions. However, the nature of the "something" is open to question. People in some occupations seem to have different interests than those in other occupations, but there is doubt about the validity of some of the inferences that are made from interest tests. The problem of "cheating" also presents a difficulty. A person may indicate he likes to go to the opera or read books because such interests seem related to the job he is seeking.

Personality Tests. These tests attempt to infer personality traits from various kinds of information. The subject may be asked to make a choice from a number of alternatives, tell stories about a series of pictures, give impressions about ink blots, or simply to talk about himself. The responses are generally analyzed in terms of a personality theory and results obtained in previous testing. The statements that were made about the validity of interest tests and the "cheating problem" also apply to personality tests.[6] However, useful information can be gained from personality tests administered and interpreted by qualified persons.

Test Validity and Reliability

Psychological tests should be viewed as supporting instruments and used with discretion. Executives should consult with qualified psychologists and be wary of those who promise too much. They should endeavor to determine test validity (do they test for the intended purpose?) and reliability (are the results consistent?) as soon as sufficient information is available. They should also recognize that a testing program may provide good results for one purpose but not for another. Psychological tests do not eliminate the need for executive judgment and should not be used to avoid responsibility. However, they can sometimes be profitably used to justify unpopular changes.

Achievement or proficiency tests to determine writing skills should probably be given more emphasis than is presently the case. Many executives lament the lack of such skills in college and university graduates. The ultimate responsibility for this situation rests with educational institutions and there is

[6]People with a Machiavellian bent might wish to read William H. Whyte, Jr.'s instructions on how to cheat on personality tests, in *The Organization Man* (New York: Simon and Schuster, 1956), pp. 405–410.

no intent to shift it to business leaders. Companies should help themselves, however, while this unfortunate state of affairs continues to exist. A solution is to ask each applicant to write a two or three hundred word essay on some subject without help from a dictionary or any other source. This may sound too simple and even "unscientific," but it seems reasonable to assume that one way to discover a lack of writing skills is to have people write.

Interviews and Other Techniques

Interviews can be used to eliminate applicants who obviously lack appropriate qualities and to gain some general impressions. An applicant who shuffles into the interview with a cigarette dangling from his mouth and speaks in an uncouth manner might not be given further consideration. However, such extremes are exceptional, which means that the alternatives are not always so evident. Interview impressions should not be used as the only basis for eliminating an applicant, and they should be carefully evaluated. Well-qualified applicants are sometimes rejected for superficial reasons. There seems to be a tendency to give preference to the man with the right "look" and a friendly and "sincere" attitude. Every interviewer should be required to study a photograph of Abraham Lincoln and listen to a few Churchillian stutters before he marks his little book.

Letters of recommendation are generally of little value because they are either extremely favorable or they say nothing. The use of rating scales does not help the matter much because standards are apt to have different meanings to different people. Average is below average to one person, and above average is average to another. A telephone or a personal conversation with someone who knows the applicant generally produces better results than letters or rating sheets. Some companies invite selected applicants for an extended visit for interviews and consultations with personnel and other executives. As was pointed out above, a great deal of subjectivity is involved in these techniques; the "perfect" woman on a date does not always make an "ideal" partner in marriage.

RECRUITMENT IN PERSPECTIVE

A high degree of uncertainty is involved in the selection of personnel for executive and other responsibilities. Mistakes cannot be entirely avoided, but they can be reduced through planning. Some companies do not give adequate attention to the problem; others "put on a good show" but do not properly use such techniques as testing and interviewing. Still others recruit in terms of immediate needs and give too little consideration to the long run. They fail to recognize that the requirements at lower levels may not serve future needs at higher levels. They might give greater emphasis to hiring persons who have potential "executive qualities" even though, for the present, they may be primarily engaged in nonmanagerial work. Furthermore, there should be less reluctance to hire the person who does not fit the stereotype expressed by such terms as "togetherness" and "other directed."

Recruitment of Experienced Personnel

Some companies have a policy of promotion from within and do not normally recruit for positions at higher levels. An oft-cited danger of bringing in people from the outside is that it has adverse motivational consequences, but the other side of the coin also has importance. Some competition from outsiders may motivate insiders to become more productive; promotions should not become a definite eventuality for those who stay around long enough. Some companies may even justify the promotion of unqualified people to show others that their opportunities will not be given to outsiders. Such a policy can be supported under certain circumstances, but it also invites dissatisfaction from those who believe that promotions, including their own, should be given on the basis of merit. Subordinates who have to work under an unqualified superior are apt to become disgruntled with their situations.

NEW IDEAS AND PERSONALITIES

Too much promotion from within or inbreeding can lead to inertia in the ranks of management. A periodic injection of new ideas and personalities is sometimes helpful in combating this problem. However, the dangers of too much disruption must be kept in mind. A necessary amount of stability should be maintained without engendering stagnation, but there are no easy or exact solutions.

THE EVALUATION OF PAST PERFORMANCE

The problems in recruiting experienced executive and other personnel are similar to those involved in hiring neophyte university graduates, with the added element of the evaluation of successes and failures in previous places of employment. Reliable information about past job performance is sometimes difficult to obtain. Letters of recommendation and information given by the candidate may provide few useful insights. Furthermore, good or bad performance in one company does not necessarily mean a repeat performance in another. A person may experience failure in one environment and outstanding success in another. The elements of circumstance and chance are sometimes as important as knowledge and skills. There is probably too much reluctance to hire someone who expresses dissatisfaction with his present situation or who has changed jobs a number of times. A man who seeks another position in the middle of his career is not always foolhardy. He may have the initiative and courage required in a company that wants to go places.

KEY EXECUTIVES

Companies sometimes seek an outstanding executive from another company because they want someone who is tried and tested for a particular purpose. They may also want to gain advantages from the personal contacts and influence of such an executive and the motivational impact of an important personage upon present personnel. A dynamic and experienced executive from the outside can help bring a company out of the doldrums and lift it to new heights. But far too much is frequently expected in too short a time and in situations that cannot be salvaged. The impossible is impossible unless the meaning of the word is changed. Good management, like good football, starts with fundamentals; an executive or a coach can be helpful if miracles are not expected. The cost of top talent is usually high. Other alternatives for the resources involved should be given careful consideration.

Executive Development Through Promotion

Some executives may be hired from the outside for purposes indicated in the previous section, but companies must generally meet much of the need for executive talent through promotion from lower positions. Career patterns in an organization can be categorized in a number of ways. Some people advance in status by becoming more proficient in such functional specialties as accounting, market research, and engineering. Others move up in scalar rank by assuming more and more executive responsibilities. A sizable proportion of line, staff, and service personnel will spend their working lives at middle and lower levels of the hierarchy. Such personnel frequently lack the capacities for higher positions or the ambition to put forth the necessary amount of effort. Many of them are content with such a career, which is in some respects a fortunate situation. There is not enough room at the top of a pyramid for everyone at the bottom, and experienced personnel is required at lower levels.

SELECTION FOR PROMOTION

A major problem is to determine which persons should be promoted or prepared for promotion to higher executive positions. Some companies attempt to classify personnel for future responsibilities at the recruitment stage. Others recruit personnel for particular positions without giving explicit consideration to promotion potential. Still others have a planned program of training and experience through which persons may advance to higher executive positions. There are no hard and fast rules for deciding which person or persons should be selected for actual or potential promotion.

PROMOTION CRITERIA

The recruitment stage provides information that may have value in later stages of a person's career. Some of this information may relate more to the requirements of the future than of the first position. Thus, the fact that X has a broad liberal arts background or a solid foundation in science may be particularly pertinent for promotion to some kinds of responsibilities. Recruitment information should be modified and magnified by subsequent information about performance. Some initial inferences may not have been appropriate in terms of later performance, and others may be supported by performance data. Subordinate performance should be systematically and periodically evaluated by superiors and others. However, the evaluation process should be carefully planned, and an attempt should be made to establish "objective" standards. As Professor Mace has pointed out, "slipshod and casual filling out of appraisal forms is potentially more dangerous than no appraisal system because of the possibly irreparable damage to the careers of men and because of the faulty management decisions resulting from misleading basic information."[7] Performance evaluations should generally be used together with other types of information such as educational achievements and test results. The idea that people change over time should always be kept in mind. Some people develop more slowly than others, and factors like family responsibility may result in a marked change in motives. Also important is that "good" or "bad" performances should be evaluated in terms of the responsibilities that are involved. An outstanding plant design engineer may not work out well in a position requiring executive talent. Furthermore, the capacities and motives required for higher positions are not the same as those required for lower positions. Performance and other kinds of information provide a basis for judgment about such matters, but they do not automatically provide the answer.

Company Educational and Training Programs

The years that followed World War II have witnessed a tremendous growth in company executive training programs.[8] Before that time the primary emphasis was on foremanship training, and little attention was given to the higher levels of management. A number of factors gave impetus to executive development through training and education. The earlier foremanship programs and the leadership training experiences of the military services and industry

---

[7]Mace, *The Growth and Development of Executives*, p. 82.

[8]Donald S. Bridgman, "Company Management Development Programs," in Frank C. Pierson and others, *The Education of American Businessmen* (New York: McGraw-Hill Book Company, Inc., 1959), pp. 537–541.

during the war demonstrated that effective leaders can be rapidly developed through training techniques. Rapid economic expansion and technological innovation created a large demand for competent executive personnel, while government, the military, and other areas of endeavor made inroads into an already short supply.

KINDS OF TRAINING PROGRAMS

Management training may be used to increase competency in a present position, to prepare people for promotion, and to provide opportunities for self-development. Training programs may be concerned with the problems at the various levels of management, such as first-line supervision, the junior executive level, middle management, and top management.[9] They may also give emphasis to the functional areas of management specialization and to particular staff, service, and technical functions. The length of the training period may vary from a few weeks to several years and may be intermittent or continuous. Training may be conducted on a part-time basis during regular employment, or it may involve full-time participation for several weeks or months. It may be administered by central management, by departmental units, or by outside organizations like universities and associations.

CONTENT OF PROGRAMS

The content of management training programs varies from company to company and with the different purposes they are supposed to serve. Some programs involve a planned sequence of different subject-matter areas; others present pertinent aspects of various fields in an integrated course; and still others offer individual courses in subjects like accounting, job evaluation, and computer programming. Much company-administered training gives primary emphasis to knowledge and skills that can be applied to particular positions. The philosophy and practices of the company tend to become a major motif in the training program, and attention is generally concentrated on conditions that pertain to the company rather than to companies in general. A course in organizing, for example, may give almost exclusive consideration to the company's organizational structure. A course in accounting may use the company's accounting system as a point of departure. University and association programs for practicing executives are generally not adapted to the conditions of a given company, but many of them are oriented toward the problems of a particular industry.

[9]The distinction between the first-line supervisor and the junior executive is that the latter is usually a university graduate who is being prepared for supervisory responsibilities. A first-line supervisor such as a foreman or an office supervisor, comes from the ranks and does not generally advance beyond this level.

EMPHASIS ON TECHNIQUES

Management training has tended to emphasize techniques rather than the fundamental knowledge from which techniques are ultimately derived It has also been more concerned with internal company problems than the economic, political, social, and cultural environment. However, the growth of training programs for higher executives has brought about some change in perspective. Greater emphasis has been given in recent years to the dynamics of the total organizational system and to the manner in which it fits into the environment. A few programs focus upon the humanities, with readings in classical and modern literature.

INSTRUCTIONAL METHODS

The instructional techniques used in management training programs are similar to those employed by educational institutions in undergraduate and graduate programs. Lectures, the case method, role playing, business games, and seminars and conferences are widely employed, with relatively more emphasis being given to student participation. The effectiveness of various techniques depends on the purpose of the program and the kind of participants. The problems of business organizations in this respect are similar to those experienced by universities and colleges.

EFFECTIVENESS OF COMPANY TRAINING

Some formal training undoubtedly improves executive performance and reduces the time required for adaptation to present and potential positions. It can be carried to an extreme. There is little in the way of objective measures to indicate exactly what is gained by various kinds of programs. Some programs are little more than superficial presentations of superficial material. They may seem like great sport, but nothing much is gained either by the participants or the companies. "Keeping up with the Joneses," company affluence, and tax deductions are probably important underlying motivations for some training programs. Programs sometimes reflect inadequacies on the part of educational institutions, for example, companies may have to teach junior executives to write the English language because high schools and colleges have not provided proper preparation. Company programs include subject matter that can be better handled by universities and colleges, and conversely. If more knowledge in the liberal arts is necessary, such preparation should generally fall within the domain of educational institutions. On the other hand, training in techniques can often be better handled by companies. Companies should generally not educate in the broader sense, and universities should not become too concerned with training for particular positions. This is not to say that definite jurisdictional lines can or should be drawn, but rather that educators and executives should give serious attention to their mutual problems and prevent wastes in limited educational and training resources.

UNIVERSITY-SPONSORED PROGRAMS

In addition to regular degree programs in which executives can participate with or without company support, higher educational institutions conduct executive programs, conferences, institutes, and courses. A number of universities offer "on-campus" integrated programs, that take a broad executive-development approach.[10] The duration of these programs ranges from two weeks to several months, the cost from $500 to over $2000 (with and without living costs), the size of the group from less than a score to over a hundred, and the participants from junior to senior executives. Program content includes such subjects as the management process, functional areas, human and public relations, and personal development (conference leadership, public speaking, and reading); instructional methods vary from exclusive use of the case method (Harvard) to combinations of lecture, case, seminar, and other techniques. Regular faculty members and specialists from business and from other universities make up the teaching staffs.

Colleges and universities have also established literally hundreds of residential and nonresidential courses in such areas as supervisory training, time study, quality control, cost accounting, computer programming, and production planning. These courses are designed to give executives specific knowledge and skill, to introduce new developments, and to refresh executive memories. Many of them serve a useful function, but some have little or nothing to offer. In more than a few instances, resources that are needed for regular degree programs are frittered away in large and small chunks.

TRAINING THROUGH DIRECTED EXPERIENCE

Companies frequently develop executive talent through what might be called "directed experience" with or without supplementary "classroom" training. In some situations, job experience is an integral part of the development program. A management trainee may be shifted from one department to another to gain a diversity of experience and, at the same time, attend formal training sessions. This approach is used in many different ways in general management programs and in the functional areas of specialization.

On-the-job training by superiors is another form of directed experience. This technique is often referred to as "coaching" and has been called "the most effective way of providing for the growth and development of people in

[10]George V. Mosher and Allison V. MacCullough, "Executive Development Courses in Universities," *Conference Board Reports*, Studies in Personnel Policy, No. 142 (New York: National Industrial Conference Board, Inc., 1954).

manufacturing organizations. . . ."[11] The purpose of coaching is to develop subordinate potential, and it involves more than a set of training techniques. Coaching represents the conscious creation of an environment within which subordinates can learn to become better executives. Subordinates must be given rope but not enough to hang the company, and they should have the opportunity to make mistakes and learn from them. Responsibilities can be increased or decreased as the situation warrants, but this process should not seem deliberate. Superiors should "instruct" and counsel, but they should not appear to be intruding or interfering. At the same time, subordinates should feel that they can take problems to the superior without a loss of self-respect and status. In many ways, the superior must be willing to sacrifice his own ego for the interests and future of the subordinate. Some otherwise successful executives are not able to assume this kind of role. The qualities that make for effective coaching are not necessarily the same qualities that make for effective leadership. Leaders are often successful for reasons other than their ability to coach subordinates.

Coaching also takes place in such situations as committee meetings and informal relationships. The McCormick Company, for example, uses committees of junior executives to provide insights into the problems at higher levels; staff or "assistant to" positions may accomplish a similar purpose.

THE IMPORTANCE OF NONDIRECTED EXPERIENCE

If the present emphasis on education and training is carried to an extreme, a man might find himself in retirement before he has a chance to perform. Educational and training programs, and this includes directed experience, simulate reality; they are not the same as reality. The "hard-knocks" type of experience is still an essential ingredient of executive development. There is a thin line between directed experience and actual experience, but the line is highly significant. The psychological properties of the two are not identical as long as there is any awareness on the part of the subordinate that experience is planned in some fashion. Conscious coaching may be the exception if the fact that it is conscious can be hidden from the subordinate. Experience in executive work involves a personal burden that cannot be shared by others. Subordinates who have not been frustrated by uncertainty or who have not felt the pangs of failure have probably yet to pass through the executive portals.

[11]Mace, *The Growth and Development of Executives*, p. 108. A comprehensive discussion of coaching methods and results is found in *ibid.*, pp. 107–175.

PART IV

Directing

11

AUTHORITY AND POWER

Authority and power are essential in complex cooperative endeavors because compulsion is frequently necessary to achieve cooperation. The nature of authority and power and their relationship to the managerial process are considered in this chapter.

The Nature of Authority

Authority and power are closely related concepts. Power may be defined as the capacity to change individual or group behavior. Brown has power if he can cause Smith to go to a poker party with the boys instead of to a dancing party with the wife. Power gives rise to behavior that differs from the behavior that would have otherwise occurred.

AUTHORITY OF POSITION

Authority is the power that evolves from a managerial position. Subordinates normally accord authority to those who occupy higher organizational positions. This authority is to a great extent unrelated to the particular person who occupies the position. Authority would arise even though the occupant does not have the personal capacity to create power. On the other hand, a person who has no authority may have a great deal of power by virtue of his personal qualities.

PERSONAL POWER

The power of executives may far exceed the amount of power (or authority) that evolves from the authority of position. The reason is that some executives have personal and professional qualities that make subordinates more willing to accept organizational responsibilities. There are also executives who actually reduce the authority accorded them by their positions. The personal qualities they possess adversely affect the extent to which subordinates accept responsibilities.

THE POWER OF SUBORDINATES

Subordinates sometimes have considerable personal power even though they may not have authority. This power can be used to challenge the authority of those in superior positions and to change the balance of power implied by the authority of position. The power of subordinates may significantly modify the planned structure of power (or authority). A superior may actually become a subordinate even though all of the attributes of his position indicate a higher status.

The Social Foundations of Authority

Society supports and sustains authority in business and other organizations. The factors that affect the authority relationship will now be analyzed.

SOCIAL CONDITIONING

Social conditioning is important in establishing and reinforcing the authority relationship. People learn to play the role of subordinate shortly after birth. The behavior of the child is initially conditioned by the intervention of his parents and continues as the child becomes subject to teachers, clergymen, scout leaders, and other authority figures. The result is that obeying a superior becomes a habitual mode of behavior for many people. The social sanctions imposed on nonconformists give strong support to authority in particular organizations.

THE SANCTIONS OF PROPERTY

Authority in a business organization is supported by the sanctions that evolve from the law of property. A subordinate who does not obey an order can be physically removed from company property by the courts and the police if he does not do so voluntarily. This action is implied whenever anyone is discharged from employment. The power to discharge has a corollary in the power to hire and grant economic and other benefits. Executives as owners or as representatives of owners can determine the use that will be made of the property rights conferred by law. They possess the power to impose sanctions in the sense that actual and expected benefits from an employment relationship can be removed in whole or in part. This power is highly instrumental in creating authority or acceptance from subordinates. It differentiates executives from others in the organization and gives a basis for the idea that authority is delegated from the top. The sanctions of property are based on authority in other parts of the society. They can be enforced by the courts, the police, and, if necessary, the military. However, the law of property has general social acceptance and is usually obeyed without the use of such instrumentalities of power. This situation did not prevail with respect to the Eighteenth Amendment prohibiting the sale of alcoholic beverages and the enforcement provisions set forth in the Volstead Act. The result of Prohibition was a large volume of illicit production offered for sale by thousands of bootleggers. There was a great deal of laxity in the enforcement of the law, and, in many instances, law enforcement personnel refused to fire on or arrest violators of the law. Thus, the failures in authority with respect to the law were given support by insubordination among those responsible for imposing sanctions.

THE IMPACT OF THE MARKET

The potency of sanctions that may be imposed by management as a result of property rights is affected by economic and market conditions. An excess of jobs over job-seekers sometimes makes a subordinate more inclined to "tell the boss to go to hell." A large amount of unemployment or the lack of particular employment opportunities tends to enhance the compulsion of the power of discharge. Present and potential benefits of an employment situation can be made more or less attractive by alternative opportunities. The possibility of being promoted to a vice-presidency or of an increase in salary is not quite as alluring if a similar or a better opportunity is offered by another organization.

UNIONISM AND COLLECTIVE BARGAINING

The power implied by property rights has found a countervailing force in the rise of powerful labor unions. Labor legislation and the strike weapon have given unions formidable power in bargaining with management. Collective bargaining is partly concerned with the manner in which the workers represented by the union will share in the distribution of income to stockholders, customers, and other interest groups. This aspect of union action is not unlike that of other organized groups with which management must contend. A "monopolistic" supplier or bank may exert as much pressure upon management as a labor union. However, there is a fundamental difference between the impact of unions upon the affairs of management and that of other groups. The interests of the workers are more closely related to matters internal to the organization because they are themselves subordinates and directly subject to managerial decisions. The power of the union is used to restrict the discretion of management in dealing with subordinates represented by the union. The trade agreement that evolves from the collective bargaining process sets forth norms that limit the actions of both parties for a given period of time. Differences involving such norms are generally resolved through a formal grievance procedure agreed to by both parties.

Many aspects of collective bargaining are applications of the political norms of a democratic society into the industrial area. The development has been lauded by such terms as "a system of industrial jurisprudence" and "industrial democracy." The difficulty is that there is frequently a difference between idealistic preachments and industrial practices. Unions and their constituents generally regard the trade agreement as a safeguard against "arbitrary" actions on the part of management. The history of labor-management relations is not without examples of management practices that would bring a ringing rebuke in the "climate of opinion" of today. But the pendulum can swing too far in the opposite direction. The restrictions imposed by unions can interfere with management's responsibility to the organization as an integrated system. Military commanders cannot be expected to assume the responsibility of fighting the nation's wars if they cannot order soldiers into battle. Soldiers might prefer not to face death on the battlefield, but they must if the nation is to survive. Industrial workers might also prefer not to face many of the hazards of the industrial order. They can and should be protected against some of them, but they cannot escape them all. Too much restriction on the power of management to make decisions can cause industrial organizations to bog down with inefficiencies. A production line might be paced at a rate that adversely affects the health of workers, but it need not be slowed to prevent a little perspiration. The welfare of the worker should be considered in making technological innovations, but it should obviously not be the only consideration. Workers should not be required to subject themselves to a hell on earth, but they and the unions that represent them should not assume that the "pie in the sky" can be obtained by merely asking.

Unionism and collective bargaining have also placed limitations upon management's power to impose sanctions. Workers have recourse in the grievance procedure if they believe their rights under the trade agreement have been violated by management actions. Thus, although management has the right to discharge and impose other sanctions for "cause," workers have procedural rights much like those extended by courts of law. The union is generally given a part in the proceedings through shop stewards and joint union-management committees. Many trade agreements make provision for arbitration by outside parties if the union and management cannot themselves resolve the dispute. The rights that are accorded by this procedure place a restraint upon arbitrary uses of power by management. However, unions and workers sometimes use the grievance procedure for other purposes. They may accumulate an unreasonable number of grievances to put pressure upon management and give the union bargaining power relative to other matters. The grievance procedure can also be used to avoid sanctions through "legalistic" strategies. It can be used to protect scoundrels as well as saints. Furthermore, management may not attempt to discipline workers for some improper acts because it involves a long sequence of power clashes with the union. The grievance procedure provides a useful instrument for those who deliberately seek to practice insubordination.

Management is sometimes forced to approach labor relations in terms of conflict with the union. A genuine desire to treat workers fairly may be thwarted by strategical and tactical considerations. Management may not make concessions it might otherwise make because they are spoils in the game of bargaining with the union. Unions sometimes view management's efforts toward better labor relations as a threat to their survival and deliberately create conflict situations to justify their existence to the worker.

PROFESSIONAL ASSOCIATIONS

Associations of professors, physicians and surgeons, engineers, teachers, nurses, and other professional groups may also limit the power of management in the organizations in which they are employed. Although such associations do not usually bargain with management in the manner of labor unions, they are often highly effective in promoting the interests of their members through political, economic, and social pressures. The techniques used range from mild forms of "moral suasion" to a vigorous pursuit of legislative favor. The manner in which an association protects the interests of a professional group is illustrated by the way in which the American Association of University Professors (AAUP) endeavors to enforce standards relating to academic freedom and tenure. The universities in which professors are employed cannot be legally forced to conform to such standards. However, the AAUP censures or "blacklists" university administrations that violate its academic freedom and tenure standards and publishes a full account of the matter in its official journal. The American Medical Association and related associations have played an important part in promoting professional standards and protecting the status of their members in hospitals and other organizational situations. The decisional discretion that may be exercised by hospital administrators over the activities of resident physicians and surgeons is generally more limited than that which may be exercised over other employees even when matters relating to medical care are eliminated.

The Status System and the Authority Relationship

Status plays an important part in maintaining authority in organizations. A person generally does not like to take orders from someone he considers to be his equal. The status system makes compliance easier because a degree of inequality is rationalized. The instrumentalities of status impute qualities that reinforce the authority relationship.

FORMAL STATUS FACTORS

Some of the attributes that make for higher or lower status form an integral part of the position a person occupies in an organization. For example, the position of president generally carries with it such objects of status as a walnut-paneled private office, carpeting, and elegant furnishings, The discussion that follows is concerned with formal or planned aspects of the status system.[1]

SCALAR AND FUNCTIONAL STATUS

The levels in a hierarchy correspond closely to the amount of status accorded a position. Persons who occupy higher positions generally, but not always, have a higher status than those in lower positions. Functional specialization may also significantly affect status. The status value of a particular function varies from organization to organization. In a production-oriented organization the production manager may have higher status than the sales manager; the reverse may be true in an organization in which marketing is strategic.

FORMAL CEREMONIES OF APPOINTMENT AND ACHIEVEMENT

Formal ceremonies are more common in military, political, educational, and fraternal organizations than in business organizations. One purpose of such ceremonies is to communicate to people in the organization and society that a particular person should be accorded the status associated with a given position or accomplishment. Ceremonies also remind those in and outside the organization that such positions as general of the army, secretary of agriculture, governor, and the president of a corporation or university are important. A university commencement announces that a certain number of students are entitled to the status accorded an academic degree and that the degree and the institution conferring it have a status value. In spite of esoteric and entertaining or at least energetic commencement speakers, the educational attainment of the graduating senior is not enhanced in any significant degree by the ceremony. In fact, some of the participants, including faculty members and university presidents, may be slightly bored with the proceedings. Nevertheless, the status implications of such ceremonies should not be taken too lightly in a world in which the power of empire is symbolized by the coronation of a

---

[1]Chester I. Barnard first gave emphasis to the importance of the status system in "Functions and Pathology of Status Systems in Formal Organizations," in William Foote Whyte, *Industry and Society* (New York: McGraw-Hill Book Company, 1946), pp. 46–83. Many of the ideas in this section were derived from this source.

queen with full pomp and circumstance. The contention is not that all ceremony is useful but that ceremony can be a useful status device.

INSIGNIA AND OTHER STATUS IDENTIFICATIONS

Military organizations are probably more pronounced in their use of status identifications. Anyone familiar with the meaning of military symbols of rank can readily ascertain the approximate status of all noncivilian personnel in a military garrison. Such symbols become a common denominator of status throughout the organization. They make possible a degree of stability in the status system and give it universality throughout the organization. The importance of this fact can be seen in an armed force of ten million persons with considerable shifting of personnel and constantly changing personal associations. A high status individual does not have to take personal action to enforce his status. The general or colonel does not have to say: "I have high scalar rank and should be accorded high status." The insignia will assure a general or a colonel proper response from lower status personnel. It provides a cue to all participants in the organization as to how they should behave toward others in the organization.

Religious and educational organizations make frequent use of formal symbols of status. The vestments worn by officiants and assistants during a religious service in the Catholic Church and many protestant churches indicates the rite and the hierarchical rank of the wearer. Academic gowns used by educational organizations during ceremonial occasions identify the degree (Ph.D., M.A., B.A.), the institution that conferred the degree, and the area in which major work was done. In the legal profession a judge is identified by a black robe, and in England wigs are worn by attorneys and judges. Distinctive attire is often worn by medical doctors, nurses, and other hospital personnel. Police and fire services use uniforms and insignia that identify rank and specialization. Uniforms and insignia are also used by the Red Cross, Salvation Army, and many fraternal organizations.

Although generally not as formalized or widely used, various kinds of status identifications can be found in business organizations. Uniforms and insignia are generally worn by plant protection personnel. Identification badges used by some companies for security reasons usually become an integral part of the status system. Such badges generally identify scalar and functional position by shape and color. One company uses round badges with two colors for top executives, one-color round badges for other executives, rectangular badges for supervisors and workers. Supervisory rank is indicated by the number of black bars on the badge. All badges have a photograph of the wearer, except those worn by top executives. The status value of these badges is indicated by the fact that many people wear them after working hours. In the restaurant industry, standard uniforms are often worn by waitresses. The chef's hat is an important status symbol in the kitchen. In the better restaurants one can readily identify the functional position and the scalar rank of all personnel from the bus boy to the chef. Hotels also use uniforms and symbols of rank extensively; bellboys are almost always uniformed. Uniforms are also frequently used by trucking concerns, public transport companies, and theatres.

THE USE OF TITLES

Scalar rank is indicated by such titles as vice-president, foreman, group chief, general, captain, bishop, mayor, governor, and maître d'hôtel. Functional designations are also vital ingredients of the organizational status system. The status distinctions inferred from the following titles are well understood by participants in organization: engineer, accountant, bookkeeper, filing clerk, private secretary, stenographer, machinist, janitor, chemist, physicist, typist, and laborer. Professional designations such as attorney, physician, C.P.A., psychiatrist, osteopath, and chiropractor have similar status implications. Academic achievement is indicated by such titles as Doctor of Philosophy (Ph.D.), Doctor of Medicine (M.D.), Master of Arts (M.A.), and Bachelor of Arts (B.A., A.B.).

THE STATUS IMPLICATIONS OF PRIVILEGES
AND SPECIAL FACILITIES

Status is also symbolized by the privileges and special facilities made available to organizational personnel. A distinction should be made between privileges and facilities as instruments of status and other organizational purposes that privileges and facilities may serve. A private office may improve the functional efficiency of an executive, and it may also be a material reward. In the following discussion, the emphasis is upon the status implications of privileges and special facilities. Someone taking a tour through the offices of any large organization will find significant differences in the physical facilities provided various kinds of personnel. The desks of top executives are usually more ornate and larger than the desks of lower-level personnel. The lowest-ranking office personnel use functional desk pens, while higher-ranking executive personnel have more elaborate marble-base desk pens. Sometimes the size of the base and the number of pens increase as one goes from lower executive ranks to the top ranks. In one concern, the top executives have real fireplaces; the next level of executives has artificial fireplaces; lower levels have no fireplaces. The carpeting in the offices of top executives is often more luxurious than the rugs, if any, at lower levels. The offices of some top executives are furnished by the best interior decorators and resemble penthouse apartments. The kind of automobile provided by the organization to various ranks may vary from Cadillac limousines (with chauffeurs) for top executives to a less opulent Ford, Chevrolet, or Plymouth for lower-ranking personnel. Less restricted working hours and longer lunch periods are privileges of rank. Access to company-owned hunting lodges and other facilities has an important status meaning. Also important is the type of traveling and entertainment facilities made available for business purposes. A similar distribution of privileges and facilities is found in universities, hospitals, churches, government, and military organizations.

RATIONALIZATION OF PERSONALITY

The status of high-ranking executives is often enhanced by a public relations program. A good press agent can emphasize the "personal qualities" of an executive and "create" attributes that confer higher status within an organization and in the society. The techniques that were used to make an "Elvis Presley" are also used to promote the "personalities" of top leaders in business, governmental, religious, and military organizations.

Authority and Power Structures

The actual structure of power in an organization may differ in a marked degree from the planned structure of authority. A good example of the extent to which the authority (or power) accorded by managerial positions may be modified is indicated in a study made by Melville Dalton.[2]

AUTHORITY VERSUS POWER: THE MILO PLANT

The formal organization chart of the Milo plant portraying the planned structure of authority is shown in Figure 11-1. The actual power of the people who occupied the positions is indicated in Figure 11-2. The power rankings were made by Milo personnel who were or had been close associates of the managers being ranked. The author of the study, Melville Dalton, who was himself a staff member, participated in the rating process by challenging rankings he thought to be out of line in terms of his own experiences. It should be noted that there were far more agreements than disagreements on what the rankings should be.

The Plant Manager, Stevens, and the Assistant Plant Manager, Hardy, are given equal rank in the power structure. Some of the reasons for this departure from the formal authority structure were the following. Stevens was clearly less forceful than Hardy and generally gave way to Hardy in executive meetings. Most of the questions at the meetings were directed to Hardy, who usually gave answers without consulting Stevens. Hardy's approval was considered to be strategic in the more important promotions. When production delays occurred, persons in charge were more concerned with Hardy's possible reaction than they were about the Plant Manager's. Stevens was considered to

[2]Melville Dalton, *Men Who Manage* (New York: John Wiley & Sons, Inc., 1959), pp. 20–31.

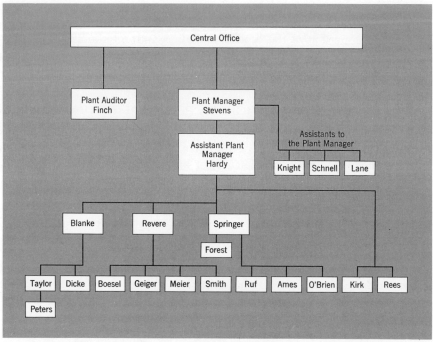

FIGURE 11-1. Milo formal structure simplified. (Reproduced with permission from Melville Dalton, *Men Who Manage*. New York: John Wiley and Sons, Inc., 1959, p. 21.)

be "unsocial and distant" in contrast to the highly personable Hardy. These and other factors were sufficient to counterbalance the authority accorded Stevens by his superior position.

The third man in the power structure was Rees, who headed the Industrial Relations section. Rees, a bright young man with a degree in aeronautical engineering, had recently taken over the section from someone who was no longer capable of managing it. One of the first things Rees did was to challenge Hardy emphatically in a meeting on incentives, asserting that the "top management" had put the system here and "by God we're going to make it work, not just tolerate it!"[3] This and other incidents, together with the fact that Rees had spent three years at headquarters, led people to view Rees as an unofficial spokesman for top management. Hardy was assumed to be more powerful because he dominated more areas of Milo life, but he did not interfere with Rees' "functional" jurisdiction. As Melville Dalton points out: "Hardy almost certainly exceeded his assigned authority over all plant processes except those

[3]Dalton, *Men Who Manage*, p. 25.

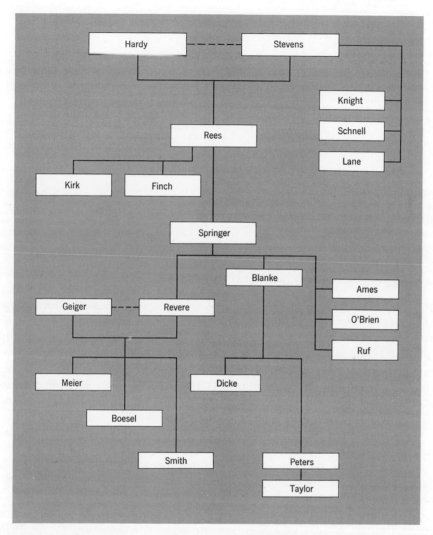

FIGURE 11-2. Milo structure of unofficial power. (Reproduced with permission from Melville Dalton, *Men Who Manage*. New York: John Wiley and Sons, Inc., 1959, p. 22.)

which Rees interpreted as lying in his sphere. Here Hardy exercised less than his formal authority."[4]

Springer, the superintendent of one of the three divisions, was placed slightly below Rees in the power ranking. He had developed a close personal

[4]Ibid.

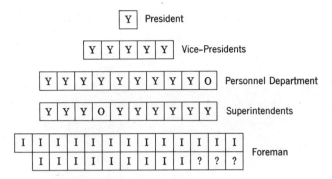

FIGURE 11-3. Legend: Y—Yankee; I—Irish; O—Others. Job-ethnic hierarchy in a New England factory. The non-Yankee at the superintendent level is a testing engineer. The non-Yankee member of the personnel group is a young Italian who does safety cartoons and acts as general errand boy. (Adapted from Orvis Collins, "Ethnic Behavior in Industry: Sponsorship and Rejection in a New England Factory," *American Journal of Sociology,* January 1946, p. 294.)

bond with Hardy during the past. The other superintendents, Revere and Blanke, recognized this relationship and often consulted with Springer when they wanted something from Hardy. Revere had the lowest rank among the superintendents partly because he "no longer aspired to dominate plant events."[5] He was not particularly interested in higher income and he was reluctant to accept more responsibilities. Hardy had given him the job because there were no other good candidates.

The rank held by Ames in Springer's division resulted from his ability to get along with the men and the union. Both Hardy and Springer appreciated the support that Ames gave them in the shop. Geiger ranked at a par with his chief, Revere, partly because he headed a major production unit. He also had strong support from Blanke, one of the other division superintendents, as the result of favors in the past. The power situation was affected by the close cooperation among Blanke, Geiger, Dicke, Meier, and Boesel because of their German descent. Knight ranked above the other two assistants to the Plant Manager because of his knowledge of internal affairs and his close personal relationship with Stevens.

INFORMAL STATUS AND POWER INSTRUMENTS

Status is a planned attribute of organizational positions which, in addition to other things, gives support to authority. It may also stem from the qualities

[5]Ibid., p. 27.

of the person who occupies a position and can serve as an important instrument of power. The nature of some of these qualities is now considered.

Ethnic and Related Factors

Attitudes that relate to nationality, race, and religion can significantly affect the way in which people react to someone. Such identities as Catholic, Jew, Negro, Indian, Japanese, Italian, and Irish are important in status evaluation. Some people are antagonistic toward persons from particular ethnic groups and will not accord them "equality." One executive may have much less power than another executive with the same authority but the "right" ethnic background.

Ethnic groups, including those who are a minority, may form alliances to preserve their power and to prevent entry by "outsiders." The cooperation among "the Germans" in the Milo plant illustrates this kind of behavior. A study of a New England factory by Orvis Collins is another case in point.[6] Figure 11-3 shows the ethnic backgrounds of the people in the management hierarchy. The upper and middle positions are dominated by Yankees and the supervisory positions by Irish. The ethnic loyalties that were involved in this situation "enforced" a policy of hiring Irishmen for supervisory positions and Yankees for the higher positions. A departure from this policy was permitted only with the complete approval of the two in-groups. The promotion of a Yankee named Peters to replace Sullivan, an "old country" Irishman, caused an immediate uproar. The social pressure became so pronounced that Peters soon failed to show up for work for reasons of illness. Peters did not again report for work and was replaced by a man named Murphy.

The problem of cooperation may cause management to consider ethnic factors in recruiting and promoting personnel. An outsider may not be able to work effectively with a particular ethnic group. An example is provided by the problems experienced during World War II with a group of Indians recruited on a reservation for work in a shipyard.[7] The supervisor to whom they were assigned reported them a sullen, unmanageable crowd, soldiering on the job. He threatened to quit if he could not be given another assignment. His boss complained that he did not know what to do with these "maladjusted employees." An employee counselor finally took command of the situation. She talked to the chief and found that he had successfully supervised a work project on the reservation. On the suggestion of the counselor, the chief was

[6]Orvis Collins, "Ethnic Behavior in Industry: Sponsorship and Rejection in a New England Factory," *American Journal of Sociology*, January 1946, pp. 293–298.

[7]E. B. Strong, "Individual Adjustment in Industrial Society: The Experience of the Navy Employee Counseling Service," *American Sociological Review*, Vol. 14, No. 3, June 1949, p. 341.

given some training and put in charge of the group. The result was reported in the following words.

The Indians went to work with a will. The supervisor wisely ignored complaints that the Indians were loafers because they took their accustomed siestas, dozing in the shade. The work was done in unexpected ways, but the results were, by the highest production standards, excellent.[8]

Although an emancipation of the distaff side of the human species has occurred during recent decades, women are still accorded an inferior rank in many respects. Most males have many reasons for not wanting female supervisors, and even the women have doubts on this subject. Age also plays a part in status evaluation, even though it does not command its former respect. Older supervisors are often more effective than younger ones, other things being equal.

Education and Experience

Education is an important status factor partly because the knowledge it presumably produces is necessary in an advanced industrial society. It is in many instances the first step in the managerial and professional ladder. Many organizations will not look twice at an applicant who has not completed at least some college. The knowledge that comes from experience may also significantly affect a person's status in an organization. Education is important, but it is not enough. Experience is generally assumed to be an essential quality of the successful man.

Administrative Skills and Related Factors

An executive who has had a great deal of experience in business or other bureaucracies is often much more effective than one without such experience. Familiarity with the ins and outs of the administrative process is highly important in this respect. Knowledge of people may also significantly influence the power structure. An executive who is personally acquainted with persons in key positions has an advantage over an executive who is not well known. A wide circle of friends, membership in a powerful clique, and support from higher executives are often strategic elements in the power structure. The adage "it is not what you know, but who you know" has much validity in the management field. The reason is that executives have to work through other people to get things done. An executive who knows many people has an important ingredient for the achievement of both organizational and personal goals.

[8]Ibid.

Sociopsychological Factors

A person with a large amount of drive often has more power than someone with less drive. Decisiveness or the ability to come to a decision may also be important in this respect. Another applicable quality is the extent to which an executive is motivated toward particular objectives. A strong desire for power and status can cause a person to expend much energy and take many risks to achieve this goal. On the other hand, there are people like Superintendent Revere in the Milo plant who have less power because they do not want to control events.

An ability to "manipulate" people is an important instrument of power in an organization. Social skills, communication capacities, and a talent for leadership can greatly enhance the power of an executive. However, it should not be assumed that effective executives are necessarily well liked. A "struggle" for power is not the same as a popularity poll. Indeed, a powerful executive is not infrequently "feared" as much as he is "liked."

Family, Clubs, Politics, and Other Factors

Family background may make a difference in the manner in which people behave toward a person. The situation that often prevails in family-controlled corporations is almost too obvious to mention. The influence of prominent families can also serve their siblings in many ways. The children of business and governmental leaders frequently have an advantage. They probably gain more from the fact that they are familiar with the intricacies of organizational behavior than they do from contacts made for them. They have learned something about "the rules of the game" and the techniques that make for success.

Fraternal and other forms of association can play a major part in the power formula. Melville Dalton cited constant references to the importance of the Masons in the Milo plant.[9] Of the 21 top managers of the plant only 2 were not Masons. Membership in the community Yacht Club was also related to progress in the managerial structure. It should be noted that membership in some clubs is possible only *after* high status is achieved. Power is both a prerequisite and a consequence with one reinforcing the other.

All of the higher managers in the Milo plant were or pretended that they were Republicans.[10] One of the executives expressed considerable anxiety when a Democratic sticker was stuck to the rear of his automobile. He hoped that his superiors had not seen it. Although there are important exceptions, business executives tend to take a conservative position in their political thinking.

[9]Dalton, *Men Who Manage*, pp. 178–181.
[10]Ibid., p. 91.

Participation in community affairs, such as heading the Community Chest, often provides a basis for higher status within an organization. The contacts that are made with influential people and the publicity that results from such activities are important in this respect. The wives of executives may also help determine their husband's place in the power structure. An executive can be helped by his wife's family background, her skills at company social affairs, and the psychological support she gives him. Social relationships among organization personnel in neighborhood groups, on the golf course, in poker clubs, and at dinner parties are often used for "politicking." Executives who do not participate in such affairs sometimes find themselves with a disadvantage. Informal alliances and "inside" information are important pawns in the power game.

A Combination of Factors

A person's power or lack of it is influenced by a combination of many factors. The part played by a particular factor is most difficult to determine. Some factors add to and others subtract from the total. Being a Catholic may be helpful, but not having a college degree may be a hindrance. A particular quality may be an advantage in one organization, but a disadvantage in another. A Republican, a Protestant, or a Mason may find himself with an asset or a liability in different situations. Some factors are not at all important in one company or locality, but highly strategic in another. Furthermore, status involves more than simply adding together a set of plus or minus attributes. A given factor may have a different value in different kinds of combinations.

THE POWER OF SUBORDINATES

Subordinates may have considerable power even though they do not have authority. The power of subordinates as individuals and as a group acts as a countervailing force upon the power of superiors. Indeed, as was shown for Stevens and Hardy in the Milo Plant, a formally constituted subordinate may actively assume the role of a superior. The factors that make for superior power also apply to subordinates. Ethnic qualities, personality, educational background, length and kind of experience, and administrative and social skills are highly important in this respect.

An important source of subordinate power, as Professor David Mechanic has noted, "is to obtain, maintain, and control access to persons, information, and instrumentalities."[11] A superior who is cut off from the informal stream of information will generally experience difficulties in performing his functions. Subordinates may also use formal rules and regulations as a weapon against a superior. They may use rules to justify inaction on their own part and to keep

[11]David Mechanic, "Sources of Power of Lower Participants in Complex Organizations," *Administrative Science Quarterly*, Vol. 7, No. 3, p. 356 (December, 1962).

a superior from by-passing "red tape" to get an important job done.[12] Subordinates may form combinations to combat or to defend themselves against particular superiors. Such coalitions sometimes involve subordinates in a number of departments and, not infrequently, include superiors who dislike one of their own kind.

The form that subordinate power can take is illustrated by the actions of Joe Cook, an office manager in a gypsum plant. Cook disliked Peele, the new plant manager, and proceeded to make him "look bad" in the eyes of the main office executives. As described by sociologist Alvin W. Gouldner:

"When the main office would telephone the plant, Cook frequently would take the call in Peele's absence. When asked to put Peele on the phone Cook would make some effort to find him, but would finally report that he couldn't contact Peele. Instead of 'covering up' for Peele—as he had for Doug [the former manager]—by pretending that Peele was in some inaccessible part of the mine, Cook would intimate that Peele had not let him know where he could be found. The main office was allowed to draw the inference that Peele was acting irresponsibly."[13]

The ultimate power of a subordinate is that he can quit his job. A subordinate who has strategic knowledge and skills and who cannot be readily replaced generally has a great deal of power. A lack of adequate rewards for the responsibilities that must be imposed to achieve organizational objectives can also put superiors in a highly vulnerable position. The ability to fire subordinates may have little meaning under such circumstances simply because it is difficult, if not impossible, to find replacements. Such a situation shows that authority in an organization is by no means absolute and that it may not be adequate for particular purposes.

THE POWER STRUCTURE: A DYNAMIC PROCESS

The power structure in an organization is in a constant state of flux. Gradual and not so gradual changes occur in individuals. Smith may decide that he doesn't want a vice-presidency. Another addition to the family can cause Jones to really go after a promotion. The recruitment and retirement of personnel always alters the power structure in some fashion. Changes in informal groups or cliques also affect the relative power of individuals and groups.

The Decision-Making Process

Decision making involves the use of authority to implement the plans that result from the planning process. The authority of position and, not infre-

---

[12]Ibid., pp. 362–363.
[13]Alvin W. Gouldner, *Patterns of Industrial Bureaucracy* (Glencoe, Ill.: The Free Press, 1954), p. 75.

quently, informally derived power translate the last step in the planning process (the selection from among alternatives) into decisions that impose behavioral requirements on subordinate personnel.

THE MANAGEMENT HIERARCHY IN ACTION

An organized decision-making process translates broad objectives into more specific objectives as one proceeds from the top to the bottom of the hierarchy. Simultaneously there occurs a transformation of objectives into plans which indicate the activities that will be necessary to achieve them. As Barnard has expressed it, the organized decisional process "is one of successive approximations—constant refinement of purpose, closer and closer discriminations of fact—in which the march of time is essential."[14] At the upper levels primary attention is given to objectives with little attention to the means for achieving them. At the intermediate levels broad objectives are redefined into more specific objectives, and a great deal of attention is given to the solution of particular production, marketing, personnel, engineering, and financial problems. The type of departmentation used at various levels determines the manner in which subsidiary objectives are defined. Thus, the organization objective may be differentiated on a product basis at one level and on a functional basis at another. Decisions at the lower levels are essentially concerned with the specific activity through which objectives are achieved.

DECISION-MAKING CENTERS

The decision-making problem may also be approached from the vantage point of each position in the hierarchy. Every executive, from the president to the foreman, is assigned a certain portion of the total decisional responsibility. The jurisdiction of each executive is defined by a two-dimensional process of delineation which was considered in the chapters on departmentation and on centralization and decentralization. For example, the executive who heads the production department has decisional responsibilities over production problems which have not been delegated to his subordinates or retained by his superior. Within the area thus defined, decisions about production objectives and methods originate with him. The apportionment of the decision-making function reduces the magnitude of the decisional problem. The executive cannot and need not comprehend the vast array of technical and human problems that make up the total executive work load. His function is to provide a solution to a relatively small part of the problem. Each executive should give primary attention to the decisional matters that have been assigned to him, but of course he need not ignore the problems of other executives. Using Adam Smith's mode of expression, by pursuing their own particular interests, execu-

[14]Chester I. Barnard, *The Functions of the Executive* (Cambridge: Harvard University Press, 1951), p. 206.

tives are led by an invisible hand to promote the welfare of the whole organization. Every executive adds a few pieces to a puzzle that cannot be solved by any one of them.

EXECUTIVE RESPONSIBILITIES IN A DECENTRALIZED DECISION-MAKING SYSTEM

A prime ingredient of cooperative planning and control is effective executive action at each position in the hierarchy. The failure of an executive to properly discharge the decisional responsibilities assigned to him may seriously disrupt the process. But executives should also refrain from making decisions that should be made by others.[15] Thus, the superior should not make decisions that ought to be made by subordinates. On the other hand, subordinates should not constantly shift their responsibilities to the superior. As Barnard has pointed out, an important problem of the executive is to determine whether he should or should not make a decision.[16] Although there are no absolute rules, decisional obligations generally evolve from three sources.

1. Decisions transmitted to an executive from higher levels in the hierarchy generally require further decisional action. As noted earlier in this section, broad objectives are redefined into more particular objectives, and objectives are translated into plans. Some superior decisions cannot be executed because they fail to take into consideration the nature of the problems at the subordinate level. Executives sometimes have to practice insubordination if they are to effectively promote what they consider to be the best interests of the organization. They often find themselves between the proverbial frying pan and the fire. A failure to respond to a decision from above is obviously a serious matter, but attempts to impose the decision may have equally serious consequences. It takes courage and social skill to successfully resolve such a dilemma. Some executives have the capacity to make insubordination appear as though it expressed absolute loyalty.

2. Decisional obligations may also evolve from appellate cases referred by subordinates. Such cases can arise from the unwillingness or the inability of the subordinate to make a decision. As Barnard has indicated, the capacity of most men to make decisions is limited and they often try to avoid decisions that involve more than a routine response to conditions.[17] Jurisdictional conflicts among subordinates, lack of information, and insubordination at lower hierarchical levels may also cause subordinate executives to solicit intervention. The executive cannot respond to every subordinate appeal for help without

---

[15]An excellent discussion of the nature of a decentralized decisional system is found in Barnard, *The Functions of the Executive*, pp. 189–194.

[16]Ibid., p. 190.

[17]Ibid., pp. 189–190.

negating the very reason for delegation in the first instance. He should seek to develop self-reliance and initiative among his subordinates by forcing them to make decisions. Subordinates should not feel free to call for a superior decision whenever difficulties darken the horizon. Superiors should generally confine their intervention to important decisional problems, matters that require a precedent, serious jurisdictional questions, and informational deficiencies.

3. Every executive has some decisional responsibilities that are not imposed by superior decisions or referred by subordinates. The nature of such responsibilities is generally defined by the formal plan of organization. The executive must determine whether changes should be made or corrective action should be taken within the subject matter area thus defined. Although he is held accountable for results, such decisions are made entirely on his own initiative. Barnard calls such decisions the most important test of executive capacity.[18] Decisional problems imposed by a superior or posed by a subordinate generally cannot be avoided. But executives can and often do avoid decision over matters that fall within their exclusive province. One reason for a failure to take action is the personal responsibility imposed by the act of decision. The fear of wrong decision is frequently more compelling than the possible adverse consequences of no decision.

THE DYNAMICS OF DELEGATION

The management literature is replete with double talk about delegation.[19] Greater delegation or decentralization has been lauded by many executives, but practice does not always reflect preachments. Executives are often more reluctant to delegate than they themselves will admit. Perhaps the most common problem in this respect is the failure to delegate responsibility over relatively minor matters. Far too many executives clutter their desks and minds with details that could be handled by a literate office boy. Some of them are so concerned with the position of the sheet music on the stand that they fail to conduct the orchestra. They frequently disrupt the work of subordinates by neglecting to develop a systematic approach to delegation. William C. Durant, founder of the General Motors Corporation, had the habit of assuming decisional responsibilities of subordinates without notice. Walter Chrysler, who headed the Buick organization and later served as GMC general manager, relates that Durant at one time sold the Detroit Buick Branch without consulting him.[20] At another time Durant hired one of Chrysler's principal superintendents without informing him about it.

[18]Ibid., p. 191.

[19]A discussion of some of these problems is found in an article by Perrin Stryker, "The Subtleties of Delegation," *Fortune*, Vol. 51, No. 3, March 1955, pp. 94 ff.

[20]Ernest Dale, "Contributions to Administration by Alfred P. Sloan, Jr., and GM," *Administrative Science Quarterly*, Vol. 1, No. 1, June 1956, p. 36.

The qualities of the superior play an important part in determining the kind of functional and social equilibrium that will be achieved in superior-subordinate relationships. The following situation, experienced and described by Sir Ian Hamilton, illustrates the importance of individual differences.[21] While serving as Deputy-Quartermaster-General with the British Army at Simla, Hamilton was constantly faced with an almost endless amount of night work. He described his boss, the Quartermaster-General, as "a clever, delightful work-glutton. . . ." When his chief was ordered back to Europe, Hamilton was asked to assume both the duties of the Quartermaster-General and the job he had been doing. He thought the task an impossible one, but decided to give it a try. To his surprise he found that when his chief departed so did the work. His twelve-hour workday was reduced as though by magic to a six-hour day. The reason was that his former chief liked to record his reasons for every decision, while Hamilton simply said "Yes" or "No." Many subordinates have experienced similar problems in working for and with superiors. They may consider the boss to be somewhat less than efficient or even a little touched in the head, but they rarely suggest that he change his work habits. If the boss likes to work early in the morning or late into the night, many subordinates are inclined to adjust their schedules. If he takes home a briefcase full of work every evening, the office will begin to sprout executives carrying briefcases. If he likes elaborate written reports, subordinates will load his desk with their literary efforts. The work habits of high-ranking executives often influence the behavior of large numbers of subordinate executives at lower levels.

The allocation of decisional responsibilities is also related to the qualities of subordinates. Some subordinates have the capacity to assume more responsibility than others. One may constantly seek to enlarge his domain and another may have opposite propensities. As Lucius D. Clay, who became chairman of the board of Continental Can, has said, "individuals with above average capacities will continually absorb the work and responsibilities of their weaker associates."[22] As a result the actual responsibilities of executives may differ significantly from those specified in the formal plan. Some executives believe that subordinates should be encouraged to add to their responsibilities and make decisions that others fail to make.[23] This idea can obviously be carried too far in a cooperative decision-making system. Anarchy would soon reign supreme if executives failed to abide by the basic pattern of responsibilities set forth in the plan of organization. However, there is generally a shadow

[21]Sir Ian Hamilton, *The Soul and Body of an Army* (New York: George H. Doran Company, 1921), pp. 235–236.

[22]Lucius D. Clay, "The Art of Delegation," in: Edward C. Bursk (editor), *The Management Team* (Cambridge: Harvard University Press, 1954), p. 6.

[23]Ibid., p. 7. This view was also expressed by a number of executives interviewed by the author.

area within which decisional responsibilities may shift between superior and subordinate. Delegation should be viewed as a dynamic rather than a static concept. Superiors frequently increase responsibilities as subordinates become more experienced. On the other hand, the responsibilities of "weak" subordinates are often reduced by redelegation to another subordinate or to the superior himself. An executive may permit a subordinate to make a decision about a certain matter at one time but not at another. A serious mistake by a subordinate may cause a superior to reassume responsibilities formerly delegated. Personal antagonism between superior and subordinate may also lead to shifts in responsibilities.

A MUTUALLY DEPENDENT SYSTEM

The management hierarchy and its adjuncts produce a constant sequence of decisions made by different executives at the same time and at different times. An executive position is both an active and a passive force relative to other positions. The decisions made at each position have an impact on other parts of the organization, but at the same time decisions are made in response to changes that result from the decisions of executives in other positions. For example a decision by the president to reduce the budget of a department presents a decisional problem to the departmental executive. Marketing decisions may create problems for the production executive, and conversely. Decisions are interrelated into a unified system by the hierarchical distribution of functional responsibility. Coordination is achieved by subjecting lower levels of the hierarchy to decisions made by higher levels. The decisional process is made dynamic through the authority relationship. However, the decisional process should not be viewed as a mechanistic system with precise differentiations and interrelationships. Unplanned or informal social interactions among executives and others are an integral part of the system. Such interactions may facilitate or impede the decisional process, but they cannot be eliminated in organizations composed of the human beings who presently inhabit this planet.

12

COMMUNICATION

Communication is an important part of the management process for two reasons. One is that organized planning requires extensive communication among managerial and other personnel. Another is that efficient communication is important in executing a planned program. In the first part of this chapter, communication is considered from the perspective of the organizational structure. Attention is then given to alternative communication media and methods and their effectiveness. The problem of constructing oral and written messages and the importance of listening and reading are considered in later sections.

Organizational Communication Channels

Although the word "channel" is generally used in a more restricted sense, the line of persons through which written or oral messages pass may be viewed as a communication channel. Some persons in a channel play a passive role with respect to the content of the message. They transmit the message to another person who may be the ultimate recipient or yet another link in the channel. Other persons add to, subtract from, modify the content, or change the form of the message before transmitting it to another person. The communication problem is an important consideration in developing the organization structure. As Chester I. Barnard has pointed out: "The need of a definite system of communication creates the first task of the organizer and is the immediate origin of executive organization."[1] The executives who occupy po-

[1]Chester I. Barnard, *The Functions of the Executive* (Cambridge: Harvard University Press, 1951), p. 217.

sitions in the management hierarchy are important links in the chain of information flow.

HIERARCHICAL COMMUNICATION CHANNELS

The hierarchical system gives direction to and imposes restrictions upon the flow of information. Decisional information flows from higher to lower levels and information about performance from lower to higher levels. Executives are required to respond to decisional information transmitted by superiors and provide information about the activities under their direction. If the "unity of command" principle is followed, a subordinate has only one superior from whom he receives orders and to whom he reports. A subordinate need not respond to the decisions of any other superior. Thus, personnel in the sales department is not subject to decisions made by the head of the production department. A functionally differentiated decision-making system modifies the "unity of command" principle by making subordinates subject to a number of functional executives. In such a system, people in the production department are required to respond to the personnel manager on matters that fall within his jurisdiction.

Information flow is also restricted by prohibitions against bypassing levels or "short-circuiting" the line of command. A superior should not directly give orders to anyone who is more than one level below him in the hierarchy. However, emergency conditions may cause a superior to take a personal hand in the affairs of subordinate executives. Restrictions are also imposed on the subordinate's freedom to communicate with those at higher levels in the hierarchy. Bypassing one's immediate superior is generally considered to be a mortal sin in organizational life, but a distinction is usually made between hierarchical decisional relationships and other kinds of contact. The following instructions from an organization publication of the Radio Corporation of America are typical in this respect.

"The organization structure and the organization chart define lines of responsibility and authority; but do not indicate channels of contact. The RCA organization permits and requires the exercise of common sense and good judgment, at all organizational levels, in determining the best channels of contact necessary for the expeditious handling of the work. Contact between units of the organization should be carried out in the most direct way. In making such contacts, however, *it is the duty of each member of the organization to keep his senior informed on*: (1) Any matters on which his senior may be held accountable by those senior to him. (2) Any matters in disagreement or likely to cause controversy within or between any units of the corporation. (3) Matters requiring advice by the senior or his coordination with other units. (4) Any matters involving recommendations for change in, or variance from, established policies. RCA could not operate without freedom of decision at many key action points down the line; yet those who carry senior responsibility must be kept in a position to exercise the direction and control for which they are held accountable. It is the job of everyone to make good use of channels of contact and communication in making this concept work throughout RCA."[2]

As was indicated in Part III, committee and staff organization influence the pattern of communication among executives. Committees create supplementary links in the communication chain and provide additional means for the dissemination of information. They may facilitate communication through the development of executive contact patterns that might not otherwise arise. For example, executives with different scalar ranks often feel more inclined to communicate with one another because a degree of equality is implied by membership on the same committee. Executives from different functional areas, such as production and sales, are given an opportunity to exchange ideas and discuss mutual problems. Staff and functional relationships represent additional elements in the hierarchical communication system. Although staff executives cannot directly transmit orders or commands, the possibility of support by superior line executives means that staff recommendations and advice cannot generally be ignored by subordinate executives. Functional decisional prerogatives give staff executives the same status as line executives with respect to certain functional matters. Thus, a staff executive may have the final word in negotiating a contract with the union or the hiring of certain kinds of personnel.

PLANNED PAPERWORK PROCEDURES

It takes a mountain of paper to conduct the affairs of organization. The flow of forms, records, and reports connects the various elements of an organization. The personnel department is constantly engaged in the task of assembling information about prospective and present employees. The accounting department is concerned with information about cash disbursements, accounts receivable, accounts payable, operating expenses, and other financial matters. Production planning and control translates sales and forecast information into production schedules. Purchasing processes requisitions and orders, receiving reports, invoices, and inventory information. Some paperwork is directly related to the production of products or services. As one writer put it: ". . . the whole complex web of production is kept alive and moving by a network of pieces of paper held together by threads of interdependent and interrelated information which stem from the planning goal and lead to the finished prod-

[2]The Four Basic Organizational Concepts of the Radio Corporation of America (New York: Radio Corporation of America, April 1954), pp. 4–5. (Italics inserted.)

uct."[3] A large volume of paperwork is also required to handle information requirements that are not directly related to production activities, such as social security and tax reports, employee medical records, and public relations material. Paperwork operations are linked together by planned procedures which guide the flow of such information within the organization.

INFORMAL COMMUNICATION CHANNELS

Managerially planned communication channels represent only a portion of the actual communication channels found in an organization. Much of the communication system is informal in the sense that it is not planned by superior executives. Subordinates modify planned channels and create channels that have not been planned. As Professor E. Wight Bakke has concluded from a comprehensive study of a large telephone company:

"Our respondents were reacting . . . not to the planned system of Communication even in those areas where it *was* planned; they were reacting to planned procedures, which they had remade; but what is equally important, they were reacting to unplanned procedures which they themselves had made."[4]

A diversity of opinion can be found on the subject of informal communication. Some executives look upon such communication as a noxious weed that should be eliminated. Others regard it as an important facilitating force in organization communication. Still others can be found somewhere between these two extremes. The problem of evaluating informal communication is partly semantic. The word "grapevine," which is often used to refer to such communication, seems to be used as a synonym for "rumor" and "gossip" by some executives. There is also a tendency to use the word to mean the dissemination of information detrimental to the interests of management. Furthermore, some executives seem to have the idea that the "grapevine" is found only among workers. Such conceptions are given credence by the fact that informal communication may spread false and harmful information, but they fail to take into account the positive role that informal communication can and does play in organizational life. Indeed, there is some question as to whether organizations can survive without such communication.

Management cannot possibly plan every communication channel that will be necessary to perform the work of the organization. The formal or planned system is the framework within which other communication channels are developed by managerial and nonmanagerial personnel. The distinction that is

[3]R. L. Forster, "Coordinating Office with Company-wide Cost Reduction," *Office Management Series Number 125* (New York: American Management Association, 1949), p. 27.

[4]E. Wight Bakke, *Bonds of Organization* (New York: Harper & Brothers Publishers, 1950), p. 84.

often made between "lines of responsibility and authority" and "channels of contact" gives emphasis to the importance of supplementary informal channels. Some organizations explicitly sanction the development of informal channels for operational purposes. Other organizations give implicit recognition to the need for such channels by permitting them to develop with little or no intervention. But not all informal communication channels are concerned with the work of the organization. Some channels evolve from the efforts of people to satisfy purely personal motives. A promoter of a football pool may develop communication channels with individuals who normally buy chances. Other individuals may periodically contact one another for an exchange of jokes or gossip. The channels normally used for organizational purposes may also be used to conduct personal affairs. A "convention-returned" sales manager may describe the attractions of a burlesque show to the production manager during a meeting on changes in product design. The president may give a dissertation on his recent achievements in golf during the weekly meeting of vice-presidents. The foreman may tell the latest "traveling salesman" joke before he informs the machinist that tolerances have been revised. Social relationships that occur outside the province of the organization also have an informational significance. A country club party or an evening of bridge involving organizational personnel is rarely terminated without some reference to the affairs of organization.

Communication Media and Methods

ORAL VERSUS WRITTEN COMMUNICATION

Executives seem generally to make greater use of oral than written communication. Operational studies of executive work behavior indicate that a large part of the executive's working time is taken up by personal contacts with subordinates and others. The average executive probably devotes between 50 and 70 percent of his time talking or listening to people. However, functional and personal factors cause a great deal of variation from the norm. Furthermore, executives have expressed a decided preference for oral communication as a means for gathering and disseminating information. A *Fortune* poll asked executives to select from among four methods the one they found most satisfying in gathering information about their business. Over 55 percent preferred calling in subordinates for verbal reports; 37 percent had a preference for inspection tours; about 18 percent selected scheduled staff meetings; less than 25 percent preferred written reports from subordinates.[5] In another study, the presidents of large corporations were asked to select the methods of commu-

[5]*Fortune*, Vol. 34, No. 4, October 1946, p. 14.

nication they preferred for the transmission of "very important policy."[6] They were asked to select from 5 alternatives the 2 methods that were most likely to get the best results. The following preferences were selected by the 51 responding presidents.

Call a meeting of management personnel and explain orally	44
Hold personal interviews with key personnel	27
Announce policy in a management bulletin	16
Explain the policy in an interoffice memo	14
Explain the policy on the telephone or intercom	1

Of the respondents 21 selected oral methods in both of their choices, and none preferred written methods exclusively. However, 30 cast their vote for a combination of oral and written methods. Written messages are often used to supplement orally transmitted information. Although executives seem to prefer the oral method for most purposes, they also recognize that repetition and review in written form can be an important facilitating instrument.[7] In a similar sense, oral communication can be used to accompany or follow up written messages.

Written media are more effective for the transmission of certain kinds of information than oral methods. Few people can effectively transmit lengthy messages containing financial, production, or other data by oral means. Messages are often distorted as they flow through oral communication chains; written media provide protection against changes in the symbolic content of messages. However, the distortions of meaning that evolve from semantic problems are not necessarily avoided. Messages may be written for purposes other than the transmission of information. Written media are frequently used to provide tangible evidence that some event, agreement, or transaction has occurred. The statement, "I'll send you a memo (or a letter) to this effect," is a common one. Many future disagreements over what was said and by whom can be avoided by written evidence. A written statement may also be used to give *de jure* status to an arrangement arrived at through oral means. Thus, an orally transmitted decision giving a person certain prerogatives and responsibilities is generally followed or accompanied by a written proclamation. Written media are also used to protect the organization in relationships involving contractual obligations; orally transmitted orders from customers, for example, can cause legal difficulties if they are not confirmed in written form. Written

[6]Paul E. Lull, Frank E. Funk, and Darrel T. Piersol, "What Communications Means to the Corporation President," *Advanced Management*, Vol. 20, No. 3, March 1955, pp. 17–18.

[7]Ibid., p. 18; Helen Baker, John W. Ballantine, and John M. True, *Transmitting Information Through Management and Union Channels* (Princeton, N.J.: Industrial Relations Section, Department of Economics and Social Institutions, Princeton University, 1949), pp. 84–85.

records are frequently necessary to satisfy the requirements of tax and regulatory legislation.

FACE-TO-FACE, GROUP, AND MASS COMMUNICATION TECHNIQUES

Oral communication on a face-to-face basis is generally considered to be more effective than other modes of communication. Face-to-face communication means that each person in a pair or group has an opportunity to respond directly to the other or others. An important advantage of this type of communication is that it encourages a two-way process of information exchange. Such a process offers a fertile ground for new ideas and a means for promoting cooperation. Disagreements and misunderstandings can frequently be resolved on the spot, which helps eliminate discord and dissension. Each party is given an opportunity to respond to and modify the views of the other. Superiors can learn something about the reaction of subordinates to a planned course of action and can use motivational and leadership techniques to break down barriers to effective cooperation. The information received from subordinates may bring about beneficial changes in a superior's orders or instructions. Face-to-face communication can help give the subordinate a sense of belonging and personal importance. The organization becomes something more than an abstract force that controls his destiny through impersonal messages from the executive suite.

Face-to-face communication may occur in a variety of unplanned and planned settings. Organizations generally rely heavily on informal contacts as a means of communication. As a top executive of a medium-sized company has said:

"The fact is that we do nearly everything on an informal basis and because all of our executives are in such close touch with each other every day, no formal conference or communications plan seems necessary. We do constantly but informally endeavor to establish in the minds of our executive staff the management policies of the company."[8]

However, many executives believe that informal communication should be supplemented by planned individual and group contacts. One reason is that the informal approach may leave out people who are less gregarious than others or who may simply not be around at a particular time. A systematic program of planned meetings between two or more individuals increases the probability that vital information will be disseminated to those who need it. Another consideration is that planned contacts give the people involved an

[8]William W. Mussmann, "Communication within the Management Group," *Conference Board Reports*, Studies in Personnel Policy, No. 80 (New York: National Industrial Conference Board, Inc., 1954), p. 3.

opportunity to make adequate preparations. Thus, a subordinate is given an opportunity to make a mental or written list of problems that require the superior's attention, and conversely. Preparation and planning may also make a committee meeting more effective than a haphazard informal meeting. The point is not that informal communication should be eliminated but rather that other techniques are generally required for adequate and effective communication. Furthermore, planned individual and group meetings can indirectly promote better communication by setting the stage for informal communication among the participating individuals.

Effective face-to-face communication cannot occur in groups beyond a certain size. Formal procedural rules and chairmanship become a more vital part of the process when the size of the group is increased to more than fifteen people. Although participation is still possible, it tends to be less dynamic and direct than in more informal situations. People are often less inclined to express their feelings and sentiments. Communication tends to become more of a one-way process of information transmission rather than a two-way process of information exchange. However, in spite of this tendency, a formal meeting that limits and directs participation can be an important communication medium. It represents a necessary compromise between the higher degree of participation possible in face-to-face communication and the completely one-way process of talks to large groups.

Speeches to mass audiences can be useful tools in the kit of communication techniques. They can be used to disseminate information rapidly and directly to large numbers of people. They make possible a degree of personal contact between organizational personnel and major executives, such as the company president. Periodic talks by executives can be important motivational devices and promote a greater unity of purpose. For example, a speech that announces some outstanding cooperative achievement or a major policy change can help make people feel that they are a part of and important in the total picture. But it should not be assumed that everyone is effective in addressing a large audience. Success in such an activity requires skills that few people possess in any great measure. The fact that the audience is captive and cannot respond presents another difficulty. Saying the wrong thing or even the right thing in a wrong way can create many misimpressions that are not easily corrected. Lower echelon executives may have to spend a great deal of time setting the matter straight. Furthermore, much of the effectiveness of even the best talks is lost by the fact that people do not have a high listening capacity.

THE DESIGN AND DISTRIBUTION OF WRITTEN INFORMATION

A large volume of written information is composed of messages that are systematically distributed in terms of functional requirements. Such messages, designed for particular purposes and distributed only to those who require them to perform their organizational duties, are frequently written on standardized forms with blank spaces for the message and instructions on preparation and distribution. A disadvantage of forms and other standardized formats is that they place a limitation on the content of the message. However, the use of forms promotes uniformity in message content and quality and reduces the cost of information processing through the economies of "mass production." These advantages are generally sufficient to compensate for restrictions imposed by forms. The problem is to design forms that provide adequate information for the majority of cases. Exceptional matters can be handled by supplementary informational channels and media, such as informal oral communication, committee meetings, or written memoranda.

Standardized messages should be distributed only to those who actually require the information in the performance of their duties. But the question as to whether a person really needs the information does not always have an easy answer. An experience in a large stock exchange house illustrates the problem that can arise in this respect.

"The head of the accounting department questioned a thirty-seven copy report, asking each of the thirty-seven executives who received it whether it was necessary, complete and so on. All answers were emphatically affirmative. The next month he kept all copies in his file and not a question was asked. After several months he discontinued preparing the report. Many man and machine hours, not to mention the paper, have been saved. The surprising thing in this situation was that no question was asked even though all the executives had had the report called to their attention."[9]

In another company, a monthly report distributed to eight departments duplicated other reports that presented the same information in better form.[10] Yet, many years passed before anything was done to stop such unnecessary duplication. Many man-hours of work and dollars of profit were wasted preparing, distributing, filing, and storing a useless report. However, a great deal of money may be lost by a failure to provide a sufficient amount of information. Effective decision making and operations require adequate information about such matters as sales volume, production schedules, material requirements, design and specification changes, purchases and inventories, operating costs, and employee performance.

Some communication problems require a greater range of choice in message construction than is afforded by forms and other standardized formats. Letters, memoranda, reports, employee and management newsletters, and various types of publications can be used to handle exceptional matters. Written messages

[9]Ben S. Graham, "Paperwork Simplification," *Modern Management*, Vol. 8, No. 2, February 1948, p. 22.
[10]Ibid.

may also be specifically designed for and directed to particular persons or groups. For example, a letter or a memo may be used to commend an individual for an organizational or personal achievement. Bulletins and newsletters may be designed to serve the needs and interests of specific groups, such as engineers, chemists, foremen, or office supervisors. Other kinds of written media involve a shotgun approach which attempts to reach a wide audience. Company magazines and newspapers, mimeographed letters and memos, and notices on bulletin boards illustrate this kind of communication technique.

ALTERNATIVE MESSAGE TRANSMISSION TECHNIQUES

Messages can be transmitted through many alternative transmission devices and systems. Thus, a particular message may be transmitted by telephone, bulletin boards, messengers, or airmail. One consideration in the selection of transmission techniques is the problem of time and distance. Telephones, telegraph, teletype, radio, and other electronic devices can be used to transmit messages over long distances. Such devices are extensively used to transmit vital information in organizations that are dispersed over a wide geographical area. Another consideration is the relative cost of alternative transmission techniques .The cost factor may determine whether long-distance telephone or first-class mail is used to transmit a message. A further consideration is that the effectiveness of the message may be reduced or increased by the mode of transmission. For example, oral communication on a face-to-face basis tends to be more effective than oral communication on the telephone. Only one of 51 company presidents surveyed about communication selected the telephone or inter-communication devices to explain important policy.[11] A large majority of the executives polled by *Fortune* reported that they used the telephone "an hour or less" on days they work in their offices.[12] However, although telephone communication may be less effective than a face-to-face approach, it may give better results than other communication media. The effectiveness of a message is also influenced by such alternatives as airmail versus third-class mail, general versus special delivery, and bulletin board posting versus an article in the company magazine.

COMBINATIONS OF MEDIA AND TECHNIQUES

Although some modes of communication seem better than others, a combination of media is necessary to provide the communication potential required for effective operation and cooperation. No one communication medium can adequately serve the diverse functional and personal problems of organizational dynamics. Also important is that a repetition of ideas in different

[11]Lull, Funk, and Piersol, *"What Communications Means to the Corporation President,"* p. 18.

[12]*Fortune*, Vol. 34, No. 4, October 1946, p. 14. Functional requirements and personality factors make for a great deal of variation from individual to individual.

forms is useful in solving some communication problems. What kind of media combination is most effective? An attempt to construct a one best combination for universal or particular application is a hopeless project. There are undoubtedly many combinations that would give equally good results. Ideally, various media should be evaluated in terms of the additional costs and the revenues they produce. However, the problems of forecasting and measurement preclude a rigorous application of the economic calculus. A great deal of communication is concerned with the manipulation of highly subtle and complex sociopsychological forces. The consequences of particular communication efforts are often indirect and not immediately apparent. But the lack of perfect solutions should not deter management from giving consideration to the problem.

The effectiveness of communication media should be systematically and periodically appraised and reviewed. Particular media should be evaluated in terms of functional and motivational requirements. The possibility that specific decisional and operating failures resulted from a lack of information should be carefully scrutinized. Attention should be given to the manner in which media changes may affect particular motivational problems. Management should endeavor to eliminate any unnecessary duplication of communication efforts. Interviews and questionnaires can be helpful in determining the nature and solution of some of these problems. For example, the knowledge that only 6 percent of organization personnel read a particular publication may well justify its elimination. The fact that a large number of people are not informed about certain company policies provides a basis for corrective action. The suggestions and opinions of managerial and operating personnel may also be helpful in planning media changes.

The personal qualities of executives should be considered in the selection of media. Executives should give recognition to their strengths and their limitations. Thus, the president should schedule weekly or monthly speeches before mass audiences of company personnel only if he is a reasonably competent speaker. It might be better for him to communicate his ideas through an informal newsletter or an article in the company magazine. Some executives may find that oral face-to-face communication is more effective for them than written memoranda. Others may find that their forte is written memoranda and formal meetings. Each executive should evaluate his communication successes and failures and plan a media program that best fits his qualities.

The Construction of Messages

The purpose of this section is to give some insights into the problem of constructing oral and written messages. No attempt is made to present a complete or detailed account of speaking and writing techniques. A person who wants more specialized knowledge about techniques can find literally hundreds of articles and books on such subjects as "how to write better business letters," "how to write better sales (credit, collection, or application) letters," "writing business memoranda," "better business and technical report writing," "more effective oral communication," and "preparing and delivering a talk." This discussion is concerned with basic ideas on the development of skills in message construction together with some of the factors that may influence their effectiveness.

KNOWLEDGE OF LANGUAGE

One aspect of communication involves the construction of oral and written messages from a language, such as English, French, accounting, and statistics. Although the message rather than the language performs the communication function, a knowledge of language is an important prerequisite for effective message construction. An understanding of words or symbols and the logic involved in combining them is a necessary first step. The potential messages that can be created by an individual are increased by his knowledge of language. A highly trained mathematician, statistician, or accountant has a far greater potential communication range than a neophyte in these specialized languages. The same thing can be said about such nonspecialized languages as English, French, and German. Language was an important barrier in the communication efforts of American soldiers in France and Germany during World War II. One could add that "never has so much been communicated with so few resources." However, language may also be a limiting factor among those who presumably speak and write the same language. Many people in the United States cannot effectively communicate because they lack knowledge of the English language, and, unfortunately, some executives and aspiring executives can be placed in this category.

THE IMPORTANCE OF VOCABULARY

Effective use of a language requires a knowledge of words and their various meanings and the contexts in which they can be used. The dictionary is helpful in achieving a better understanding of word meaning, but, as Bergen and Cornelia Evans have emphasized, the only way to really understand words is to experience their use in as many contexts as possible.[13] This idea indicates the importance of reading, writing, and conversing as instruments of effective vocabulary formation. How much and what kind of vocabulary should the executive possess? The executive should undoubtedly have a larger vocabulary than the average of the population, and higher executives generally require a more extensive vocabulary than lower level executives. The range of specialized areas of knowledge and the diversity of social situations with which

[13]Bergen Evans and Cornelia Evans, A *Dictionary of Contemporary American Usage* (New York: Random House, 1957), p. v.

the executive must contend make a large vocabulary a highly essential attribute. The executive's vocabulary should include a knowledge of technical terminology and the language of ordinary communication, but the relative emphasis that should be placed upon the two types of language is difficult to determine. Clarence B. Randall, former president of Inland Steel Company, has stressed the importance of the language training of a liberal education.

"The communication of ideas is obviously a function of general education. One learns the effective use of the written word by studying the great literature of the past, and by infinite practice under skilled instruction. One learns to speak by hearing the spoken word of the masters, and by daily practice under guidance. Moreover, general education places emphasis on the speaking and writing of language as generally employed. This is not true in the technical institutions. There the inevitable emphasis is upon the particular terminology in that subdivision of science to which the scholar is devoting himself. Each specialist tends to express himself in the language of his own subject, and this goes so far sometimes that specialists in different branches of science all but lose the capacity of communicating with each other."[14]

It seems evident that people should learn the specialized language of their particular branch of knowledge. The difficulty is that often they cannot adequately read or write the English language. A student sometimes attains high academic achievement in the language of the accountant, mathematician, chemist, and engineer, but he requires a kind and sympathetic professor to pass "some highly useless and impractical" elementary English courses. If something must be sacrified in the educational process, it would seem better for those who aspire to any sort of executive career to learn a little more English and a little less technical jargon. However, too little knowledge of the technical and professional languages can also be a problem. The two goals should not be considered as mutually exclusive; the problem is to achieve a better balance in some high school and university curricula. A major barrier for many students is a negative attitude toward any attempts to change the language habits that were learned from parents and home town cronies.

THE PROBLEM OF GRAMMAR

Grammar is concerned with the classification of words, changes in word form, sentence structure, and the function of words. The grammarians of the past were often highly dogmatic in their views of how people should speak and write the language. They were concerned with what ought to be in terms of a rather rigid predetermined system. Much more attention is presently being given to the manner in which the language is actually used. Although

---

[14]Clarence B. Randall, "A Businessman Looks at the Liberal Arts," *The Randall Lectures* (White Plains, N.Y.: The Fund for Adult Education, 1957), p. 11.

formal grammatical logic is still important, the grammarian has been more willing to accept usage as a determinant of correctness. But the criterion of usage, if carried to an extreme, would sanction a large variety of modes of speaking and writing. The grammar of uneducated people could be called as correct as that of the educated. From the viewpoint of expressing meaning, "bad" grammar is frequently as effective as "good" grammar. However, grammar is only partly concerned with the problem of effective communication. The usage of formally educated people has been a major determinant of what is deemed to be proper in the formal sense. An important by-product is that language usage has important social implications. In the words of the Evanses:

"There are some grammatical constructions, such as *that there dog* and *he ain't come yet*, that are perfectly intelligible but are not standard English. Such expressions are used by people who are not interested in "book learning." They are not used by educated people and hence are regarded as "incorrect" and serve as the mark of a class. There is nothing wrong about using them, but in a country such as ours where for a generation almost everybody has had at least a high school education or its equivalent few people are willing to use expressions that are not generally approved 'as correct.' "[15]

The executive should use "correct" grammar because much of his work and life involves interaction with university graduates, but executives must also communicate with people whose mode of speaking and writing does not conform to this standard. Persons who speak differently in this respect sometimes have communication difficulties. The reaction of the one might be: "How can anyone who speaks in such an 'uncouth' manner have anything worthwhile to say?" The other might think: "He speaks fancy cause he's got 'book larnen' but he don't know nothing about practical things." They fail to communicate because each is evaluating in terms of inferred personal qualities rather than message content. An approach to this problem is to speak in the language of the person or persons being addressed. Politicians sometimes deliberately speak the language of "hill country people" or "street corner society" to get their messages across, but this technique can easily seem contrived when used by people who have never had close personal contact with the environment concerned. A person who has always spoken "proper" English should generally not attempt to speak the language of people who speak in a different manner. Also important is the social precept that a person should not depart too far from the role he is supposed to play. People expect an executive to talk like an executive for the same reason that most children frown when their parents mimic their speech.

[15]Evans and Evans, *A Dictionary of Contemporary American Usage*, p. v.

CONSTRUCTING THE ORAL OR WRITTEN MESSAGE

The problem of message construction is to select a combination of words that most effectively transmits meaning. Message content is frequently controlled by planned message forms and formats. An application form or a purchase requisition indicates the kind of information that should be included in the message. Financial statements and reports are generally written in a standardized format. Many organizations make use of "canned" sales talks, ghost-written speeches, form letters and memoranda, and professionally written press releases. But the problem of message preparation cannot be entirely delegated to the professional, and the discretionary element cannot be completely eliminated by planned forms and format.

There is no easy road to effective speaking and writing. Books and articles on techniques can be helpful in overcoming some difficulties. They often present ideas that are useful to someone who must prepare sales letters, credit letters, public relations material, reports, and various kinds of oral presentations. Dictionaries and grammars are also important facilitating instruments in preparing messages. But a purely techniques-and-rules approach is not generally effective without a background of skills in speaking and writing. Such skills are partly developed through university courses in public speaking, debate, group communication, creative writing, and technical and business writing. Membership on student committees, holding an office in a fraternity, dormitory, or departmental club, participating in teas and other social events, and informal contacts with fellow students and faculty also afford excellent opportunities for developing communication skills.

A message should contain sufficient information to cover the subject matter and achieve the objectives of the speaker or writer. An important determinant of content is the capacity of the message recipient to impute meaning. A few words may be adequate for some people, but many words may not be enough for others. A supervisor may simply say to Jones: "The washrooms need cleaning." But Smith may have to be given detailed instructions on how to clean the washrooms, where to find the proper equipment, and also be told that cleaning activities should begin immediately. Another consideration in message construction is the importance of attracting and keeping the attention of the listener and reader. Humor, analogy, and illustrations are sometimes used to make conversation and speeches more interesting. The opening sentence in sales and other letters is often designd to catch the interest of the reader. Pictures, charts, color, indentations, and variations in type can be used to make written material more attractive.

Many books and articles on technique properly warn against the use of redundant and superfluous words or phrases. However, such words or phrases can sometimes be justified on the basis of social and business customs. For example, a failure to include a complimentary close ("Sincerely yours," "Yours truly," or "Cordially yours") in a letter might be viewed as bad form by a recipient. These words are not information in the ordinary sense, but they may imply a great deal.

The speaker or writer should give consideration to the problems of the other person in designing his message. For example, a subordinate should not involve the superior in a long rambling conversation if others are waiting to see him or when he is busy with an important matter. Written memoranda or reports should be written in a manner that reduces the work-load of the reader. Many reports are far too long and written to impress rather than to inform. A brief summary at the beginning of the report, a table of contents, and the use of appendices for detailed data are usually appreciated by a busy executive who must digest a large number of reports. Messages can generally be improved if people do a little more planning and thinking before they speak or write. Too many people dash off a letter or a memorandum, compile reports, and utter sounds from the mouth in an unorganized and makeshift fashion.

INDIVIDUAL AND GROUP DIFFERENCES

Differences in background, interests, and motives should be considered in preparing messages to particular persons and groups. The employees in the factory should generally be approached differently than those in the office. Communicating with a group of foremen is not the same problem as communicating with vice-presidents or engineers. This idea also applies to communication with different individuals; a technique that works well with the production manager may not give good results with the sales manager or the credit manager. Such problems can be partly attributed to differences in functional responsibilities and professional or vocational interests. In addition, there are the unique personal qualities of individuals and the norms developed by social groups. Thus, one production manager will not react in exactly the same manner as another production manager or a third production manager, and so on. The foundry workers, foremen, or vice-presidents in one company do not generally have the same group norms as the foundry workers, foremen, or vice-presidents in another company. An ideal solution might be to design a different message for each individual or group in the organization. However, the extent to which this approach can be carried into practice is limited by considerations of time, effort, and cost. Another restricting factor is the lack of sufficient knowledge about psycho-sociological dynamics of particular individuals and groups. But in spite of these limitations executives give implicit, if not explicit, recognition to individual and group differences in their communication efforts. They usually develop a great deal of insight about the probable reactions of their subordinates and employ appropriate techniques.

AUTHORITATIVE COMMUNICATION: GIVING ORDERS

An order differs from an ordinary message because it involves the authority relationship. It imposes an organizational responsibility on its recipient and carries with it a threat of sanctions for nonconformity. But the fact that a subordinate is required to respond does not repudiate the ideas presented in previous paragraphs about message construction. An order is in one respect simply an oral or written message from a superior to a subordinate. Like any other message, an order should contain words that transmit the desired meaning and motivate the recipient.

Order-giving techniques may range from a direct order or command to an approach that indirectly implies that something should be done. Between this polarity are techniques inferred by the words "request," "suggest," "recommend," and "persuade." It is sometimes difficult to determine whether a message from a superior is an order or not. But the fact that it comes from a superior gives a message an imperative quality, however subtle, that invites a different kind of response than ordinary messages. The technique that should be used in giving orders varies with the kinds of personalities involved, the social situation, and the circumstances under which they are given. The use of such words and phrases as "please," "would you do this for me," and "I would appreciate" works wonders with many subordinates, but a tough foundry or construction worker might respond better to an order prefaced by a little lusty swearing. The norms developed in a particular social situation are important in this respect. Soldiers expect the first-sergeant to behave in a somewhat uncivil fashion and would probably not respond well to a highly courteous and tactful sergeant. A sergeant should behave like a sergeant, not like the manager of a haberdashery. Order-giving techniques may also vary with the environmental situation; an emergency, for example, often necessitates a more direct approach. The following general guides were prepared by one company to help superiors adapt their orders to particular situations.

A *request* doesn't offend the sensitive worker, while a direct order often antagonizes.

The *direct order*—if not used too frequently—stands out emphatically. It tends to shock a worker out of his lethargy, and may save a dismissal.

A *request* may partly melt the hard-boiled man, and is worth trying before a direct order.

The *implied order* usually gets best results from the dependable worker. But it is *not* for the inexperienced or unreliable.

The first time an error is made, *a request* to correct it adds the friendliness that keeps a man on your side. The *direct order* may be advisable on repetition of the error.

The *direct order* is appropriate for the chronic violator—and if most of your orders have been requests, the change to a direct order will carry emphasis. The *call for volunteers* often is a challenge and produces good results where the job is disagreeable, calls for special effort or involves unpopular overtime. But *don't* use it to escape responsibility for making assignments in the best interests of production.

To develop ability and judgment in a promising employee, the *implied* or *suggestive order* is a good way of trying him out and putting him on his own. Close follow-up may be required, however.

The emergency usually requires a *direct order.*[16]

Courtesy, tact, and finesse are frequently more effective than a direct approach to order giving, but executives should not become "wishy-washy" in their dealings with subordinates. Subordinates generally expect the superior to give orders and behave like a leader. Subtle motivational techniques in order giving facilitate cooperation but only within certain limits. A failure to take a positive approach to order giving may result from inadequacies on the part of the superior. Some people do not like to tell other people what they ought to do, a deficiency that seems often to be rationalized in the name of human relations techniques. A so-called democratic approach is sometimes a sophisticated way to avoid responsibility.

Message Reception Problems

The construction of oral and written messages is only one part of the communication process. The best message is of little avail unless the person at the receiving end listens or reads and makes an effort to understand. We often speak without listeners and speak when we ought to be listening. And we frequently fail to find readers for the avalanche of words that make up the memoranda, letters, and reports of the organizational world. A partial solution is to speak less and say more and to write shorter, fewer, and better messages. But a great deal more attention should also be given to the development of listening and reading skills.

TOWARD MORE EFFECTIVE LISTENING

Listening requires as much, if not more, mental effort and concentration than speaking. It is true that some speakers and subjects are not worth the effort, but listening can reap a large harvest of ideas and help promote cooperation. Effective listening involves more than hearing the words spoken by

[16]Reproduced in: M. Joseph Dooher and Vivienne Marquis (editors), *Effective Communication on the Job* (New York: American Management Association, 1956), p. 106.

another person. The listener should look beyond the words for the meaning and sentiments the speaker is attempting to convey.

A major barrier to effective listening is the tendency of the listener to evaluate in terms of *his* rather than the speaker's frame of reference. The listener's prejudices and beliefs, cued by the words or the person of the speaker, partially or completely inhibit any exchange of information between the two parties. Each party is essentially talking to and about himself rather than to the other person. As the psychologist Professor Carl R. Rogers has said:

"Although the tendency to make evaluations is common in almost all interchange of language, it is very much heightened in those situations where feelings and emotions are deeply involved. So the stronger our feelings, the more likely it is that there will be no mutual element in the communication. There will be just two ideas, two feelings, two judgments, missing each other in psychological space."[17]

Such words as Herbert Hoover, Franklin D. Roosevelt, Republican, Democrat, income taxes, government, and Communist can create an emotional reaction that blots out anything else the speaker may have to say. People often react adversely to the speaker because he is identified with a particular organization or cause. Thus, some people cannot listen to anything Lyndon Johnson has to say, and others have similar difficulties with Richard Nixon. Walter Reuther might have had a problem in getting a point across to an audience of N.A.M. members, and L. R. Boulware might not find too many listeners at a U.A.W. convention. This sort of barrier to effective listening can be partially overcome if people make an effort, in the words of Professor Rogers, "to see the expressed idea and attitude from the other person's point of view, to sense how it feels to him, to achieve his frame of reference in regard to the thing he is talking about."[18] The solution may sound simple, but it is not easy to bring about. Logical argument is generally not very successful in changing sentiments. Most people evaluate because they do not want to change their prejudices and beliefs. Little progress can be made unless a person has a genuine desire to become a better listener. Understanding the problem is also a major step toward a solution, and success in overcoming it is another element in the cure. But people should not expect too much in too short a time; a bad listener, like an alcoholic, overcomes his problem on a day-to-day basis. Third-party intervention may also help overcome emotional

---

[17]Carl R. Rogers and F. J. Roethlisberger, "Barriers and Gateways to Communication," *Harvard Business Review*, Vol. 30, No. 4, July–August 1952, p. 47.

[18]Ibid., p. 47. Professor Rogers then considers some of the barriers to this kind of understanding and techniques for overcoming them.

barriers to communication. This technique is often used in labor-management disputes, marital difficulties, and international conflicts.

OTHER LISTENING PROBLEMS AND TECHNIQUES

Most people can think a great deal faster than a person can speak. A person can listen to a conversation, speech, or lecture, and, at the same time, periodically ponder about last night's poker game, a certain blonde bombshell, a forthcoming football game, the household budget, or picking green peas. Unfortunately, the mind often wanders too far and loses the speaker completely. A good listener does not let his mind drift away from what the speaker has to say. The following suggestions from an article on listening problems and techniques by Ralph Nichols and Leonard A. Stevens can be helpful in this respect.

"Try to anticipate what a person is going to talk about. On the basis of what he's already said, ask yourself: 'What's he trying to get at? What point is he going to make?'

"Mentally summarize what the person has been saying. What point has he made already, if any?

"Weigh the speaker's evidence by mentally questioning it. If he tells you facts, illustrative stories and statistics, ask yourself: 'Are they accurate? Do they come from an unprejudiced source? Am I getting the full picture, or is he telling me only what will prove his point?'

"Listen 'between the lines.' A person doesn't always put everything that's important into words. The changing tones and volume of his voice may have a meaning. So may his facial expressions, the gestures he makes with his hands, the movement of his body."[19]

People sometimes listen for words rather than ideas and may even attempt to memorize the specific sequence of words used by the speaker. A more effective approach is to grasp the main ideas the other person attempts to convey. The details should be synthesized into higher order ideas and meanings. If the listener needs to relate the ideas to others, he should translate them into more specific terms in his own mode of speaking. People may also reduce their listening capacity by taking detailed notes. University students, for example, sometimes attempt to write down every pearl the professor casts before them. They divert too much energy to the act of writing and become frustrated by an inability to record everything. A better approach is to listen carefully and then write down only the leading ideas. If necessary, such notes can be elab-

---

[19]Ralph Nichols and Leonard A. Stevens, "You Don't Know How to Listen," *Collier's*, July 25, 1953, p. 19. This article deals with a variety of listening problems and offers some useful techniques.

orated after the speaker has relayed his message. The ability to remember the ideas presented in a talk or conversation is often enhanced by subsequent review and reconstruction.

People can generally present many "good" reasons for not listening. They behave much like the heavy smoker who feels he ought to quit for health reasons but who finally decides to keep the habit because "there is no real proof that cigarettes cause lung cancer or heart trouble" or "my uncle smoked fifteen cigars a day and lived to be ninety-two." A bad listener may rationalize his habit in some of the following ways: "I couldn't hear because the people behind me were making too much noise." "What can she tell me about raising children? She doesn't have any and she probably won't because no sane man would marry her." "How can an idiot like that give advice on foreign policy?" "He was way over my head the minute he opened his mouth." "What does he know about economics? He doesn't have a Ph.D." "I couldn't understand a word he said because he talked like a man with a mouth full of mush."

Such comments may reflect actual listening difficulties and express legitimate reasons for not listening, but they are often used to soothe the conscience of the lazy listener. People sometimes seem to expend more energy avoiding the problem than it would take to become a reasonably good listener. They may even go to great lengths to make the speaker believe they are listening or have listened. An eager and intense look and a periodic comment or a question is the usual technique. The inappropriateness of some of their queries does not bother them in the least because they have not listened to anything the speaker said. Such techniques do not generally fool the speaker and those who were listening. But more important than this is the loss of information that might have served vital vocational and personal goals. Furthermore, a genuine understanding of others is possible only by listening to what they say and feel.

THE IMPORTANCE OF LISTENING IN THE SUPERIOR-SUBORDINATE RELATIONSHIP

Listening is as important as order-giving skills in obtaining appropriate behavioral responses from subordinates. Some executives unduly stress the importance of order giving in their relationship with subordinates. They assume that a breakdown in communication can be credited either to their failure to properly explain what and why something should be done or to inadequacies on the part of the subordinate.[20] A frequent consequence of this approach is that the superior continues to explain to the point of exasperation, with the subordinate becoming less and less inclined to understand. Professor F. J.

---

[20]Rogers and Roethlisberger, "Barriers and Gateways to Communication," pp. 50–52. Professor Roethlisberger presented this portion of the discussion.

Roethlisberger believes that better results can be achieved if the superior gives less emphasis to explaining and more emphasis to listening. Such a technique will give the subordinate the feeling that he is understood and accepted as a person and that his sentiments are important. The subordinate frequently assumes a more cooperative attitude and may even willingly accept a condition or a command that imposes an extreme personal burden.

AN EFFECTIVE OPEN DOOR POLICY

Executives sometimes have little information about the actual state of affairs at subordinate levels. The sociopsychological restraints of an authoritarian system cannot and should not be completely eliminated, but such restraints can seriously interfere with the planning and control process if they become too extreme. Subordinates, whether they be vice-presidents or foremen, should feel that they can express sentiments without the threat of direct or indirect sanctions. Disagreements by a subordinate with a particular departmental or company policy does not necessarily imply insubordination. Effective communication with subordinates requires a willingness to listen with an open mind to the ideas and sentiments they express. It involves more than a perfunctory statement that "my door is always open." Subordinates must feel that the man behind the door wants to hear what they have to say and that he will do something about their complaints and suggestions.[21] However, it should not be assumed that the superior should make every change suggested by a subordinate. Some complaints are highly unreasonable, and some suggestions unsound. But, even though the subordinate cannot be satisfied through direct action, he often responds favorably to the interest and recognition implied by a superior's willingness to listen. There is also evidence that "talking out a problem" to a good listener can help ease emotional tensions and frustrations. Another important consideration is that listening helps keep communication channels open. Superiors must listen if they want knowledge about subordinate attitudes and activities.

FASTER AND BETTER READING

Executives frequently complain that they do not have sufficient time to read the memoranda, letters, and reports that flow into their offices. They also lament their inability to keep up with the professional, business, and trade literature. The development of reading skills is one approach to the solution of this problem. The average reader reads at the rate of about 250 words per minute, very good readers from 500 to 600 words, and a few exceptional per-

[21]A comprehensive discussion of the nature of the problem and some techniques that can be used to solve it are presented by William Foote Whyte in *Human Relations in the Restaurant Industry* (New York: McGraw-Hill Book Company, Inc., 1948), pp. 217–234.

sons read at the rate of 1000 or more words.[22] But effective reading involves more than the speed at which something can be read. It also requires an ability to comprehend the meaning transmitted via the words. Improvements in reading speed must not result in reduced comprehension if anything useful is to be gained. However, there is evidence that higher reading speeds do not generally reduce the degree of comprehension and may somewhat increase it.[23]

How do people become more proficient readers? Some people are skillful readers because they read a great deal. They practice the preachments of the experts in reading techniques without conscious effort. Better reading habits can also be developed by reading-improvement courses, an approach used with good results by universities and business organizations. For example, a reading course given to executives and other personnel in a number of motion picture studios increased reading speed from an average of 250 to 300 words per minute to somewhat over 800 words per minute with a rather significant increase in comprehension.[24] Equally impressive results have been achieved in many other cases.

What are some of the basic elements that make for more effective reading? Reading is partly a matter of moving the eye over written material. Many reading-improvement courses give emphasis to techniques that increase the span of print taken in by the eye. Use is sometimes made of various types of optical instruments and reading-training films. This approach can help correct habitual eye movements that make for reading inefficiencies, but the idea that reading is essentially a mental process should not be neglected. As Professor Nila B. Smith has emphasized, "the eye movements are simply symptoms of the mental process which a person uses while reading."[25]

Effective reading, like effective listening, requires a great deal of mental effort and concentration. A fast reader reads by lines, paragraphs, and even pages rather than one or a few words at a time. However, the basic problem is to grasp and retain the thoughts expressed by the words. A good way to start a reading venture is to make a quick survey of chapter headings, table of contents, the introductory chapter, graphs and illustrations, and the preface. Such a survey gives the reader some insight into the nature of the content and a basis for deciding whether a more detailed reading is worth the effort. It also provides a mental framework into which more detailed content can later be placed. Another good reading technique is to learn to read by paragraphs.

[22]Nila Banton Smith, *Read Faster—and Get More From Your Reading* (Englewood Cliffs, N.J.: Prentice-Hall, Inc., 1958), p. 3. This book contains many useful ideas and techniques that can be used to improve reading speed and comprehension.

[23]Ibid., pp. 364–366.

[24]Ibid., p. 363.

[25]Ibid., p. 21.

The paragraph generally contains one leading idea around which supporting details are organized. The problem is to find this idea rapidly and then go to subsidiary ideas if necessary. Reading the main idea in each paragraph is sufficient for some purposes. If the details are important, reading proficiency can be increased by mentally organizing subsidiary ideas and facts around the central idea of the paragraph. Watching for directional words is helpful in guiding the reader. For example, words like "furthermore" and "likewise" suggest further elaboration of what has gone before; such words as "but" and "however" give warning that something is to be qualified. The really fast reader knows how to glean the essential ideas by skimming. These readers generally have a comprehensive knowledge of language and subject matter and have great facility in making a synthesis. Completely ignoring the trimmings, they seek out only the really essential or specific ideas and facts.

Even the best reader does not and cannot read everything at the same rate of speed. Some written material contains more meat or less chaff than others; a scientific article, for example, may require a slow sentence by sentence approach. Variations in reading speed also result from differences in reading objectives. Some things are read for details, others for the essential ideas, and still others to find a specific fact. A person who reads novels at a fast clip might slow down considerably with a book or an article in economic theory. But an economist can often read publications in theoretical economics as fast as other people read novels. The degree to which a person is motivated to read something is also a determinant of reading speed. A football or baseball enthusiast may read the sports section in rapid order but slow down considerably for other parts of the newspaper. Some university students read twenty pages of the latest issue of *Playboy* in a much shorter span of time than a five-page assignment in a management book. The kind of psychological barriers that impede effective listening also influence reading capacities. Many people respond negatively to an author's ideas because they evaluate in terms of their values rather than his. Some labor leaders would experience mental torture in reading a publication prepared by the National Association of Manufacturers. Similar trepidations might engulf an executive who ventures into the literature of the AFL-CIO.

13

MOTIVATION

The problem of motivation presents a major challenge to management. It is often difficult to obtain appropriate behavioral responses from subordinates. This chapter is concerned with some basic ideas about motivation and the manner in which they can be used to solve the problem.

The Matter of Motivation

The ability to make effective motivational decisions requires knowledge about the motives which bring about purposeful behavior. The decision maker must have insights into the manner in which people will respond to particular conditions. Human behavior must be susceptible to the concept of causality if control is to become a possibility.

HUMAN MOTIVES: PHYSIOLOGICAL DRIVES

Motivation has its roots in motives within a person which induce him to behave in a particular manner. Human motives evolve partly from the physiological conditions that create sensations of hunger, thirst, pain, and sexuality. These motives will normally cause a person to respond by seeking food or water, eating or drinking, etc. Physiologically induced motives are modified by the customs and norms that prevail in a group or society. For example, babies are generally fed on a socially determined schedule that modifies the time and potency of "natural" hunger pangs. A similar kind of change is involved in the learning that eventually eliminates the need for diapers.

HUMAN MOTIVES: CONDITIONED RESPONSES

Many human motives are acquired by a conditioning process that begins the day a baby is born. When people tend to react in a repetitious fashion, generally they are making a "conditioned process." In Pavlov's classic conditioning experiment, a dog was conditioned to respond to the sound of a bell as though it were a piece of meat. The ringing of the bell was followed by an offer of meat. The sight of the meat gave rise to the salivary mechanism in the dog. Eventually the dog would salivate at the sound of the bell and continue to do so for some time even though behavior was not reinforced by a reward of meat. The bell provided what psychologists call secondary reinforcement in spite of the fact that it does not directly satisfy the hunger motive. However, the secondary reinforcement tends to become weaker unless it is itself reinforced by the primary reward or reinforcement.

In other experimentation, chimpanzees have been conditioned to respond to poker chips with which they could later purchase food.[1] They would accumulate a large number of chips even when they could not be spent until a later date. They learned to distinguish between chips with different values and to select chips in harmony with thirst and hunger drives. Human beings seem to behave like chimpanzees in the way in which they respond to money. Money is an important reward for most people even though it does not directly satisfy their needs. It is a secondary reinforcement or reward which induces appropriate behavioral responses so long as it can be used at some future time to satisfy more basic human motives. Few people will accumulate or hoard money that has no value in the market for goods and services.

CULTURAL NORMS AND HUMAN MOTIVES

Man has an advantage over animals in his ability to create a culture which can be handed down from one generation to the next. A culture may be roughly defined as the totality of norms that govern behavior in a society. Cultures embody the achievements of the past and give humans greater capacity to cope with their environment. Man does not have to constantly begin anew; he has a store of knowledge from which he can draw.

Cultures are transmitted from one generation to the next through formal and informal modes of instruction and indoctrination. Basic human needs make for similarities among cultures, but there are significant differences in ways cultures solve particular problems. For example, polygamy and monogamy are different approaches to the satisfaction of sexual and survival needs.

---

[1]John B. Wolfe, "Effectiveness of Token-Rewards for Chimpanzees," *Comparative Psychology Monographs*, Vol. 12, No. 5, May 1936, pp. 1–72; John T. Cowles, "Food-Tokens as Incentives for Learning by Chimpanzees," *Comparative Psychology Monographs*, Vol. 14, No. 5, 1937–1938, pp. 1–96.

Beef, pork, horse meat, and dog steak are acceptable means for satisfying hunger pangs in some cultures, but they are taboo or disapproved in others. Hindus do not like beef, Moslems abhor pork, and Englishmen are not apt to relish a rare dog steak. Some societies abandon or kill their aged; others provide them free medical care and pay them pensions.

Cultural variations make for differences in human motives. Australian aboriginals would not respond to the rewards that motivate Americans, and conversely. There may also be significant differences in the motives of people from the same basic culture. Studies of underprivileged people in a large metropolitan area in the United States indicate they have widely divergent motives from those found among people with a middle-class background.[2] The motives of executives from lower-class backgrounds differed from executives born into high position.[3] Many other contrasts exist within broader cultural classifications and influence the way in which people respond to responsibilities and rewards.

Many cultural norms arise because man is a social being. Humans need affiliation—contact with their own kind. Gregariousness may be an intrinsic human motive or it may have been acquired over a long period of socializing. Some aspects of social behavior may have evolved from such basic physiological drives as sexuality and survival. Biological families and the various kinds of kinship groupings may have gradually brought about broader social systems. The economic and other benefits that could be derived from cooperative endeavor helped reinforce human social propensities. Social living gives rise to cultural norms and human motives which strengthen social bonds and help preserve the society. The need to defend the society against outsiders may give rise to aggressiveness. Dominative motives may be encouraged for those who are to perform the leadership functions that are required. A feeling of deference may be fostered so that certain individuals can more effectively fulfill the role of subordinates.

Many different kinds of human qualities make for effective social functioning and survival. Some are appropriate for some social goals and not for others. Achievement motives, for example, may promote a great deal of economic progress, but they may also engender high levels of social conflict. Societies have experienced difficulties because they did not have people with the appropriate motives for a particular purpose. S. L. A. Marshall, in an analysis of combat motivation during World War II and the Korean war, noted that many soldiers did not fire on the enemy. An important reason was the soldier's background, which Marshall described in the following words.

[2]Allison Davis, "The Motivation of the Underprivileged Worker," in William Foote Whyte, *Industry and Society* (New York: McGraw-Hill Book Company, 1946), pp. 84–106.

[3]W. Lloyd Warner and James C. Abegglen, *Big Business Leaders in America* (New York: Harper & Brothers Publishers, 1955), pp. 59–107, 144–176.

"He is what his home, his religion, his schooling, and the moral code and ideals of his society have made him. The Army cannot unmake him. It must reckon with the fact that he comes from a civilization in which aggression, connected with the taking of life, is prohibited and unacceptable. The teaching and the ideals of that civilization are against killing, against taking advantage. The fear of aggression has been expressed to him so strongly and absorbed by him so deeply and pervadingly—practically with his mother's milk —that it is part of the normal man's emotional make-up. This is his great handicap when he enters combat. It stays his trigger finger even though he is hardly conscious that it is a restraint upon him. Because it is an emotional and not an intellectual handicap, it is not removable by intellectual reasoning, such as: 'Kill or be killed.' "[4]

Some of the norms and motives that were developed during past periods and for particular purposes can become anachronistic with changing conditions. The motives that are necessary to obtain the proper behavioral responses differ in some degree as societies go from war to peace, from handicraft to mass production, from economic scarcity to abundance, and from ruralism to urbanism. Too much lag in modifying motives can cause an unduly large amount of conflict and disruption in a society. It can also give rise to an excessive amount of frustration, anxiety, conflict, and other psychological problems for individuals.

HUMAN MOTIVES: SIMILARITIES AND DIFFERENCES

There are similarities as well as differences in human motives. Cultural anthropologists have listed universal needs from which particular cultural norms appear to have evolved. Psychologists have also prepared listings of basic needs which reflect the motives that result in human activities. An analysis of human needs may begin with basic physiological drives—such as hunger, thirst, and sexuality—and attempt to relate these drives to the various motivational elaborations that exist in human societies. Many human motives seem to be an outgrowth of simple and complex forms of conditioning which substitute secondary rewards or reinforcements for the real thing. Some of these motives have evolved from the past and persist even though the reason for their existence may be lost to conscious awareness.

The impact of cultural norms on human motives is influenced by the extent to which the norms are enforced by social sanction. Actual social behavior is not always in accord with cultural norms. The behavior of small groups and individuals may depart from cultural norms and social patterns of behavior. The enculturation and socialization processes do not bring about anything approaching complete conformity. Human motives are apt to differ significantly

[4]S. L. A. Marshall, *Men Against Fire* (New York: William Morrow & Company, 1947), p. 78.

in societies with freedom of religion, press, and speech. Differences in families, churches, schools, and other kinds of association make for a diversity of motives.

Human beings have a far greater capacity for reflective and creative thinking than their animal counterparts. Chimpanzees can be conditioned to respond to poker chips, but their ability to learn or create complex sets of symbolic relationships is limited. Man can choose to be a nonconformist, developing norms and patterns of behavior that depart from the dominant patterns of the society. Some uniformity in human motives makes for more successful social living and cooperative endeavor. But there is also a need for diversity in societies characterized by complex divisions of labor. Social and organizational specialization demands people with different motives to fit into diverse roles and tasks. Banks, churches, armies, universities, laundries, hospitals, and restaurants cannot all be manned by people cut from the same cloth. The organizational problem is to put a round peg into each round hole and a square one into each square one. The social problem is to have a sufficient supply of people who have appropriate motives for the jobs that need to be done.

PREMISES FOR MOTIVATIONAL DECISIONS

The problem of motivation should be viewed from the perspective of the cultural norms of the society in which the organization is situated. Although basic physiological and social needs make for uniformities in motives, there are many differences in the motives of people from different cultural backgrounds. The cultural heritage of Americans, for example, makes them more reluctant to accept authoritarianism than other groups. The emphasis on a democratic approach in the political sphere tends to be transferred to religious, economic, and other kinds of social endeavor. Emphasis should also be given to the manner in which cultural changes may affect motivation. The permissive educational philosophies of recent decades have undoubtedly influenced attitudes toward responsibility and authority. The shift from an economy of scarcity to an economy of abundance has significantly marked American attitudes toward consumption and saving, consumer credit, retirement, and leisure. Freudian and Darwinian ideology, the trade union movement, the Great Depression, the political philosophy of the New Deal, World War II, full employment, the specter of communism—these phenomena have modified American beliefs and hence American motives.

THE THEORY OF DOUGLAS McGREGOR

Some motivational assumptions are widely accepted as entirely valid even though they provide only a part of the answer. Douglas McGregor has categorized such assumptions under the label of Theory X, which he called the traditional view of direction and control.[5] One assumption is that the average human being has an inherent dislike for work and will avoid it if possible. Another is that the dislike for work means that most people must be threatened with sanctions to get them to put forth the effort necessary to achieve organizational objectives. Still another is that people generally prefer to be directed, attempt to avoid responsibilities, have relatively little ambition, and want security most of all. McGregor believes that recent research in the behavioral sciences has shown that the assumptions of what he calls Theory Y may be more valid than the precepts of Theory X.[6] The assumptions of Theory Y are described by McGregor in the following words.

"1. The expenditure of physical and mental effort in work is as natural as play or rest. The average human being does not inherently dislike work. Depending upon controllable conditions, work may be a source of satisfaction (and will be voluntarily performed) or a source of punishment (and will be avoided if possible).

"2. External control and the threat of punishment are not the only means for bringing about effort toward organizational objectives. Man will exercise self-direction and self-control in the service of objectives to which he is committed.

"3. Commitment to objectives is a function of the rewards associated with their achievement. The most significant of such rewards, e.g., the satisfaction of ego and self-actualization needs, can be direct products of effort directed toward organizational objectives.

"4. The average human being learns, under proper conditions, not only to accept but to seek responsibility. Avoidance of responsibility, lack of ambition, and emphasis on security are generally consequences of experience, not inherent human characteristics.

"5. The capacity to exercise a relatively high degree of imagination, ingenuity, and creativity in the solution of organizational problems is widely, not narrowly, distributed in the population.

"6. Under the conditions of modern industrial life, the intellectual potentialities of the average human being are only partially utilized."[7]

Theory X assumes that the personal goals of employees are incompatible with organizational objectives. It places major reliance on the use of authority as an instrument of command and control. Theory Y asserts that people have much to offer an organization if they can only be persuaded to accept its objectives. It attempts to take full advantage of the personal and professional

---

[5]Douglas McGregor, *The Human Side of Enterprise* (New York: McGraw-Hill Book Company, Inc., 1960), pp. 33–43.

[6]Ibid., pp. 45–57.

[7]McGregor, *The Human Side of Enterprise*, pp. 47–48. Italics in original were deleted.

potential of employees. The use of authority is assumed to impede the development of this potential, although authority may be necessary if people will not cooperate. The basic difference between the two theories is that Theory Y opens the door to motivational techniques that are precluded by sociopsychological restraints imposed by Theory X.

MASLOW'S HIERARCHY OF NEEDS

Abraham Maslow has developed a theory of human motivation in which human needs are arranged in the form of a hierarchy.[8] At the bottom of Maslow's hierarchy are the basic physiological needs, which are the starting point for most motivational theories. Security, or safety needs, expressed by such phenomena as job tenure and insurance, are found at the second level in Maslow's need hierarchy. The third level is taken up by what Maslow calls "the love and affection and belongingness needs," which may be generally categorized as social needs.[9] Next in line are the esteem needs, which involve both the need for self-esteem and the need to have the esteem of others (prestige and respect). At the apex of the Maslow hierarchy is the need for self-actualization or a need to fulfill what a person considers to be his mission in life. Self-actualization may take many forms: to be an ideal mother; to be an outstanding golfer; to be the top student; or to be the highest paid university professor or business executive.

According to this theory of motivation, lower level needs must be satisfied before higher needs become important. Maslow contends physiological needs to be the most potent of all needs. An individual "who is lacking food, safety, love, and esteem would most probably hunger for food more strongly than for anything else."[10] All other needs tend to be pushed into the background or to become nonexistent. However, after physiological needs are satisfied, they are no longer an important motivating instrument. In Maslow's theory, higher needs emerge as lower level needs are satisfied—safety needs follow physiological needs, social needs come after safety needs, and so on.

Human motives cannot be as neatly categorized as Maslow would have them. A need may become less important as a motivational factor after it is satisfied, but it probably retains some degree of potency by the fact that the rewards involved can be withdrawn. The higher needs undoubtedly play some part in motivation even when lower needs are not fulfilled. However, Maslow's theory of motivation has importance in spite of such modifications. All of the needs in Maslow's hierarchy should be taken into account in planning a motivational system. The relative potency of the needs at the various

[8]A. H. Maslow, *Motivation and Personality* (New York: Harper & Row, 1954), pp. 80–106.

[9]Ibid., p. 89.

[10]Ibid., p. 82.

levels may vary a great deal from one situation to another. Differences among individuals, social groups, organizations, and societies are important in this respect. The principal consideration is that management should attempt to take advantage of the higher needs as well as the more obvious lower ones. Douglas McGregor's Theory Y involves such an approach to maximizing human motivation.

HERZBERG'S MOTIVATION-HYGIENE THEORY

The motivation-hygiene theory developed by Frederick Herzberg is based on a large number of interviews that sought to determine the attitudes that people have toward their jobs.[11] The participants were asked to describe when they felt *good* about their jobs and when they had *bad* feelings about their jobs. Herzberg found that the good feelings were generally related to the content of the job, such as personal satisfaction with the job, the accomplishment involved in the job, and the potential for growth. The bad feelings about the job were for the most part related to context factors, such as company policies, administration and supervision, working conditions, salary, the status situation, and job security. The context factors were categorized as dissatisfiers or *hygiene* factors; the content factors were called satisfiers or *motivators*.

Herzberg believes that industry has been too concerned with hygiene factors, which have the effect of reducing dissatisfaction but which do not motivate. The road to better motivation, according to Herzberg's theory, is to make the job more meaningful and satisfying. Whenever possible, jobs should be made to offer a greater sense of responsibility, achievement, recognition, and growth potential. Herzberg's theory is closely related to Maslow's hierarchy of needs. The hygiene factors correspond to Maslow's lower levels of need and must be dealt with if dissatisfaction is not to cause difficulties. Once these needs are fulfilled, as in Maslow's theory, the job content factors become the motivators or the self-actuating factors. Management cannot ignore such context factors as salary and fringe benefits because a failure to do so would be to invite disruptive dissatisfactions. But, salary and fringe benefits do not motivate in the positive sense. Only the job itself can do that.

OTHER THEORIES OF MOTIVATION

The theory of Chris Argyris points to a basic dichotomy between the needs of the individual and those of the formal organization.[12] Argyris believes that

[11]Frederick Herzberg, "One More Time: How Do You Motivate Employees?" *Harvard Business Review*, January–February, 1968; Frederick Herzberg, Bernard Mausner, and Barbara Snyderman, *Motivation to Work*, Second Edition (New York: John Wiley & Sons, Inc., 1959); and Frederick Herzberg, *Work and the Nature of Man* (Cleveland: World Publishing Company, 1966).

[12]Chris Argyris, *Integrating the Individual and the Organization* (New York: John Wiley & Sons, Inc., 1964).

people are inclined by nature to expend psychological energy toward some purpose and that their personal needs tend to have a priority over the needs of organizations. People will use their energy to subvert the ends sought by the organization if management fails to recognize their needs. Argyris suggests that management move away from a traditional approach, through which people are made to feel submissive and dependent, toward an approach that seeks to improve interpersonal relationships and satisfy the need for self-actualization.

The research of D. C. McClelland has shown that some people appear to have an achievement motive not possessed in the same degree by others.[13] They have a high degree of self-motivation and do not respond in the same way as those who do not possess this motive. People with a high achievement motive appear to make accomplishment an end in itself. Research conducted by Rensis Likert at the University of Michigan has given a great deal of attention to the impact of leadership and supervisory styles on motivation.[14] Likert feels that participative techniques that recognize the behavioral implications of informal groups give better results than an authoritarian approach. Other motivational theories could be noted, but the above incorporate some of the basic ideas on the subject.

HIDDEN HUMAN MOTIVES

People are not always consciously aware of the motives that give rise to behavioral responses. Attempts have been made to determine the nature of hidden human motives through various techniques. Nondirective interviews have obtained insights about people's inner motives, fantasy life, and "unconscious" motivation. Projective techniques, such as the Rorschach Ink Blot Test and the Thematic Apperception Test (TAT), have also been helpful in gaining knowledge on motivation. In the Rorschach test ten white cards showing unstructured ink blots are presented to the subject. From the manner in which he interprets the blots the subject's inner motives are inferred. In the TAT the subject is asked to tell a story about each picture, depicting probable action situations, shown to him. Somewhat underrestrained statements about what interview and projective techniques can do are found on the cover of a recent best seller.[15] The book announced that it would give the startling answers to such questions as: Why do men think of a mistress when they see a convertible in a show window? Why are women in supermarkets attracted by items

---

[13]David C. McClelland, J. W. Atkinson, R. A. Clark, and E. L. Lowell, *The Achievement Motive* (New York: Appleton-Century-Crofts, Inc., 1953); David C. McClelland, *The Achieving Society* (Princeton, N.J.: D. VanNostrand Co., 1961).

[14]Rensis, Likert, *New Patterns of Management* (New York: McGraw-Hill Book Company, 1961); Rensis Likert, *The Human Organization: Its Management and Value* (New York: McGraw-Hill Book Company, 1967).

[15]Vance Packard, *The Hidden Persuaders* (New York: Pocket Books, 1958).

wrappcd in red? Why wouldn't men give up shaving even if they could? Why are automobiles getting longer and longer? It is interesting to note that about two-thirds of the cover of the book is colored red.

Depth psychology has offered some insights about human behavior. And even though it has not provided universally applicable answers, depth psychology has demonstrated that the cause and effect of human behavior has many, and frequently indeterminate, intermediate stages. The reasons for individual and social behavior are not always what they appear to be. Executives should not be surprised to find that many of their assumptions about how people will respond to particular situations were wrong.

Motivation: The Burdens and Benefits of Organized Endeavor

The analysis that follows takes advantage of the behavioral research of the recent past. It considers the basic problem of motivation in terms of the burdens and benefits of organized endeavor. Executives should not impose unnecessary responsibilities, and they should attempt to reduce the burden of the responsibilities that are necessary. At the same time, they should make an effort to enhance the benefits or rewards that may be derived from the acceptance of responsibilities.

ADAPTING AND ADJUSTING RESPONSIBILITIES

One approach to the authority problem is to reduce the responsibilities of subordinates. For example, the territory of a salesman can be changed if he does not like the idea of being away from wife and children for long periods of time. Workers who are reluctant to work on the night shift can be given day work. Executives who do not like to live in a large metropolitan area can be assigned to the Iowa City plant. Some such adjustments are frequently possible, and they may favorably influence authority. The problem is partly a matter of taking advantage of individual differences in subordinates. The burdens imposed by the organization are reduced if such differences are taken into account in assigning responsibilities. Thus, the fact that Brown does not like to live in a metropolitan area and that Smith does should be taken into consideration. But some of the psychological hazards and handicaps that make up organizational responsibilities cannot be avoided. The superior may be forced to use the power of discharge against subordinates who do not perform the responsibilities that are necessary to maintain the organization. However, the defining of "necessary" may be subject to a diversity of opinion. For example, military training during World War II included the digging of what seemed to be an infinite number of foxholes in some rather solid soil. Some officers had the opinion that such responsibilities need not have been imposed because one enemy mortar shell will cause even an untrained civilian to dig deep and well. Other officers disagreed and contended that such responsibilities were necessary to condition recruits to accept the hardships and discipline of combat. The relationship between a superior's decision and the achievement of the organizational objective may be highly indirect. The appropriateness of decision must be judged in terms of many technological and socio-psychological factors which seem to work in combination. There is generally no simple cause and effect solution to the problem.

RESPONSIBILITIES RELATING TO PURELY PERSONAL CONDUCT

Superiors may also impose responsibilities that relate to personal habits as well as work habits. For example, the subordinates of one executive are "compelled" to drink anywhere from five to seven very dry martinis before they are permitted to sup at his table. The subordinates of another dare not touch the stuff if they have inclinations to cash in on the company pension program. Changes in political and church affiliations have occurred because of real or imagined pressures from above. The social relations among the wives of executives may also be influenced by the hierarchy, with the social status of the wife frequently reflecting in some manner the position of the husband.[16] The wives of superiors have been known to affect appointments and promotions within an organization. The behavior of the subordinate's wife at social affairs is sometimes scrutinized by both the superior and his wife. Some careers have been cut short by the fact that the wife could not or did not properly play the part expected of her. Every subordinate must judge for himself the extent to which he will conform to the behavioral requirements of superiors. Although some degree of conformity is generally expected, subordinates should not assume that refusal to conform always results in disaster. The norms of superiors have been significantly modified by subordinates who directly or indirectly impose their conceptions of appropriate behavior. Conformity frequently goes far beyond the expectations of superiors.

ORGANIZATIONAL VERSUS PERSONAL AFFAIRS

The validity of norms that relate to personal behavior in nonorganizational situations has been questioned. Some executives contend that what a man does after working hours is his own business. However, there is no clear-cut line of demarcation between organizational and personal affairs. An obvious consideration is that personal conduct outside the organization may have implications in the area of public relations. A subordinate who is picked up for disorderly conduct in a public bar might properly be discharged, particularly

[16]William H. Whyte, Jr., "The Wives of Management," *Fortune*, Vol. 44, No. 4, October 1951, pp. 86 ff.

if the matter is given wide publicity. Another consideration is that a person's private conduct may infer qualities that relate to behavioral requirements of the organization. For example, a failure to show some deference toward a superior at a social gathering may indicate a lack of respect for persons in authority. Still another consideration is that personal compatibility is related to teamwork within the management hierarchy and in the organization generally. Some degree of conformity to the mores of the group is a necessary feature of the total organizational life. A person to whom the personal habits of associates are repugnant will experience some difficulty in working with them. Such reasoning can also be applied to the wife who is not happy in social relations with company personnel and their wives. Her unhappiness with the situation might well have some bearing on the husband's performance in the organization. A nagging wife can cause a man to dislike a job that he likes for other reasons.

THE BENEFITS OF ACCEPTANCE

Subordinates will accept the burdens imposed by superiors as long as the benefits or rewards are adequate. Authority may be favorably affected by actions that reduce burdens of organizational responsibilities. The discussion thus far has been concerned with this approach to the problem. Attention is now directed to the problem of increasing the rewards of acceptance. The rewards that may be used to maintain or enhance authority take many forms.[17] Some of the more obvious rewards are wages, salaries, bonuses, profit sharing, vacations and holidays with pay, health and retirement plans, and insurance programs. Somewhat less obvious are such rewards as reserved parking space, longer lunch periods, private offices, titles of rank and function, and other special prerogatives and privileges. These rewards can generally be categorized as formal or organizational instruments. They may also be viewed as penalties through the idea that they may be withheld.

The organizing and planning processes place limitations upon the discretion of the superior to allot responsibilities and rewards. One limitation results from the fact that monetary and other rewards available to achieve particular objectives are limited. The superior can influence the share allotted to his sphere of operations to the extent that he participates in planning. The amounts budgeted for wages and salaries in a department are generally affected in some degree by the superior's recommendations. Some superiors make better bargains in this respect than other superiors, which gives them an advantage in maintaining authority. The wages and salaries available in a particular department may be higher than necessary to induce subordinates to accept the

[17]For a comprehensive listing of different types of reward and penalty in organizations: E. Wight Bakke, *Bonds of Organization* (New York: Harper & Brothers Publishers, 1950), pp. 124–125.

responsibilities involved. Another limitation upon the discretion of superiors is imposed by the allocation of responsibilities and rewards in terms of positions. The organization of managerial positions into a hierarchy represents one aspect of this kind of limitation. The situation is subjected to further systematization by job evaluation, salary and wage classifications, employee rating systems for promotion and other changes in classification, and objective standards established by the planning process, such as sales quotas and time study rates. Although superiors play some part in the hierarchical process through which decisions about such matters are made, the discretion that may be exercised by particular superiors is limited by the actions of management as a group.

An organized approach to the allocation of responsibilities and rewards limits the discretion of the superior, but it does not eliminate him as a vital force in the superior-subordinate relationship. The superior may be forced to justify his actions in terms of the requirements of the system, but he wields a big stick through the power to recommend changes in classification and promotions in position. A subordinate's career can be affected far into the future by an adverse report or rating. Subordinate complaints about "unfair" actions by their superiors are not easy to effectuate. Bypassing one's immediate superior is generally frowned upon by higher executives, and such action may not be a good idea even when a formal appeal mechanism exists. Few soldiers register complaints about their noncommissioned and commissioned officers to the inspector-general. Some superiors have memories like the proverbial elephant; formal action against them can have dire consequences for the subordinate.

SOCIAL SATISFACTIONS AND SANCTIONS

Some of the burdens and benefits of organizational association are a product of social interaction among subordinates. The superior should understand the nature of the social system and the manner in which it may influence subordinate behavior. The foundation stone of the social system in organization is the small or primary group. Professor Charles H. Cooley, who first gave emphasis to the primary group as a sociological concept, presented his idea in these words.

"By primary groups I mean those characterized by intimate face-to-face association and cooperation. They are primary in several senses, but chiefly in that they are fundamental in forming the social nature and ideals of the individual. The result of intimate association, psychologically, is a certain fusion of individualities in a common whole, so that one's very self, for many purposes at least, is the common life and purpose of the group."[18]

[18]Charles Horton Cooley, *Social Organization, A Study of the Larger Mind* (New York: Charles Scribner's Sons, 1909), p. 23. For a discussion of primary groups and their significance: ibid., pp. 23–31.

The first comprehensive study of a primary group in an industrial situation was the Hawthorne Study which was discussed in Chapter 2. A vast amount of subsequent research has elaborated on the importance of such groups in molding organizational behavior.

The primary group evolves from interaction or doing something in close personal association with others over a period of time.[19] Interaction may be verbal or nonverbal. A baseball thrown from the pitcher to the first baseman, two persons shaking hands, a helper giving a board to a carpenter, and a waitress giving a menu to a customer are examples of nonverbal interaction. People engaged in a discussion or conversation are interacting verbally. The boundary lines of a primary group are determined by plotting the interaction that takes place among people. A plotting of interactions in an organization would show many clusters of interaction. The people within such clusters interact more frequently with one another than they do with others in the organization. Each cluster of interactions indicates the boundaries of primary groups and cliques that may arise within such groups. An individual may and generally does belong to more than one primary group. He may belong to a group composed of people in his office or factory work area, a group with whom he eats lunch in the company cafeteria or executive dining room, a group commuting on the same train, and many others. The people in a primary group share common sentiments, feelings, and convictions about various things. They develop group norms of behavior which are ideas about how people in the group ought to behave. They rank the individuals in the group and tend to identify themselves with the group.

Individual, Group, and Organizational Goals

The group plays an important part in shaping the behavior of subordinates from vice-presidents to factory and office workers. The penalties that may be imposed by the group for failure to conform to its norms may significantly influence a subordinate's response to organization responsibilities. A subordinate may refuse to obey an order because he fears the penalties of the group more than penalties that may be imposed by the superior. Thus, producing beyond the group output norm or informing on fellow subordinates may give rise to more severe penalties from the group than any that the superior might exact. Even the penalty of discharge is sometimes preferred because the group can make life in an organization a living hell. However, the impact of the group upon subordinate behavior is influenced by the psychological make-up of the individual. Some subordinates make a religion out of the group and adapt their behavior to group norms even though they may fail to reap other rewards. Others are at the opposite pole and behave in a highly "individualistic" pattern. For example, about 10 percent of the employees in one industrial

[19]George C. Homans made a noted contribution to primary group theory in *The Human Group* (New York: Harcourt, Brace and Company, 1950).

situation consistently violated group output norms and were generally not responsive to group pressures.[20] The majority of subordinates fall somewhere between the two extremes. They are attracted by the social and other satisfactions that may be derived from conformity to group norms. At the same time, they do not ignore the rewards that can be conferred by the superior even though conflict with group norms may be involved. Individuals who are highly motivated by the prospect of advancement are generally more inclined to conform to the norms of those who occupy higher positions in the hierarchy. Their behavior may be significantly conditioned by such norms in spite of the fact that they do not frequently interact with higher executives. The ambitious subordinate may be caught in a web when the norms of higher groups conflict with the norms of fellow subordinates. His chances for advancement are enhanced by conformity to the norms of those above him, but they are also affected by his ability to get along with his peers.

Some superiors view the group as a disruptive force in their efforts to achieve organizational goals. Their ideal subordinate is the "rate buster" or individualist who does not respond to group pressures. The difficulty is that most people are not social isolates in a culture that gives so much emphasis to "togetherness" and social conformity. Whether people ought to behave in this manner is an interesting philosophical question. The superior may be able to reshape human behavior to some extent, but he should not attempt the impossible task of remaking mankind. Man seems generally to have propensities to socialize with his fellow man for reasons that need not be explored here.[21] Such propensities undoubtedly further the goals of organization more than they hinder them. An organization could not come into being without individuals willing to work in conjunction with other individuals. Organizations of complete "individualists" do not exist except in the minds of some economic and political theorists. Organization is a social process through which human beings cooperate to achieve a common purpose. It forces individuals into a context in which some degree of social behavior cannot be avoided. However, the socializing process through which organizational goals are pursued may be used to promote purposes other than those of the organization. It also provides an "organized" basis for opposing goals that seem detrimental to the interests of organizational members.

Groups as Positive Instruments of Leadership

The superior should not ignore the positive role that primary groups may play in promoting organizational goals. The following conclusion by the Army Studies in Social Psychology during World War II is pertinent in this respect.

[20]Melville Dalton, "The Industrial Rate Buster: A Characterization," *Applied Anthropology*, Vol. 7, No. 1, Winter 1948, pp. 5–18.

[21]Ralph Linton makes some interesting comments on this matter: *The Tree of Culture* (New York: Alfred A. Knopf, 1957), pp. 29–30.

"The group in its informal character, with its close interpersonal ties, served two principal functions in combat motivation: it *set and enforced group standards* of behavior, and it *supported and sustained* the individual in stresses he would otherwise not have been able to withstand."[22]

Psychological research by the Army Air Forces among air combat units came to the conclusion that "the primary motivating force which more than anything else kept these men flying and fighting was that they were members of a group in which flying and fighting was the *only accepted way* of behaving."[23] A good commander was interested in the welfare of his men with respect to such things as food, living conditions, recreation, medical care, promotions, and awards. However, these factors "did not seem in themselves of primary importance in keeping the men flying and fighting."[24] The test of effective leadership, according to the researchers, was the ability to create and maintain group solidarity and group norms that promoted desired ends.

Similar conclusions were made by a research group from the Harvard School of Business Administration in a study of labor turnover and absenteeism in the California aircraft industry.[25] The aircraft industry had experienced a tremendous expansion in plant and personnel to meet the production demands of World War II. A major difficulty was the occurrence of over 175,000 terminations of employment between March and October of 1943. Statistical data indicated that some work centers had much less labor turnover and absenteeism than others. An intensive study was made of a work center composed of nineteen workers with an excellent attendance and production record. The workers in this center behaved as a group rather than a disunited collection of individuals as was found in other work centers. The researchers concluded that group solidarity had an important bearing on the problem being studied. The worker who attended regularly did so because he had a close identity with his group. He enjoyed the human association and took pride in group accomplishments. The group in turn imposed sanctions against individuals whose behavior threatened satisfactions that evolved from group living. The sanctions of the group seemed more effective in controlling absenteeism than direct action by management. A major factor in the development of this kind of teamwork was that the immediate superior recognized the importance

[22]Samuel A. Stouffer, et al., *The American Soldier*, Vol. II (Princeton, N.J.: Princeton University Press, 1950), pp. 130–131.

[23]John C. Flanagan (editor). *The Aviation Psychology Program in the Army Air Forces*, Report No. 1 (Washington, D.C.: U.S. Printing Office, 1948), p. 208.

[24]Ibid.

[25]Elton Mayo and George F. Lombard, *Teamwork and Labor Turnover in the Aircraft Industry of Southern California*, Business Research Studies, No. 32 (Boston: Division of Research, Graduate School of Business Administration, Harvard University, October, 1944).

of group solidarity and gave attention to human as well as technical problems.

The importance of the group is also evident in these events that occurred in a Chicago restaurant. A waitress, named Jo, decided to quit because she disliked the hours. The waitress' sister, Ellen, who worked in the same restaurant, told the supervisor that she was leaving too. The supervisor tried to get the sister to stay, but was told: "Miss Jenkins, Jo and I have always worked together, and that's the way we want it to be." The matter seemed settled. The more Miss Jenkins talked to Ellen about staying the more resistance she got. The next day Ellen had changed her mind. Why? In her own words: "I'm staying. They talked me into it. Jo's quitting, but I'm going to stay awhile. Yes, it was the girls, Ann and the rest of them, they went to work on me. They told me I was foolish to quit. Well, I thought it over, and I thought after all I'll never have such a good bunch of kids to work with. I've been here eight months so I might as well stay another four and make it an even year."[26] The restaurant retained an experienced waitress. The satisfactions offered by the group were more important than the inducements offered by the superior.

Social satisfactions represent an important aspect of the totality of benefits that may evolve from organizational association. They may compete with other rewards in the sense that an increase in one results in a reduction in another. Thus, the amount that can be paid in wages and salaries is reduced if socializing (such as extended coffee breaks) reduces productivity. However, socializing may increase productivity without increasing the cost side of the ledger. The following situation illustrates this idea. The comptroller of a plant, who was in charge of the office workers, was concerned about social activity during working hours. He related the problem to Professor William F. Whyte in these words.

"You know, I've just come back from a visit to the main office, and I want to tell you, the contrast is really unbelievable. They have an office force several times as large as ours, and it's all in one big room. But you could stand in that room any time of the day and hear a pin drop. Now, down here the place is in an uproar a good deal of the time. Of course, I realize that people sometimes have to talk to each other to get their work done, but I know lots of times when they are talking it can't be just about the work. I wonder, Dr. Whyte, do you think I should ask them to quiet things down? [Whyte asked how well the work was done.] Oh, I'm more than satisfied with that. Two years ago when I came here we had 62 people in the office; we now have 57, and still we are handling 40 per cent more orders than we were when I

[26]William Foote Whyte, *Human Relations in the Restaurant Industry* (New York: McGraw-Hill Book Company, Inc., 1948), pp. 136–138.

started. Why, last week they put out a volume of orders that I didn't think was possible. Whenever we have an emergency, I only have to ask them to put out a little extra effort, and everybody pitches in. Now, I'll bet you that, man to man, the main office doesn't begin to put out the volume of work we do right here. . . . But I don't know. It doesn't seem right. The place is in an uproar. . . ."[27]

The comptroller did not take action to eliminate the uproar, but he continued to worry about the unbusinesslike atmosphere it created. His worry about the situation expresses the cultural precept that work is work and play is play and the two should not be mixed. Had he taken action to "correct" the situation, the result might well have been a reduction in output and a negative attitude toward him and management generally. The argument is not that organizations should be turned into social clubs but that the socializing involved in working with others may reduce the burdens and increase the benefits of organizational association. The superior cannot completely control the social situation, but he can take care not to destroy satisfactions that enhance the cooperative process.

STATUS AS AN INSTRUMENT OF MOTIVATION

The status system is an instrument of motivation; status is extremely important to most people. It is something the organization can offer to promote a greater degree of cooperation. The possibility of a loss of status is likewise available as an inducement to greater cooperation. This negative aspect of status, however, is generally a less effective motivational instrument.

Abilities and Aspirations

The status system should be closely related to the abilities and aspirations of people in an organization. When high status is conferred indiscriminately, the significance of status is reduced for people who have high status and those who seek higher status. An army with more generals than privates does not have an effective status system. An unduly large number of vice-presidents has a similar effect. Another problem arises when equal status is conferred on those who are not equal in ability. If two persons, who are not equally good accountants, are given the title of senior accountant, the result is frequently a great deal of friction and dissatisfaction. It should also be remembered that management is not the only judge of qualities. The informal social system may reverse a status decision by management by refusing to give it recognition from a behavioral standpoint. Since status is determined by an ability to get along well with others, the status of two people who are equally qualified

[27]Eugene Staley (editor), *Creating an Industrial Civilization* (New York: Harper & Brothers Publishers, 1952), p. 220.

from a technical point of view may actually be unequal. For this reason, social skills deserve consideration in making status decisions.

Ideally the status system should reflect the differing aspirations of people in an organization. Such an equilibrium would maximize satisfaction in this respect and greatly facilitate cooperation. If the aspirations of a great many people cannot be satisfied by the existing status system, one possibility is to upgrade status by manipulating the instruments of status. Such a policy, however, presents a danger because status is relative. The result may be a net loss in the satisfactions offered by the system. Another approach is to strive for more realistic aspirations. Young college graduates, for example, often have unrealistic expectations about the role they will play in industry. Better use can probably be made of the employment interview and the orientation period to correct such difficulties. Sometimes people can be given the recognition they desire through other channels, such as a photographic contest, a hobby club, or athletic programs. Sufficient emphasis should always be given to the importance of a person's present role in the organization and the role he may play in the future. Future possibilities should, however, be realistically appraised, or the satisfactions created today may result in greater dissatisfaction later.

Conferring Recognition: de Jure or de Facto

Serious status problems are created by giving an individual recognition or promotion without conferring upon him the formal symbols and instruments of status. To make the man a division head without giving him the title of vice-president may create many personal and organizational problems. His scalar rank is equal to other division heads, but his status is not equal. Placing someone in a functional or scalar position without full status credentials should be done only on a temporary basis. Withholding formal status recognition may result in "jockeying for position." The individual feels insecure and attempts by political and opportunistic means to gain his rightful "place in the sun." Another serious problem may be caused by a long delay in filling a vacancy. To "keep them guessing" generally does not motivate the candidates in the direction of higher productivity. It often leads to all sorts of connivance, which does not serve the organizational ends. This kind of policy may cause a valuable executive to resign if he is not promoted. The longer he "campaigns" for the vacancy, the greater will be the possibility of resignation to "save face" before friends and followers. Some of the candidates for a vacancy may be unknown to management. Individuals may assume that they are qualified and being considered when such is not the case. Management should recognize such a possibility and make every effort to determine the possible candidates and reassure them that they have not been overlooked for the future.

The Deadwood Problem

The effectiveness of the status system can be seriously reduced by "bad" appointments. A short period of opportunism in making appointments or of failures in forecasting human propensities can plague the organization for many years. Universities sometimes have problems with professors who lose interest in teaching and research after they attain status. Corporate executives, governmental officials, and military officers are sometimes not unlike professors in this respect. Over a period of time an accumulation of such appointments can destroy the motivational significance of the status system and seriously disrupt teamwork. Who wants status if any idiot seems to achieve it? Why make an effort if no effort seems to be necessary? Executives should carefully scrutinize the appointment process at all times. It may be better to tax the present somewhat by a lack of personnel in order to safeguard the future welfare of the organization.

The problem of "deadwood" is complicated by the fact that a decision to confer higher status is not readily reversed. The difficulty increases when high status personnel, such as presidents, vice-presidents, generals, and admirals, are involved. When a person is removed from a position, the integrity of the appointing officials is at stake. For that reason, an executive is often "protected" even when it seems evident to others in the organization that an error in judgment was made in the appointment. Another important factor is the normal reaction to anything that tends to upset the status quo. The removal of an executive or a foreman even when justified may establish a "dangerous" precedent in the organization. The difficulty of reversing a status decision is further enhanced by "alliances." The removal of one executive may involve the removal of other executives. This problem may make necessary the retention of an incompetent executive to prevent a serious disruption in the executive ranks. To mitigate some of the above difficulties, the high status person is generally asked to resign and is not infrequently given a bonus.

The Problem of Status Anxiety

Many status problems are caused by management's failure to understand the significance that status has for people and to recognize a problem as a status problem. People do not always respond as a presumably rational person should. It is a serious mistake to assume that such behavior is not as it ought to be and, therefore, something to be ignored. The difficulties that can arise in this respect are well illustrated in a case reported by Roethlisberger.

"The personnel of a certain department was moved from one building to another. In the new location, because of lack of space, it was found necessary to seat four people across the aisle from the remainder of the group. It happened that there were three women in the department who were to be transferred to other work. These three were given desks across the aisle so that their going would not necessitate a rearrangement of desks. The fourth person, a man, was also given a desk there, simply because there was no other place for him to sit. In choosing the fourth person, the supervisor was undoubtedly influenced by the fact that he was older than the rest of the group and was well acquainted with the three women. But, beyond that, nothing was implied by the fact that he was chosen. Now see how he interpreted this change. He felt that his supervisor regarded him as one of the women. The women were being transferred to other types of work; consequently he too would be transferred before long. Two of the women were being transferred to jobs in the shop. He, himself, might be transferred to the shop; and there was nothing he dreaded more. Having dwelt on speculations like this for a while, the employee recalled with alarm that his name had been omitted from the current issue of the house telephone directory. This omission had been quite accidental. The house telephone directory, however, constituted in this concern a sort of social register. Names of shop people below the rank of assistant foreman were not printed unless they were employed in some special capacity requiring contacts with other organizations. With the exception of typists and certain clerical groups, the names of all office people were listed. The fact that his name had been omitted now took on new significance. It tended to reinforce his growing conviction that he was about to be transferred to an unimportant shop position. He became so preoccupied with the problem that he could not work. He was completely demoralized."[28]

Some people might conclude that the man was "not very rational." That such a response is not an isolated case is indicated by the "status anxiety" expressed by a number of college professors when they were incorrectly listed in the university catalogue.

Who Else Calls Him Tony?

People generally view their situation in relative rather than absolute terms. Thus, the status value of calling a superior by his first name is closely related to the number of people who assume this prerogative. John P. Marquand illustrated this idea well in the novel *Point of No Return*. The characters are Anthony Burton, president of the Stuyvesant Bank, Charles Gray, a young executive working for Burton, and Nancy, his wife.

"Look here, feller," Mr. Burton said, and he blushed when he said "feller," "why not cut out this sir business? Why not just call me Tony?"

That was in 1941 but Charles still remembered his great joy and relief, with the relief uppermost, and that he could hardly wait to hear what Nancy would say.

[28]F. J. Roethlisberger, *Management and Morale* (Cambridge: Harvard University Press, 1947), pp. 34–35.

"You know, Charles," Mr. Burton had continued, "Guthrie Mayhew and I have quite an idea. We're going to get hold of Tommy Mapes on the New Haven and see if he can't get us a special car on the eight-thirty. How about getting aboard? My idea is to call it the *Crackerbarrel*."

"Why, thanks," Charles had said. "I'd like to very much, Tony."

He had worked late that night and he could not remember what train he had taken home, but Nancy had been asleep when he got there.

"Nance," he said, "wake up. I've got something to tell you. Burton's asked me to call him Tony." And Nancy had sat bolt upright in her twin bed.

"Start at the beginning," Nancy had said. "Exactly how did it happen, and don't leave out anything."

They must have talked for a long while, there in the middle of the night. Nancy had known what it meant because she had worked downtown herself.

"Now wait," she had said. "Let's not get too excited. Who else calls him Tony?"[29]

Nancy's last statement is also pertinent when applied to other things, such as a salary increase, a private secretary, a private office, an invitation to the boss's home, and a longer lunch period. A walnut-paneled office for one assistant vice-president will certainly cause comment if other assistant vice-presidents have ordinary offices. It is sometimes better to leave the walnut-paneled office vacant. Difficult status problems may be caused by wage and salary differences among those who consider themselves to be equal in qualification and contribution. One executive, for example, expressed delight with a salary increase. A few days later he found that a fellow executive had received a much larger increase. The result was dissatisfaction, which was not in the least compensated by the fact that he did get a significant raise. Management should be able and ready to defend its wage and salary policy; it should not and cannot depend on secrecy as a means for controlling this source of status difficulties. In some cases such a problem may result from an individual's unrealistic appraisal of his qualifications and accomplishments. Management may not be aware that a status problem exists. The solution to such difficulties lies in the maintenance of effective communication. Maintain a real "open door" policy. *Listen* to what your subordinates have to say. Let them tell you *their* problems. One of them may be a status problem.

The Telephone Directory as a "Social Register"

The primary purpose of the company telephone directory is to facilitate the mechanics of internal telephone communication. However, the listing of names in the directory may have important status implications. The telephone direc-

[29]John P. Marquand, *Point of No Return* (Boston: Little, Brown and Company, 1949), p. 20.

tory sometimes becomes a sort of "social register" which confers higher status upon those who are listed. Since many people in the organization are not listed, the appearance of a person's name gives a degree of distinction. The status value of a listing is also influenced by the fact that high status people, such as the company president, are listed with low status personnel.

Office Layout as a Status Factor

The arrangement of desks in an office is a matter of efficient workflow in the eyes of the industrial engineer. To people in the office, the position of a desk may have status implications. The desks in the front row may have different status value than those in the rear of the office. Proximity to the supervisor's desk or office and the type of desk may also have status implications. For example, one walnut desk among metal desks can create a status problem.

The Status Value of Meat and Vegetables

In his study of the restaurant industry, Professor William F. Whyte found that different foods had different status values to the employees.[30] The preparation of fish ranked lower than the preparation of chicken or meat, and working with odds and ends had less status value than working with large slices. Highest in the vegetable field were luxury or decorative items such as parsley, chives, and celery; next came green beans and then spinach and carrots; after white potatoes came onions, which occupied the bottom of the scale. One worker made it quite clear to the researchers that she did not usually peel onions. The fish station in one restaurant presented an interesting status problem. The working supervisor, Gertrude, was a skilled and valuable employee in the kitchen. The importance of her work was enhanced by the wartime meat shortage. In spite of these facts, her position occupied the bottom of the status hierarchy because of the attitudes that the employees had toward fish.

A Blue Serge Suit and Dungarees

Clothing may be an important status symbol even when management makes no demands in this respect. Miller and Form found that the clothing worn by people in a small garage symbolized their status.[31] The owner generally worked in a business suit. The stock and order clerk removed his coat and worked in his shirt sleeves. The head mechanic also removed his coat, but he wore a nonfunctional white smock. The mechanics wore full-length blue jumpers; the apprentices and clean-up men wore overalls or discarded clothing of darker hues. The mode of dress was not formally planned or enforced by management, but it was scrupulously observed. Social sanctions were applied

[30]Whyte, *Human Relations*, pp. 35–41.
[31]Delbert C. Miller and William H. Form, *Industrial Sociology*, 2nd ed. (New York: Harper & Brothers Publishers, 1964), p. 483.

against anyone who attemptcd to risc above his status by wearing clothing "inappropriate" to his job. The same type of differentiation in the clothing worn by people of different statuses can be seen in every organization. Were this not the case, organizations would probably give greater attention to formalized status identities such as uniforms, insignia, and the like.

A Man's World

Professor William F. Whyte found that many status problems in restaurants arise when lower status individuals seek to originate action from those who have higher status. He found a great deal of friction between the bartender and the waitresses in one restaurant. The waitresses, in ordering the bartender to mix drinks for customers, were violating his conception of the role he should play in a man's world.[32] A possible solution to such a problem is indicated by the way a bartender in another restaurant handled the problem. This bartender lined up the orders and mixed enough of a particular kind of drink for all the orders. He would then call on the waitresses to get their orders. In this way the waitresses responded to him rather than the reverse. The bartender was dominating the scene as he thought a man should. Age, seniority, skill, sex, and pay were important factors in the status situation. Countermen disliked taking orders from waitresses. Highly paid and skilled cooks often resented taking orders from lower status men and from waitresses. Whyte found that some of the friction and tension between countermen and waitresses was eased by having the waitresses place orders on a spindle.[33]

These problems are not confined to the restaurant industry. One industrial plant found itself faced with a wildcat strike when a woman (who was well qualified) was given a job in an exclusively male department. A male tool-crib attendant in a manufacturing department composed primarily of women may result in a conflict situation. A young supervisor, who may be otherwise well qualified, in a department composed of older people may create serious status difficulties.

Titles and Rank Are Important

Management could give greater attention to the formal instruments of status than is sometimes the case. The expression, "We don't emphasize titles or rank in our organization," may reflect a healthy situation. But it may also ignore the positive role that titles denoting rank and function, formal ceremonies, insignia, and other status identifications can play in motivating managerial and nonmanagerial personnel. The formal status system should be given periodic scrutiny and viewed as a positive element of executive control.

[32]Whtye, *Human Relations*, pp. 78–79.
[33]Ibid., p. 69.

RESPONSIBILITIES AS REWARDS

Purposeful activity and the product it produces may become important sources of satisfaction. Some people enjoy accounting, selling, typing, operating a lathe, managing, and the many other responsibilities that make up organization. The world would truly be a vale of tears if work were actually the burden it is so often assumed to be. Much of what people say about work is the product of the learned and habitual responses that make up the culture. The idea that work is a burden is impressed upon people from early childhood. People seem generally reluctant to admit they enjoy work for the same reason most children say they dislike school. A distinction should be made between what people say about work and the satisfactions that may actually be involved. Most sinners are against sin even when they are caught in the act.

A great deal has been written about the satisfactions that were presumably removed by the breakdown of crafts into routine and repetitive factory operations. The craftsman produced a complete product which gave evidence to the skills he possessed. The satisfactions that evolved from these creative efforts have not been measured by strictly scientific techniques, but it is generally assumed that work was more satisfying under such conditions than those that exist in modern factories. The technological and organizational innovations that reshaped the work of manufacture have also remolded the office. The modern office is much like a factory and the office worker has in many respects suffered the fate of the craftsman. A similar statement can be made about the manager who, unlike the "entrepreneur" of economic theory, performs only a portion of the total task of managing. Such consequences cannot be avoided as long as man seeks to reap the advantages of cooperative endeavor. Much of the work in modern organizations is undoubtedly as satisfying as the work performed by the craftsmen of old. However, some tasks do not seem to meet the requirements that give rise to a "pride of craftsmanship." The more routine and repetitive jobs are particularly vulnerable in this respect.

Some subordinates thrive on responsibilities and gain as much satisfaction from them as from monetary and other inducements. Even those who seem to dislike work and gripe a great deal may be motivated by an increase in responsibilities. Attention should also be given to techniques that make work more interesting and satisfying. Routine and repetitive tasks can sometimes be made less burdensome by enlarging the responsibilities involved in a position or job. Another approach is to limit the time an individual is assigned to such work, and still another is to change or increase responsibilities over a period of time. Superiors should not neglect the important part that words of appreciation and commendation can play in making work a more satisfying experience. Subordinates, whether vice-presidents or production workers, like to feel that they are needed and that they are doing a good job.

The satisfactions afforded by "pride of craftsmanship" have a parallel in another important source of satisfaction. Henry Dennison, the New England industrialist, wrote many years ago, "there may be a team craftsmanship which can make an even stronger appeal."[34] Such satisfactions stem from the idea that subordinates are members of a team producing an important product or performing a vital service. Superiors and organizations generally should emphasize the development of pride in team accomplishment. The satisfactions that may have been lost through a breakdown of the craft can often be replaced by the satisfactions of successful cooperative effort. Subordinates should be given an understanding of the manner in which they fit into the big picture. An effort should be made to provide a perspective that transcends the job and to give their efforts a meaning that has social significance.

The concept of team craftsmanship, which involves pride in the objectives of team or group effort, may encompass the entire organization. It may be carried a slight step further by the idea that people may assume a personal loyalty to a particular organization irrespective of the objectives pursued Thus, a person who takes pride in producing automobiles may take particular pride in the fact that he is a member of the General Motors Corporation. Such statements as "I am a Yale man," "I boost the Cornhuskers," "I am a member of the Carpenters Union," "I am a Congregationalist," and "I am an American" suggest an identity with organizations that have characteristics distinguishing them from other organizations of a similar type.[35] Differentiating characteristics may be deliberately developed, or they may evolve as a by-product of techniques used to achieve other purposes. Organizations become unique "personalities" through such instruments as names (Ford Motor Company or Union Carbide), trade names (Wheaties or Lucky Strike), songs (I'm a Rambling Wreck from Georgia Tech), buildings (architectural form and size, such as tallest building in Chicago), advertising copy, traditions, quality products, a good labor policy, and many others. Every aspect of organizational operations may play a part in creating the image people have of an organization.

Motivation: A Dynamic Concept

The problem of motivation should be viewed in terms of a combination of complementary and competing factors. A motivational system must satisfy many different human motives if the organization is to survive. A lack of knowledge about motives precludes any kind of perfect solution to the prob-

[34]Henry Dennison, *Organization Engineering* (New York: McGraw-Hill Book Company, Inc., 1931), p. 86.
[35]Bakke, *Bonds of Organization*, p. 152.

lem. Fortunately, there are automatic adjustments which can help compensate for failures in motivational decisions.

BURDENS AND BENEFITS: AN INTEGRATED APPROACH

A strict dichotomy between the burdens of organizational responsibilities and the benefits of acceptance cannot be maintained in actual practice. Burdens are benefits for some subordinates, and benefits may become burdens. Thus, as was pointed out in the previous section, organizational responsibilities may take on the properties of reward through "pride of craftsmanship" and "team craftsmanship." The social pressures imposed by the group may turn an organizational reward into a penalty. Production beyond group output norms that results in higher wages or promotion may give rise to countervailing penalties by the group. The penalties that may be invoked from such external sources as unions, professional associations, religious organizations, and wives are also important in this respect. For example, a worker who refuses to participate in a slowdown "ordered" by the union may be rewarded by his superior but be penalized by union leaders and members. Rewards for the performance of responsibilities that interfere with a subordinate's obligations to his church may become a penalty. A higher salary or a promotion may not be worth the fires of hell to people with strong religious propensities. A promotion that involves a tranfer to another city can become a penalty if the subordinate's wife dislikes the idea. Even a vice-presidency may not be sufficient compensation for tirades of discontent at home. General economic and particular market conditions can have considerable impact on organizational rewards. A salary increase may mean very little if other companies are offering 20 percent more for the same kind of work. The threat of discharge is less potent when there are more jobs than job seekers.

Subordinates generally view their situation in terms of the totality of burdens and benefits accorded them. They also tend to balance present burdens and benefits with those that may be offered in the future. A subordinate may accept burdens in the present for expected future benefits. He may also forsake a satisfactory relationship in the present for a lack of future opportunities. Subordinates are never completely satisfied or dissatisfied with a particular departmental or organizational association. They tend to react to a combination of burdens and benefits, each of which plays some part in the conception they form about their situation. Particular burdens and benefits add to or subtract from the totality of satisfactions, but there does not seem to be a simple cause and effect relationship between the elements and the whole.

MONETARY AND OTHER INCENTIVES

The problem of motivation may be viewed in purely monetary terms. The customer exchanges money for products and services; stockholders and creditors exchange money for an expected monetary return over a period of time;

suppliers exchange material things for money; employees and executives exchange work for wages and salaries. Such exchanges are generally made on the basis of monetary values determined by market and institutional forces. The importance of money as an instrument of motivation is sometimes undervalued. Money has a universal appeal because it embodies the means for satisfying almost every human motive. It can be exchanged for an evening at the theatre, Roquefort cheese, brown shoes, a dinner date, a week in Paris, a case of bock beer, an umbrella, a regimental tie, or a management book. The motivational problem is greatly simplified by a money system. Large-scale organized endeavor would be impossible without it.

Cooperative behavior is social and gives rise to social satisfactions which also have important motivational properties. The prospect of achieving higher status in an organization and in the society is another part of the picture. Also significant to many people are the satisfactions that come from the achievement of organizational and professional goals. Organizational behavior is motivated by some combination of these incentives. One individual generally requires a different combination than another. Some people are more highly motivated by money than by social satisfactions, status, or craftsmanship. Others accord a relatively lower rank to the values expressed by monetary rewards. There is little likelihood that a large number of people would respond well to only one of these incentives. An organization that seeks to motivate primarily through monetary incentives or social satisfaction would undoubtedly experience difficulties.

MODIFYING MOTIVES: PERSONNEL REPLACEMENTS AND OTHER ADJUSTMENTS

Some adaptation to the incentives available in particular organizations is provided through recruitment and resignations. The recruitment process tends to bring in people who are inclined to respond favorably to particular combinations of incentives. Forced or voluntary resignations can also serve an important function in this respect. People willing to accept prevailing policies will stay; those unwilling to do so leave. There are obvious limits to this kind of adaptation. An organization may become so unpopular that it cannot attract sufficient personnel to maintain itself.

Organizations often change the motives of their personnel through education or indoctrination. They frequently spend large amounts of money to build a favorable image through advertising and other means. Stockholder and employee relations programs are highly important instruments for molding the motives of organizational participants. The inculcation of appropriate motives is also an integral part of many executive development programs.

14

DYNAMIC LEADERSHIP

Leadership may be defined in terms of the totality of functions performed by executives as individuals and as a group. Every chapter in this book is concerned with some aspect of leadership thus defined. Leadership is viewed from a more limited perspective in the discussion that follows. It is approached from the vantage point of the particular superior-subordinate relationships that make up the management structure. The responsibility of the superior is to direct behavior into channels that promote the achievement of organizational and departmental goals. However, the benefits that can be accorded subordinates for the burdens imposed by the superior are limited. To put the matter in economic terms, a given amount of revenue must be produced with a given amount of wage and salary cost. The wages and salaries paid to subordinates should equal their marginal revenue product under equilibrium conditions. However, such an equilibrium can be disrupted by variations in leadership capacity. Some superiors are able to produce more revenue with a given amount of wage and salary costs than others. In other words, the fact that *A* instead of *B* occupies a particular position may significantly influence the manner in which subordinates respond. The difference can be attributed to leadership or the capacity to make subordinates more willing to accept the burdens imposed by the organization. Executives can be said to have working capital in the form of the authority that evolves from their positions.[1] They may add to or subtract from this working capital through leadership or the actions they take with respect to factors that influence subordinate behavior.

[1] George C. Homans, *The Human Group* (New York: Harcourt, Brace & Company, Inc., 1950), p. 425.

Leadership: A Problem of Techniques

Much of the literature on leadership techniques has been concerned with relatively simple systems of superior-subordinate relationships. Leadership studies have stressed leadership in informal groups and the problems of first-line supervision. Such studies have provided a basis for the development of improved techniques. However, the leadership problems in complex hierarchies may differ in important respects from those found in simple systems.[2] The restraints imposed by a hierarchical system may force the leader to depart from what might otherwise be regarded as appropriate leadership techniques. Leadership in a formal hierarchical system is partly a matter of manipulating organizational instruments through which authority is maintained. Purely personal leadership qualities are important, but they are not always primary.

MAINTAINING THE AUTHORITY OF POSITION

An executive is a leader by virtue of the position he occupies in the hierarchy. Position is also a source of authority because, as Barnard has pointed out, people generally "impute authority to communications from superior positions. . . ."[3] The authority accorded an executive is not necessarily related to any personal leadership abilities he may possess. Some degree of authority may result even when the person occupying the position violates every known precept of personal leadership. Executives should recognize the importance of position in the authority relationship and promote "the authority of position" by appropriate actions.

Proper performance of the decisional responsibilities of the position is important in maintaining authority. The executive may consult his subordinates about possible alternatives, but he should make the final decision on matters that fall within his jurisdiction. Subordinates generally expect the leader to lead even when they have taken part in the proceedings. This idea has significance apart from its implications relative to personal leadership. The executive maintains the authority of position by creating the presumption that only he has the right to communicate decisions about certain matters. The ideas contained in a decision may have come from subordinate line and staff personnel, and it may sometimes appear that the executive is a pilferer of ideas. However, a failure to impress on others that his position gives him a monopoly on decisional information may have even more adverse consequences.

An executive in a hierarchical system should help maintain the authority of

[2]George C. Homans gives recognition to the difference in developing "rules of leadership": ibid., p. 425.

[3]Chester I. Barnard, *The Functions of the Executive* (Cambridge: Harvard University Press, 1938), p. 173.

executives in other positions. Thus, a superior should not communicate decisions involving matters that have been delegated to subordinate executives. He may make suggestions, exert influence, and even make the decision, but it is important that he not give the impression that he rather than the subordinate made the decision. The decision should be communicated by the subordinate if it falls within his jurisdiction. All this is another way of saying that executives should respect the formal channels of command. They should not give themselves or others the license to openly subvert the integrity of the formal system of "authority."

Much communication in the management hierarchy is informal, and some such communication bypasses the formal channels of authority. Informal communication frequently compensates for the informational inadequacies of the formal chain of command. It provides an important means through which information pertinent to decision can be considered and communicated without a repudiation of the authority of position. Decisions are generally communicated formally by the appropriate executive even when the nature of the decision is already well known informally. Such action may seem like an anticlimax, but it helps maintain authority.

An open challenge to the authority of position cannot generally be tolerated even when the challenger is right by other standards. General Billy Mitchell was "right" about the future significance of air power in warfare, but he was "wrong" in publicly questioning the authority of his superiors. In other words, he did not abide by the accepted norms of behavior in the military hierarchy. An organization can be destroyed if incompetent executives are able to maintain their positions by imposing sanctions. Many might contend that generals other than General Mitchell should have been demoted and court-martialed, but an organization can be destroyed by a breakdown in the system of authority. Discharging subordinates for failure to obey decisions they know to be wrong and defending an incompetent superior may seem unfair; however, such actions are sometimes necessary if the system of authority is to be maintained.

IMPERSONALIZING THE AUTHORITY RELATIONSHIP

The lives of subordinates may be greatly affected by the superior's power to impose sanctions. Superiors can obviously take advantage of the situation and invoke norms that are not related to the requirements of the organization. Tendencies in this direction cannot be avoided as long as organizations are composed of human beings, since some aspects of every superior-subordinate relationship involve responsibilities that relate to personal goals rather than organizational goals. But too much use of organizational power to serve the whims and fancies of a superior can disrupt teamwork and have adverse motivational consequences. Such power should be used to serve organizational interests and should not be destroyed by dissipation. Many subordinates reared in the traditions of the American culture are psychologically predisposed against the idea that the superior-subordinate relationship is a master-servant relationship. The behavioral norms that form a basis for imposing rewards or penalties should generally be susceptible to rationalization in terms of organizational responsibilities. The authority relationship becomes impersonal to the extent that the subordinate views his role and that of the superior from such a perspective. In other words, the acceptance of decisions by superiors becomes an obligation imposed by the organization rather than a personal obligation. Such a construction of the situation facilitates the maintenance of authority and explains why subordinates often obey the orders of a person they would disobey under other circumstances. Also important is that the burden of the superior is made less difficult by the idea that decision making is an organizational responsibility. The organization rather than the superior becomes the culprit when decisions repugnant to subordinates have to be made.

MOTIVATING SUBORDINATES THROUGH PARTICIPATION

Leadership in cooperative endeavor may be authoritarian, democratic, or *laissez faire*. An authoritarian leader makes all the decisions without subordinate participation. The *laissez-faire* leader, if he can be called a leader, gives the group complete freedom in determining activity. The democratic leader falls somewhere in the middle of the two extremes. He actively solicits suggestions from subordinates, frequently acts on their advice, and gives them a range of discretion in performing their activities. This terminology is used to categorize leadership techniques and does not necessarily relate to similar terminology in the political field. Thus, a leader in a "democracy" may use authoritarian techniques to promote the will of the people.

Democratic leadership techniques can produce good results. The participation involved in democratic techniques can motivate through "ego-involvement" in a group purpose. The social satisfactions made possible by greater freedom of action may also be important in this respect. The nature of cultural and social conditioning undoubtedly play a part in the response that people make toward leadership. An arbitrary leadership approach seems generally to be frowned on by people who have been reared in the traditions of "government by law" and "due process."

Actual leadership situations are rarely completely authoritarian or completely *laissez faire*. Laissez-faire groups seem to develop informal leadership and, in some instances, an informal hierarchy of leaders. Formally organized authoritarian systems, such as the hierarchies of business organizations, usually become somewhat democratic through formal and informal modifications. Subordinate participation may be promoted through such formal devices as commitees, or it may evolve through informal interaction. However, a limitation is imposed by the concepts of work division and specialization. If carried to an extreme, subordinate participation repudiates the logic of hierarchical organization. What does the superior do if subordinates do most of the work? A lack of knowledge on the part of subordinates also places a limitation on participation. The superior cannot always act on the suggestions and ideas of subordinates. Motivational difficulties may result if subordinates, rightly or wrongly, begin to feel that their views are not taken into consideration. It might have been better not to invite participation in the first instance. Furthermore, it should not be assumed that subordinates always want to play an active role in the superior's realm; many people shun responsibilities and seem willing to let others assume the burden.

KEEPING SUBORDINATES INFORMED

Inappropriate behavior by subordinate personnel may result from a failure to provide them with sufficient information. Superiors sometimes fail to recognize the nature of the difficulty and attempt to "reestablish" authority by imposing penalties. Such actions can create serious motivational problems and cause subordinates to question the superior's capacities. Although the difference is not always apparent, superiors should distinguish between informational and authority problems. Measles are not cured by skin grafts or by taking out the appendix.

Subordinates should have knowledge of or access to knowledge about the norms defining appropriate behavior and the consequences of conformity or nonconformity. The functional requirements of the position and formal company policies should be explicitly set forth. Also important is information about the informal norms that pertain to the position. For example, the superior might discreetly point out that the president of the company likes well-dressed executives and that a certain residential section is "a nice place to live." Subordinates can acquire many insights from fellow subordinates who often provide information the superior cannot "admit" in his official capacity. The superior's wife and the wives of other executives can also serve an important informational role. The idea that communication is a two-way process should not be neglected. A lack of knowledge about norms can often be attributed to listening or reading failures on the part of the subordinate. It may also result from an inability to learn some of the more implicit and subtle rules of organizational living. Some people do not have sufficient social skills to respond to cues that may be obvious to others, and they may fail to advance in the organization or even be discharged for reasons they do not understand. Such consequences may seem unjust unless viewed in terms of organizational interests.

CONSISTENT INTERPRETATION AND ENFORCEMENT

Superiors should generally be consistent in interpreting and enforcing norms. Subordinates cannot adapt their behavior to norms that are not susceptible to being learned. Unfair norms consistently enforced are sometimes more just than fair norms enforced in a capricious fashion. Erratic enforcement can create feelings of frustration, futility, insecurity, and distrust. A major problem is that some norms have highly subjective qualities. Professor E. Wight Bakke has concluded from empirical information on this matter, "the great bulk of behavior traits for which participants are rewarded and penalized is subject to personal judgment and not to objective standards."[4] Significant variations may occur in the manner in which norms are interpreted and enforced by different superiors. An appropriate mode of behavior for one superior may be inappropriate for another. Such variations may result from different conceptions of how best to achieve departmental or organizational objectives. They may also reflect differences in the personal backgrounds and goals of superiors.

Too many changes in superiors over a short period of time can have serious disruptive consequences. Each change requires some degree of adaptation on the part of subordinates with resignations, discharges, or transfers for those who cannot adapt. This problem can be partly solved by leadership training programs to promote more uniform standards. Uniformity is also imposed by the fact that lower levels of the hierarchy are subject to control from higher levels, and, to some extent, subordinate executives are molded into the image of the superior. Promotion from within gives impetus to this phenomenon. It is generally more difficult to adapt to a superior who comes from the outside, since the norms in one organization often differ from those found in another. Variation in the interpretation and enforcement of norms cannot be avoided if personality differences exist. Such differences should not always be viewed in terms of good or bad leadership. Even a superior who violates many of the so-called rules of leadership may be successful if his approach is consistent enough to permit subordinate adaptation.

UNDERSTANDING THE SOCIOPSYCHOLOGICAL ENVIRONMENT

An important prerequisite for effective leadership is knowledge of the sociopsychological environment. The psychological makeup of subordinates has an important bearing on the way in which they will respond to organizational responsibilities and rewards (or penalties). Some subordinates may be positively influenced by particular modes of leadership, and others may react in an

---

[4]E. Wight Bakke, *Bonds of Organization* (New York: Harper and Brothers Publishers, 1950), p. 129. A discussion of this problem is also found in: ibid., pp. 107–115.

opposite direction. The behavior of subordinates may also be significantly molded by the norms imposed by informal groups. The superior should become familiar with the nature of group norms and their pertinence to the problems with which he must contend. Some such norms may give support to the goals of the organization, and others may present difficulties. Superiors should listen to what subordinates have to say and make an effort to understand their conception of a situation. They cannot effectively control or change behavior without an understanding of the factors that may influence behavior. Also important is knowledge about the sociopsychological situation at higher positions in the management hierarchy.

CONFLICTING ORGANIZATIONAL AND PERSONAL GOALS

A hierarchical system is subject to conflicts about the appropriateness of organizational goals and conflicts between organizational and personal goals. Such conflicts can be resolved through decisions from superiors that can be enforced through the power to impose sanctions. But the power to impose sanctions should not be viewed in absolute terms. Subordinates may also impose "sanctions" through a refusal to cooperate. They may be fired, but they can also quit. Superiors are sometimes forced to adapt organizational goals to the personal goals of subordinates. Barnard's idea that executives should not make decisions that will not be obeyed involves this kind of problem.[5] It may be better to modify a decision than to be faced with an open challenge to authority. Such a challenge destroys authority and cannot generally be tolerated. A superior may be forced to fire a subordinate he would rather retain, a situation that can frequently be prevented by taking into consideration the possible reaction of subordinates to a decision. However, the fact that the superior must respond to decisions from higher levels may present difficulties in this respect. The superior is sometimes caught between the proverbial frying pan and the fire. Dire consequences may result if he openly disobeys his superiors, but obeying them may bring about serious difficulties with subordinates. Some might argue that obeying higher superiors is the best way out of the dilemma. They fail to recognize that subordinates can destroy a superior's career by a failure to give him support. This dilemma is generally resolved by adjustments that operate in both directions. As Professor Bakke has written, "the modification of the formal system by the inventiveness and adjustments of the very 'human' people in the organization, in response to personal and social as well as to operational needs, is extensive."[6] Such modifications are made at every level of the management hierarchy. Each superior-subordinate relationship involves a fusion of organizational and personal goals and an adaptation of one to the other. Much of this adaptation occurs with the tacit consent of

[5]Barnard, *The Functions of the Executive*, p. 194.
[6]Bakke, *Bonds of Organization*, p. 61.

higher levels, the result of which is a variation between the formally established norms and those that are actually enforced. Superiors may also deliberately distort decisional information from higher levels to compensate for problems at subordinate levels.

Some appropriate actions by superiors are highly indirect and may even seem contrary to the best interest of the organization. For example, a superior may recommend that an XYZ typewriter be purchased because a secretary has a preference for that particular brand. This typewriter may be less efficient and more expensive than another as measured by the standards generally used in purchasing, but the decision may better serve the organization than a more "logical" decision through direct and indirect motivational consequences. The superior can often gain more support from subordinates by showing a regard for the things that are important to them. As Professor Homans has noted about the superior, "it is only when he has shown by his actions that he accepts group norms that he can induce the group to adopt his own norms."[7] A superior may even respect group norms that conflict with those of the organization. However, he is sometimes forced to take action that reduces his effectiveness with subordinates as a group or as individuals. For example, he may have to impose penalties on a subordinate who is an informal group leader or who is well liked by fellow subordinates in order to maintain the authority of position even though the offense may not be serious from other points of view.

Considerations
Leadership: Strategic and Tactical

The specific action that should be taken in a particular situation cannot be determined without a knowledge of the many factors that are involved. Appropriate action in one situation may not be appropriate in another. The following discussion develops an understanding of some of the strategies and tactics that can be used to enhance authority.

THE USE OF SPECIFIC SANCTIONS TO ENFORCE AND REINFORCE AUTHORITY

The effectiveness of specific sanctions is related to the degree to which subordinates are satisfied with the totality of benefits accorded by organizational association. The threat of discharge is less effective if many subordinates are on the verge of quitting. It may be more effective if employment in the organization or under a particular superior is highly valued. Specific sanctions are not often required when they are most effective because subordinates are

---

[7]Homans, *The Human Group*, p. 426.

generally less inclined to disobey orders. On the other hand, they may have to be used a great deal when they are least effective because subordinates are less apt to obey. There is a limit to the extent to which specific sanctions can be used to maintain authority. Specific sanctions, if properly used, can help reinforce authority, but they should not be viewed as the primary instrument of authority.

The relationship between authority and specific sanctions is somewhat paradoxical. The use of such sanctions indicates a breakdown of authority. Authority cannot be maintained if sanctions are constantly required. The organization ceases to exist if every subordinate must be discharged for failure to accord authority. Sanctions should not often be required to enforce a superior's orders. The use of severe sanctions, such as discharge or demotion, should be a rare rather than a regular occurrence. However, superiors should not take a completely negative attitude toward such sanctions. Some seem to have the idea that the need to impose sanctions can be avoided by "human relations" techniques. It is sometimes assumed that discharging a subordinate represents a failure on the part of the superior rather than the subordinate. Such a conclusion may be correct in some instances but certainly not in all.

A periodic use of specific sanctions to enforce decisions or reinforce authority may be good strategy on the part of the superior. Poker players who always bluff, traffic police who never make arrests, nations which are not disposed to fight, and professors who do not flunk students tend to become less effective in pursuing their purposes. The examples that are made of the few may have a pronounced sociopsychological impact on the many. The following story about Frederick the Great, the Prussian military leader, illustrates this idea.[8] While making the rounds of his camp after "lights out," Frederick found a light coming from one of the tents. He entered and saw a Captain Zietern in the act of sealing a letter. The officer fell on his knees and begged to be forgiven. "Take a seat," said Frederick, "and add a few words to what you have already written." Captain Zietern obeyed and wrote as dictated, "To-morrow I die on the scaffold." The next day he was duly executed in the interests of discipline. The penalty may seem rather harsh for the offense involved, but not if it was necessary to maintain the security of the camp from enemy attack. The act of one man could have meant the death of thousands of soldiers. The execution of Captain Zietern also had a meaning beyond his act or fate. The authority of future orders with respect to "lights out" and other matters was undoubtedly reinforced.

A superior may sometimes deliberately seek an example with which to reinforce authority. Otherwise faithful subordinates frequently develop "bad habits," such as staying out too long for coffee, too much tardiness and ab-

[8]Sir Ian Hamilton, *The Soul and Body of the Army* (New York: George H. Doran Company, 1921), p. 100.

senteeism, or simply a lackadaisical attitude with respect to a number of matters. The situation can often be corrected with a little talk by the superior, but some situations may require more extreme measures. Appropriate action may consist of a general warning and a dismissal to make it stick. The superior might simply fire the first man who strays from the straight and narrow. However, this approach may result in the discharge of someone who is vitally needed. Such a consequence cannot and should not always be avoided, but a more selective approach may better serve the organization. One method is to pick a subject the organization can well do without and try to get him to hang himself. The person selected should not be too well liked by other subordinates. A word of warning: the superior must be able to justify his actions on some rational basis. He must not seem arbitrary or unjust to those who remain in the organization.

Two considerations are basic in the use of specific sanctions. One is the attitude of the subordinate or subordinates directly affected by discharge and other disciplinary actions. Another is the manner in which the use of sanctions may influence the behavior of other subordinates. The first consideration is relatively less important when the sanction of discharge is employed. However, the superior should attempt to make a dismissal as palatable as possible for public relations reasons. A discharged employee can help give the organization "a bad name" and create dissatisfactions among employees with whom he may interact socially. The superior should also recognize that some sanctions are equivalent to discharge. Such sanctions as a demotion or a reprimand may cause a subordinate to take a negative attitude toward the organization. The consequences that a sanction can have upon the future behavior of the subordinate concerned should always be considered. It is sometimes better to discharge or not take any action than to impose a lesser sanction.

RAPID CONDITIONING THROUGH SANCTIONS

Superiors may deliberately impose many specific sanctions in an arbitrary fashion to rapidly condition subordinates to accept their decisions. Some aspects of military training illustrate this mode of developing authority. The recruit is conditioned to respond to decisions without question by a sequence of severe sanctions for nonconformity. Sanctions may even be imposed without "cause" with more severe sanctions for those who question the "unfairness" of the situation. The subordinate soon learns that the burdens of disobedience are far greater than the burdens of obedience. He also learns that the superior is "right" even when he is "wrong." The process is relaxed after a period of time partly because sanctions have fulfilled their purpose and partly to take advantage of the rewards implicit in a reduction in disciplinary action. A severe disciplinarian may seem less severe to subordinates than a lenient superior who becomes a little less lenient. However, superiors in business organizations may experience difficulties in using sanctions in this fashion. The majority of subordinates may quit the first time a superior begins to act like a first-sergeant. It is much more difficult to escape the long arms of the military police, and any attempts in this direction may have dire consequences, to say the least. Soldiers do not generally like confinement in a military prison, and they do not have unions to protect their interests. The chaplain is helpful, but he is apt to "give unto Caesar the things that are Caesar's." Yet, in spite of the differences in the ultimate power of the two organizations, superiors in business organizations should not ignore the possibility of using the above approach in a more restrained manner.

THE STRATEGY OF THE LENIENT SUPERIOR

Some superiors are more lenient in enforcing decisions and organizational policies than others.[9] A failure to enforce strict discipline may result from psychological propensities that make the superior reluctant or unable to impose his will on others. The superior who has a psychological need "to be liked" may attempt to reap this reward by catering to subordinates. He may use his position and the power it involves to supplement inadequacies in personality and social abilities. Subordinates are sometimes inclined to take advantage of the situation and use the superior to gain unwarrantable personal ends. However, in spite of this limitation, the lenient superior may be a more effective leader than a severe disciplinarian. As Professor Blau points out, "leniency in supervision is a potent strategy, consciously or unconsciously employed, for establishing authority over subordinates, and this is why the liberal supervisor is particularly effective."[10]

The lenient superior goes along with many minor and some major infractions of official organizational policies. The fact that such policies can be enforced gives the superior a basis for imposing sanctions that would not otherwise exist. He can at any time turn to more rigorous enforcement, which subordinates are not apt to welcome. Such a relationship tends to produce a sense of obligation to the superior for the "favors" he has accorded. For example, if the superior looks the other way when Jones arrives at work an hour late, Jones is inclined to return the favor by doing something for the superior. Respecting the norms of the group tends to bring about a similar kind of relationship.[11] The fact that the superior does not listen to a "squealer" shows the group that he respects their norm against such behavior. The superior builds up a reserve of good will with individuals and the group which can be used to good advantage when he really needs support. Subordinates will tend

[9]Peter M. Blau, *Bureaucracy in Modern Society* (New York: Random House, 1956), pp. 70–74.
[10]Ibid., p. 71.
[11]Homans, *The Human Group*, pp. 426–428.

to go out of their way to show their appreciation for the consideration shown them. They will also tend to protect the superior against adverse action by higher management. Thus, they may put in extra effort to get a job done to make their superior look good to his superiors. They attempt to maintain what to them is a satisfactory personal relationship.

A strategy of leniency is limited by the necessity for the superior to conform to substantive and procedural standards imposed and enforced by his superiors. The superior also has the responsibility of making decisions in the area delegated to him. It should not be assumed that the lenient superior forsakes his responsibilities to the organization. Leniency becomes lunacy if it is carried to an extreme or practiced without purpose. The strategy of leniency is to exchange one set of values for another. The superior must use the good will he creates to serve the ends of the organization. However, he should not view the problem as one of equal exchange or seem to be manipulating in a deliberate fashion. The fine art of leadership is to manipulate subordinates without their knowing it; in most instances an effective leader is not himself aware that he is engaged in this sort of game. Human beings tend unconsciously to justify or rationalize their actions through moral precepts with which they can live.

Somewhat related to the strategy of leniency is the idea of shifting the blame for unpopular responsibilities and rewards to the "system" or higher superiors. Subordinates may be less inclined to take a negative attitude toward the superior if they can vent their aggression upon someone or something else.[12] They may even develop a closer bond with the superior in their "fight" with a common "enemy." However, this approach, like that of leniency, is limited by restraints imposed by organizational responsibilities. The superior cannot entirely escape the fact that he represents the organization.

THE ENIGMA OF LEADERSHIP

Superiors should not expect to find any sort of perfect solution to the leadership and authority problems. They must contend with a complex interrelationship of sociopsychological factors that do not remain constant over time. As Barnard has pointed out, leadership may in practice mean an almost infinite number of possible combinations of variables.[13] It involves skills that cannot be neatly categorized into a logical pattern for purposes of education and training. Many leaders are highly effective or ineffective for reasons they and others do not fully understand. They seem to violate some of the intellectually derived precepts of leadership for the same reason that many aspects of physical phenomena do not fit the theories of the physicist.

---

[12]Blau, *Bureaucracy in Modern Society*, pp. 77–78.

[13]Chester I. Barnard, *Organization and Management* (Cambridge: Harvard University Press, 1952), p. 84.

There is a constant demand from executives, students, and others for definite answers. This demand has been instrumental in bringing forth studies that provided specific techniques of leadership. Some such studies probably caused Barnard to write that "leadership has been subject to an extraordinary amount of dogmatically stated nonsense."[14] The purpose of the preceding discussion was to promote an understanding of the leadership problem and provide an approach to leadership. To paraphrase Professor Homans, the leader does not need a definite set of rules but a method of analyzing the organizational situation in which he must act.[15] There are many unanswered problems which have yet to be given scientific solution. But there may be some merit in knowing that knowledge is far from complete. The ignorant man who knows it all probably causes more damage than the intelligent man who knows so little.

[14]Ibid., p. 80.
[15]Homans, *The Human Group*, p. 424.

PART V

Controlling

15

THE CONTROL PROCESS

The planning process translates the profit norm into a variety of interrelated subsidiary standards or norms. Budgets, standard cost data, mechanical drawings, purchase specifications, procedures and methods, quality standards, and wage incentive standards represent some of the ways in which standards are set forth. Such standards are communicated to subordinate managerial and operating personnel who are expected to carry them out by delegation (to lower levels) or by performance. The intended result is a change in the behavior of subordinates through authority or acceptance by subordinates. Nothing further would be required if communication were perfect and authority complete, but such an ideal is not and cannot be achieved in human organization. For this reason, information about the performance of subordinate managerial and operating personnel is a vital ingredient of effective executive action. This information forms the basis for control decisions to create greater conformity to planning decisions.

THE PROBLEM OF MEASUREMENT

Control involves a comparison of planning and performance information to evaluate the proficiency of subordinates. However, a favorable or unfavorable relationship between plan and performance should not always be accepted at face value. A lack of conformity to plan can result from inappropriate plans rather than inadequate performance. Planning decisions frequently have to be revised because of errors in judgment and forecasts. Whether the plan or the nonconforming subordinate is the villain is sometimes difficult to determine. Subordinates are sometimes penalized for the superior's planning failures rather than their own performance failures.

The logic used to formulate planning and performance information should be the same. For example, the premises used in preparing budgets should be the same as those used to compile accounting and other performance data. The mechanical drawings used for inspection purposes should contain the same specifications as those used to plan operations. A similar statement can be made about oral and written messages prepared in the English language. A major difficulty in this respect is the deliberate and nondeliberate (semantic) distortion of information. The intent of superiors may not be properly communicated because subordinates impute a different meaning.

Executives should recognize that a comparison of planning norms and performance information may not adequately measure efficiency. The words or data in messages do not necessarily express the actual state of affairs. A great deal of knowledge about environmental, technological, and sociopsychological factors is necessary to understand the significance of messages about plans and performance.

FEEDBACK AND OSCILLATION

The purpose of a control system is to determine whether the performance of an organization or a department is in accord with planning goals and norms. The possibility of planning errors also requires a constant inflow of information about such environmental forces as product markets, resource markets, and innovation. Control or feedback information indicates planning inadequacies and variations from plans. It provides a basis for adjustments in organizational behavior and proper adaptation to environmental changes.

A thermostat used to regulate the temperature of a house is a good example of a control or feedback system. The desired temperature is communicated to the system by setting an indicator. The furnace responds by turning on or off as the actual temperature varies by some amount from the desired level. Thus, it begins to heat at 69°F and shuts off at 71°F. A good thermostat will keep a house at fairly even temperature, but a badly designed thermostat will send the temperature into violent oscillations.[1] A similar situation can arise from feedback failures in business and other organizations.

A lag in the flow of information about an environmental change and a failure to take prompt action can cause a sequence of adjustments in wrong directions. A company faced with severe fluctuations in the demand for its products may find itself increasing production when it ought to cut production, and conversely. Production schedules may never be in accord with the actual market situations because information about an increase or reduction

---

[1]The problem of feedback and oscillation in physiological, mechanical, and other feedback systems is considered by Norbert Wiener, *Cybernetics* (New York: John Wiley & Sons, 1948), pp. 113–136.

in demand is received or acted upon *after* demand has again moved in an opposite direction. Although the transformation period, lead time requirements, and planning considerations limit adaptability, an organization can often increase its survival power if information about an environmental change is received in sufficient time. Similar problems can arise with respect to factors that are internal to the organization. For example, a relatively minor morale problem can become a serious labor relations problem because a lack of information precluded prompt corrective action. Top management may not become aware of the problem until a horde of union officials storm "the executive suite" with loud voices. Such a development might have been avoided by timely information about the problem. Costly consequences can also result from inadequate information about such matters as the quality of production, customer complaints, industrial accidents, a shortage of personnel, and research and development difficulties.

THE COST OF CONTROL

Some degree of control information is necessary for effective managerial action. However, there is a level beyond which additional information is too costly from an economic standpoint. The revenues or savings that result from a correction of planning and performance errors must be at least equal to the cost of obtaining the required information. Some companies undoubtedly spend far too much money for budgeting, accounting, and other types of control information. Others are too niggardly in this respect and would reap rewards from additional information facilities. The difficulties of measurement and differences in the control problems of particular companies preclude an exact solution or a universal formula. But executives should not ignore the problem because they may be wrong by a few cents or a few hundred dollars. They should give constant attention to the problem and carefully scrutinize present and proposed control devices.

SUPERVISION AS AN INSTRUMENT OF CONTROL

The importance of supervision or direct observation of a subordinate should not be neglected. Every executive below the apex of the hierarchy, whether he be a vice-president or a foreman, is subject to supervision from a higher level. Observing a subordinate's behavior under various conditions is sometimes the best way to evaluate his performance or potential. Much of the process is informal and indirect and becomes an aspect of the sociopsychological dynamics of the superior-subordinate relationship. However, a superior cannot constantly keep watch over his flock if he is not to be overwhelmed with work. There are also good motivational reasons for not carrying supervision to an extreme. Accounting and other indirect control devices make possible a greater degree of decentralization and tend to give more personal freedom to subordinates. The control process generally involves some combination of supervision and indirect techniques.

PLANNING AND CONTROL DECISIONS

Control decisions enforce conformity to the behavioral pattern planned by management. Planning makes the rule; control enforces it. The control function is similar to the judicial function in political organizations. It cannot be legitimately exercised without prior planning decisions that stipulate the kind of behavior expected from subordinates. Control decisions bestow rewards or impose penalties for conformity or nonconformity to norms that define appropriate behavior. The problem of control is fundamentally the problem of motivation. Organizations cannot long survive if they must constantly use firing squads or layoffs to achieve cooperation.

Budgetary Control Systems

Budgets are frequently used to set forth standards that are used as instruments of managerial control. Some organizations have a comprehensive budgetary system encompassing every phase of planning and operations. The various budgets are quantitatively and logically related and form an integrated system. Other organizations have partial budgeting systems concerned with particular aspects of the planning problem. For example, budgeting activities may be confined to the preparation of a sales and a production budget.

KINDS OF BUDGETS

The planning or operating budget is concerned with forecasted relationships between revenues and costs. The budgeting process generally begins with the preparation of the sales forecast, which becomes the *sales budget* after official approval. Companies with income sources other than sales (such as interest from investments and royalties) may prepare a budget estimating such income. The sales budget provides the data necessary to prepare the *production budget* and other subsidiary budgets. The production budget sets forth the quantities of finished products that must be produced to satisfy the sales forecast and provide the inventories desired at the end of the budget period.[2] The information contained in the production budget can be used to prepare materials budgets, purchase budgets, and the labor budget.

The *materials budget* lists the kinds and quantities of raw materials, parts, and supplies required to produce the finished products specified in the produc-

---

[2]The quantities specified by the production budget will be higher or lower than sales budget estimates by the difference between inventories at the beginning and inventory levels desired at the end of the budget period.

tion budget. The *purchase budget* specifies the quantities of materials that must be purchased to meet production and inventory requirements together with estimates of purchase costs. Possible changes in material prices, necessary inventory levels to meet production schedules, and the market supply situation should be considered in constructing this budget. For example, an anticipated rise in the market price of raw materials or a possible shortage in supply may warrant a higher volume of purchases during the early part of the budget period. The *labor budget* specifies the amount of direct labor necessary to meet production schedules. Required hours of direct labor can be multiplied by estimated wage rates to obtain total and per unit labor cost. This information can be used by financial executives to estimate the funds needed to meet payrolls during the budget period. The personnel department can use labor budget information to plan recruitment, layoffs, and training. The factory overhead budget encompasses manufacturing expenses or burdens that cannot be directly allocated to particular products. Included in this budget are indirect labor costs, indirect materials costs, and such miscellaneous expense items as rent, heat, power, light, insurance, and depreciation. A considerable portion of total manufacturing expenses can be attributed to the activities of service departments, such as the time study department, the maintenance and repair department, the production planning department, and the inspection department. These departments generally prepare *service department budgets*, which set forth the estimated cost of providing their services at the projected volume of production.

The *distribution expense budget* takes into account the estimated costs of selling and delivering company products, such as advertising, sales promotion, direct selling expenses, packing and delivery, and record keeping. Estimated distribution expenses are generally subdivided in terms of departmental responsibility, such as sales territory, branch and home offices, and other modes of departmentation. The *administrative expense budget* is essentially concerned with the expenses that result from the performance of general management functions. Included in this budget are top executive salaries and traveling expenses, corporate directors' fees, professional service fees, and office expenses.

The budgets described above contain the basic information necessary to construct an estimated profit and loss statement, a projected balance sheet, a cash budget, and other financial budgets. The estimated profit and loss statement, which is usually broken down into months and quarters, indicates the profit potential of the overall company plan. The estimated balance sheet shows the financial consequences of the operating plans and investment at the end of the budget period. Such estimates can be used to evaluate the effectiveness of plans from both an operating and a financial point of view. Appropriate planning adjustments can be made if the projections indicate unsatisfactory consequences or if actual results begin to show unanticipated variations from budget estimates.

Two highly significant subfinancial budgets are the *cash budget* and the *capital additions budget*. A lack of sufficient liquidity is an important reason for business failures. The primary purpose of the cash budget is to prevent a possibly disastrous depletion of funds needed for operations. The cash budget is an estimate of cash receipts and cash disbursements during the budget period. Its preparation involves estimating the amount of cash that will be collected from accounts receivables for a specified period (usually a month) and the backlog of cash available from previous periods. The labor budget, the materials budget, and the various expense budgets provide information about cash requirements at various times within the budget period. Difficulties that arise from variations in the relative flow of cash receipts and disbursements can generally be overcome by building up liquid reserves and the use of short-term bank credit. Capital additions budgets detail planned expenditures for additional plant, machinery, and equipment, improvements in existing facilities, and replacement due to depreciation and obsolescence. Many companies prepare a long-term capital additions budget encompassing a period of years. Such a budget is highly tentative because it involves a long-range forecast of product and money market conditions, assumptions about the consequences of company operations during the intervening period, and a distant projection of planning strategy. But in spite of the difficulties, a long-term capital additions budget gives emphasis to the importance of systematic forward planning and helps to focus the attention of management upon the problem. Short-term capital additions budgets can be used either separately or in conjunction with long-term budgets to specify planned expenditures during the current period.

LENGTH OF THE BUDGET PERIOD

The length of the budget period is influenced by such factors as the time necessary for a complete merchandise turnover, the duration of the production cycle, the timing of financial and purchase operations, and the pattern of seasonal variations. The extent to which the future can be accurately forecasted is a consideration, together with the willingness of management to engage in systematic forward planning. The length of the accounting period and the scheduling of tax liabilities may also play a role in setting the budget period. Such factors as the timing of legislative appropriations and charitable contributions are often important in nonbusiness organizations.

Some organizations budget ahead for a period of a year with quarterly and monthly breakdowns at the time the budget is prepared. Others divide the budget into quarters with a monthly breakdown only for the quarter that immediately follows. Quarterly revisions are made in the budgets if the original forecasts and estimates are not in accord with the actual course of events. Forecasting and planning difficulties cause some companies to make monthly revisions in budget values. A progressive or continuous budgeting system is sometimes used under such conditions. An annual, semiannual, or quarterly budget is maintained by adding another month after each monthly revision of budget estimates. Some budgets may involve longer or shorter time periods than the basic forecast and operating budgets. Plant expansion, research and development, and financial planning budgets may be set up for three-, ten-, or even twenty-year periods. Such budgets may be integrated with annual budgets or have an essentially independent status. Some special purpose and project budgets are adjuncts to the overall budget structure and have a life-span of only a few weeks or months.

FIXED AND FLEXIBLE BUDGETS

Too much budget inflexibility over too long a period of time can be extremely hazardous. The organizational and departmental goals set forth in budgets are based on forecasts and estimates that are not always accurate. An unanticipated decline in sales or cost increases often dictate corrective changes in existing plans and budgets. However, budgets should not necessarily be adjusted the moment a miscalculation becomes evident. Too many modifications can create more difficulties than they correct. Some degree of stability is necessary for effective planning and operations. Organizations generally attempt to mitigate the disruptive impact of too many changes by making periodic budget adjustments on a monthly or quarterly rather than a daily basis. Administered budget flexibility is essential under conditions of uncertainty and change. A failure to make appropriate planning changes can seriously impair survival power in a dynamic environment. Budgets should always be subordinate to the requirements of effective planning. They should not be permitted to stifle initiative and infuse stagnation.

Another approach to the problem of change is to use budgets with a built-in flexibility. Some budget values can be made to change with changes in the volume of business. A flexible or variable budget is premised on the idea that some cost or expense items vary with different levels of sales, production, or activity. Such costs as depreciation, insurance, and plant maintenance generally change less with changes in output than direct labor and direct material costs. The basic problem in constructing a variable budget is to determine the degree to which cost or expense items vary with output. Accounting records, statistical measures, and engineering estimates can be used to classify costs into various categories and calculate their amounts. However, it should not be assumed that every item can be rigidly classified as either fixed or variable. Many costs fall somewhere in between the two extremes, and they may also have different degrees of variability in different companies. Direct labor costs, for example, will tend to be less variable (or more fixed) in a company that maintains a large nucleus of permanent employees during seasonal slack periods. A step-budget method or a formula method can be used in a flexible budget system. The step-budget method results in a different budget for various levels of output. The formula method makes possible the computation of budget values for any level of output by adding fixed and variable costs. Thus, to use a simplified example, if fixed costs total $10,000 per month or quarter and variable costs $10 per unit, the budget amounts would be $20,000 for 1000 units, $30,000 for 2000 units, $40,000 for 3000 units, etc.

THE BUDGETING PROCESS

The budgeting process generally begins with a meeting of the budget committee composed of top executives. The budget committee evaluates the manner in which various external and internal factors may affect the achievement of organizational goals. The final result is an estimate of the sales and production volume for the forthcoming period. Such estimates are sometimes given tentative approval by the chief executive, a top planning committee, or the board of directors. The executives who give such approval are frequently members of the budget committee and participate in the deliberations of the committee. The information provided by the budget committee will be the basis for the formulation of subsidiary budget estimates. The heads of line, staff, and service departments usually participate in the preparation of departmental budgets. A budget director, the controller, or the chief accountant is often given the responsibility for administering and implementing the budget program. Such a person serves in a staff capacity and performs advisory, scheduling, liaison, informational, and supervisory duties. The budgeting process is generally accompanied by a great deal of formal and informal consultation among executives. Differences of opinion and conflicts of interest are always present and must be resolved by compromise or compulsion. Effective budgeting involves more than the manipulation of accounting and other kinds of quantitative data. The budgeting process is fundamentally the planning process, and the budgets that are finally approved are messages about objectives and plans.

BUDGETS AS CONTROL INSTRUMENTS

The performance of managerial and operating personnel can be measured by a comparison of budget estimates with accounting and other data. However, a great deal of discretion should be used in interpreting the significance of such comparisons.

Accounting as an Instrument of Managerial Control

Accounting is a specialized language system that is used to measure the consequences of organizational activities and to communicate such information to executives and others. The logic of accounting has evolved over a long period of evolutionary and analytical development. Although records of business transactions can be traced to ancient Babylon, the modern method of double-entry bookkeeping was probably invented during the fourteenth century. The double-entry system is premised on the idea of an equation of business transactions and that every transaction represents a duality of elements. Something that has tangible or intangible value is received, but, at the same time, an equivalent value is given up. The value of each transaction is expressed in monetary units and results in increases and decreases in assets, liabilities, and net worth (owners' equity).

THE ACCOUNTING PROCESS

The information that flows into the accounting system is initially recorded into journals or books of original entry. Postings are made from journals in accounts which are combined in some systematic order into ledgers. Accounts are frequently arranged in the order that they will appear in such financial statements as the balance sheet and the income statement. They may also be classified alphabetically, by departmental units, according to geographical area, by budget classifications, and in other ways. Systematic numerical or alphabetical codes are often used to identify accounts in large and complex accounting systems. The problems of systematization and coding become particularly pertinent in companies that utilize electronic data-processing equipment. The changes that occur in assets, liabilities, and net worth as the result of business operations are recorded in the accounts as *debits* and *credits*. Debit has reference to the left side of an account and indicates increases in assets, decreases in liabilities, decreases in net worth, decreases in income, and increases in expense. Credit refers to the right side of an account and indicates decreases in assets, increases in liabilities, etc. The fact that every entry involves both debits and credits in equal amounts means that the two sides of an account or a system of accounts must always be in balance. A lack of balance can result only from errors.

FINANCIAL STATEMENTS AND REPORTS

The basic problem of the planner is to a achieve a favorable balance between revenues and costs. An accounting system accumulates information about the revenue and cost consequences of planning and operations. This information is presented to management and other interested parties in the form of financial statements and reports. The *balance sheet,* the *income statement,* and the *statement of retained earnings* (or surplus),[3] together with supporting schedules that may be appropriate, are generally sufficient to appraise the

---

[3]There has been an increasing tendency to discontinue the use of the word "surplus" because it has been subject to misinterpretation by nonaccountants. C. A. Moyer and R. K. Mautz, *Intermediate Accounting* (New York: John Wiley and Sons, Inc., 1962), p. 310.

overall financial and operating condition of an organization. The balance sheet indicates the nature and amounts of assets, liabilities, and net worth at a given date as illustrated in Figure 15-1. The income statement reports income, ex-

FIGURE 15-1

BROWN AND COMPANY
Balance Sheet
December 31, 1971
ASSETS

Current assets:

Cash and receivables		$ 30,145	
Inventories:			
Raw materials	$ 27,278		
Work in process	20,550		
Finished goods	31,150	78,978	
Unexpired insurance		1,485	
Supplies		517	
Total current assets			$111,125

Property, plant and equipment:

Land		$118,500	
Buildings and equipment:			
Cost	$790,000		
Less accumulated depreciation	379,500	410,500	
Total property, plant and equipment			529,000
Total assets			$640,125

EQUITIES

Current liabilities:

Notes payable to bank	$20,000	
Accounts payable	39,750	
Accrued expenses	1,885	
Total current liabilities		$ 61,635

Long-term liabilities:

Bonds payable, 5% due 1980	$200,000	
Deferred Federal income taxes payable	20,000	
Total long-term liabilities		$220,000
Total liabilities		$281,635

Stockholders' equity

Capital stock—$10 par	$200,000	
Additional paid-in capital	130,000	
Total contributed capital	330,000	
Retained earnings	28,490	
Total stockholders' equity		$358,490
Total equities		$640,125

penses, and profits (or losses) for a given period of time. It also details some of the elements that make up total income and expenses as illustrated in Figure 15-2. The statement of retained earnings provides the connecting link be-

FIGURE 15-2

BROWN AND COMPANY
Income Statement
Year Ended December 31, 1971

Sales (net)		$1,999,975
Cost of goods sold		
Inventories, Dec. 31, 1970	$ 74,155	
Material, labor, and other variable costs	791,205	
Fixed costs (excl. deprec. & amort.)	350,390	
	1,215,750	
Inventories, Dec. 31, 1971	79,749	1,136,001
Gross margin		863,974
Operating expenses (detail omitted)		749,994
Net operating income		113,980
Other expenses		
Interest-bonds		9,975
Net income before federal income taxes		104,005
Federal income taxes		51,030
Net income after federal income taxes		$ 52,975

tween the other two statements, explaining the increases (from net income) and decreases (from net losses or dividends or both) in undistributed income during the period. Accounting information may also be detailed and classified to highlight specific aspects of business operations. For example, reports about such matters as manufacturing costs, purchases and inventory changes, sales returns and allowances, salary and wage schedules, cash requirements, and bad debts may be helpful in solving particular planning and control problems. The importance of financial reporting to stockholders, creditors, employees, and governmental agencies should also be emphasized. Such reports are necessary to satisfy the personal and institutional interests of those who contribute resources to the organization and to meet the requirements of the law.

ANALYTICAL METHODS USED BY ACCOUNTANTS

Accounting and financial experts use various methods in evaluating accounting information.[4] One approach is to study the absolute amounts of particular items in the various statements to determine what significance they may have.

[4] A discussion of analytical methods and the interpretation of accounting information is found in Moyer and Mautz, *Intermediate Accounting*, pp. 482–498.

Another is to compare the same statements for two or more dates or periods or for different organizations, departments, geographical areas, etc. Such comparisons sometimes indicate important developments and problems to which management should be alerted. For example, a marked increase in certain expense items over a period of time may warrant managerial action. Percentages may be used to show the relationship between various elements of accounting information. Particular expense items or net profit may be expressed as a percentage of sales or some other base. A comparison of percentages over a period of time or with industry and other information is sometimes used in determining problem areas. The fact that advertising expenses increased from 3 percent to 6 percent of sales or that net profit declined from 9 percent to 5 percent of net worth may have significance. A similar technique is to translate relationships into a ratio of one figure to another, that is, the ratio of current assets to current liabilities is 2 to 1. Accountants have given a great deal of attention to "ratio analysis" or a study of the relationship between various elements of accounting information. Some ratios or percentages have particular significance in evaluating financial and operating results.[5] For example, the ratio of current assets to current liabilities or the total of cash and receivables to current liabilities (the acid test) provides information about the organization's capacity to meet its current obligations as they mature. A ratio of net profit to net worth and net profit to sales, particularly when compared over a period of time and with other pertinent information, can afford important insights about organizational performance and return on investment. However, accountants and executives should be wary of placing too much emphasis upon the mechanics of ratio analysis to solve their problems. As Moyer and Mautz have written:

"There is far more to both accounting and business than can be compressed into a few ratio results or into a single index as some would do. Ratio analysis is a useful tool to make accounting reports of business operations and conditions more readily understandable, but, unless the analyst knows (a) precisely what the ratio is intended to point out, (b) what a satisfactory ratio is for that company under the conditions that exist, and (c) any possible errors in the underlying data that might affect the ratio results, he is very likely to arrive at erroneous conclusions. And, unless all the financial data presented have been studied with a view toward comprehending the full significance of the data and their interrelationships, he may find himself tending to rely too much on

---

[5]A list of ratios that are commonly used in the analysis of accounting information can be found in books on accounting principles. Some typical ratios are: current assets to current liabilities, merchandise to current assets, total liabilities to net worth, net profit to net sales, net sales to net worth, and net profit to total assets.

a single fact or relationship which may be more than counterbalanced by other factors that he has overlooked."[6]

THE MEANING OF ACCOUNTING INFORMATION

Financial statements and reports are important instruments of managerial planning and control, but the information they provide cannot be understood without knowledge about the nature of accounting data, the manner in which the data are classified and combined, and accounting terminology. Executives must have an understanding of the language system if they are to understand the messages that are derived from it. They should also recognize that accounting reports, like messages in any other language, portray an abstract or incomplete picture of the reality of business operations. The significance of accounting information can only be determined by relating it to the environmental and organizational factors that affect organizational dynamics. For example, the information that net profits (as a percentage of sales or net worth) have declined over a period of time has little meaning without an understanding of the casual factors. Declining profits may indicate planning failures, or they may point to the need for control actions. But they may also evolve from environmental changes that cannot be attributed to a lack of effective planning and control. Lower profits may actually reflect greater rather than less managerial and operating efficiency.

THE ACCURACY OF ACCOUNTING INFORMATION

The accounting profession has given a great deal of attention to the development of theories and techniques to improve the accuracy of accounting information. Much progress has been made in this respect, but a number of difficult problems preclude any sort of perfect solution.[7] A major problem is that the monetary unit (dollars) in which accounting information is expressed is not a constant measure of value. An analysis of accounting statements over a period of time can lead to erroneous conclusions unless price changes are taken into consideration. Estimating depreciation expenses and inventory values are difficult problems under conditions of inflationary or deflationary

[6]Moyer and Mautz, *Intermediate Accounting*, pp. 484–485.

[7]A comprehensive discussion of some of these problems can be found in: Howard C. Greer, "What Are Accepted Principles of Accounting?" *The Accounting Review*, Vol. 13, No. 1, March 1938, pp. 25–31. A similar critique was made in an address by Marquis G. Eaton, delivered before the Illinois Society of Certified Public Accountants, June 7, 1957, printed in: *Financial Reporting in a Changing Society* (New York: American Institute of Certified Public Accountants). The relationship between accounting concepts and data and managerial problems is given careful scrutiny by Joel Dean in *Managerial Economics* (Englewood Cliffs, N.J.: Prentice-Hall, Inc., 1951).

price movements. Net profits may be overstated or understated by large amounts unless appropriate adjustments are made in financial statements or by interpretation. Price fluctuations also create difficulties in appraising planning and operating efficiency. Profits or losses may evolve from unanticipated price changes rather than from effective managerial action or the lack of it.

Government regulations and tax legislation may directly or indirectly affect the manner in which business profits are determined. For example, the Interstate Commerce Commission and the Internal Revenue Code implicitly or explicitly stipulate accounting procedures and standards deemed appropriate for their particular purposes. The "profits" that evolve from such accounting practices may differ significantly from the "profits" that result from nonregulated accounting practices. Some companies give formal recognition to this distinction by following generally accepted accounting practices for financial and business operations and maintaining separate sets of information for tax and other purposes. Thus, a company may follow normal schedules for depreciation in its regular accounting system but compute depreciation on the basis of a "fast write-off provision" to take advantage of tax legislation. Other companies follow the accounting practices prescribed by government regulations and make appropriate adjustments for private use. However, the important consideration is not the way in which such problems are handled in the accounts, but a recognition on the part of executives and others that "profits" are not always what they seem to be.

The accounting profession has given constant consideration to improvements in measurement and reporting techniques. Like others in the business world, the accountant must contend with the uncertainties of a dynamic economy. Much accounting information is directly or indirectly based on forecasts and estimates that may be repudiated by actual events. Some accountants and economists have recommended a modification of accounting methods to handle such problems as price changes. One suggestion is the use of index numbers to reflect changes in price levels, and another is to completely revalue assets if major price changes occur.[8] However, the problem of determining appropriate index numbers and the vagaries of price movements present many practical difficulties. The accuracy of accounting data is also limited by the failure to fully compensate for such intangible elements as goodwill and trademarks. Accountants generally use objective measures, for example, cost and purchase price, to value these assets. However, actual values may be appreciably more or less than the amounts stated in the accounts. The validity and applicability of accounting information is also affected by computational limitations that make necessary a considerable amount of "averaging" and abstracting of data. Also important is that there may be a lengthy time lag between accounting

[8]Moyer and Mautz, *Intermediate Accounting*, pp. 520–521.

reports and the events they represent. Recently developed mathematical techniques combined with electronic data-processing equipment are sometimes helpful in overcoming this difficulty.

Accounting provides highly useful information for planning and control purposes. But financial statements and reports can also communicate misinformation if their nature and the forces they represent are not properly understood. Executives should understand what accounting can do and what it cannot do. They should recognize that interpretation involves more than a mechanistic appraisal of accounting data.

FINANCIAL REPORTS AND REPORTING SYSTEMS

Accounting is a meaningless language unless the messages derived from it provide information that facilitates the solution of organizational problems. The informational requirements of executives, stockholders, creditors, regulatory agencies, tax authorities, and employees differ in both nature and scope. Accountants should take cognizance of such diverse needs and interests in designing financial statements and reports. They should make allowances for differences between industries and companies in planning the reporting system.

Executives and accountants should recognize that the information potential of accounting is restricted by a number of considerations. A highly organized language system, accounting can communicate meaning more precisely than English, but its information potential is more limited. The accountant is restricted in what he can communicate to executives and others by the logical constraints of his language. He should understand the capacity of his language and recognize that some kinds of information cannot be derived from accounting. A further limitation is that message recipients sometimes lack a sufficient knowledge of the language. Nothing is gained from messages that will not be understood by those who receive them. Accounting messages may have to be simplified and supplemented by the use of another language.[9]

Financial reporting should be viewed as a dynamic rather than a static problem. The individual reports and the system of reporting that gave good results in the past may not adequately reflect the informational needs of today. Prosperity and recession, changes in product and resource markets, product line changes, expansion programs, technological innovation, and legislation

[9]Other factors may also restrict the discretion that can be exercised in constructing accounting messages. A high degree of uniformity is imposed by the need for comparative analyses of financial and accounting data within an industry or the economy. The development of professionalism among accountants and the requirements of education have also been important in this respect. The appropriate content of accounting messages is sometimes stipulated by the message recipient. For example, governmental tax and regulatory agencies generally set forth specific informational requirements. Banks, investment firms, credit rating concerns, insurance companies, and executives frequently request particular kinds of accounting information and indicate the manner of presentation.

may significantly affect the kind of information required for effective managerial action. The steps taken by one company to adapt its reporting system to changing conditions are described by the comptroller of a railroad.

1. While inventories of reports had been taken periodically, there was no mechanism for maintaining them on a current basis. Our minimum starting requirement was to be able to know *at all times* what information was available. Our first problem, therefore, was to provide a current inventory of reports and a mechanism for maintaining it—in other words, *a perpetual inventory* of reports.

2. Obviously, the proper time to start designing a new fire engine is not when your house is on fire. Our second problem, therefore, was to conform the existing reporting system to *current* management needs.

3. We determined that there was a need for familiarizing our accounting organization with management problems at all levels. Only by doing this could we expect it adequately to fulfill its responsibility (a) for identifying data which were pertinent to those problems, and (b) for interpreting these data in language which would be understood by our management people. The development of these analytical and interpretive functions was related to our third problem: to convert our accounting and financial *statements* into useful and "used" management *reports.*

4. We recognized that the existing report structure, even when conformed to current needs and made more useful through analytical and interpretive services, would not necessarily fulfill future needs. Therefore, means had to be devised to keep us continuously conversant with the control techniques, programs, and objectives of our various sales and operating departments. This was a prerequisite to being able to design more effective new reports and reporting systems responsive to their foreseeable future needs.

5. Lastly, the report production process had to be simplified and expedited to the end that all management reports could fulfill the prime management requirement of being *completely timely.*[10]

The ideas presented in the above quotation have general applicability and pinpoint some of the basic requirements of effective reporting. Electronic data-processing and operations research may facilitate the solution of the time problem.

COST ACCOUNTING

Cost accounting, which is generally categorized as a specialized branch of accounting, is concerned with the accumulation and analysis of cost information. The basic problem of cost accounting is to allocate costs on some kind of

[10]Roger F. Brown, "Financial Data Reporting During Organization and Methods Transitions," *Reporting Financial Data to Top Management, Special Report, No. 25* (New York: American Management Association, Inc., 1957), pp. 112–113.

unit basis, such as products, services, subassemblies, parts, projects, and departments. Cost accountants generally use the following cost classifications in accumulating and allocating cost information.

Direct Material

Included in this category are the costs of materials that go directly into the product or are readily traceable to the product.

Direct Labor

Includes labor costs that can be charged to the production of a particular product.

Factory Overhead

This category takes into account all cost items that cannot be directly charged to a product, such as indirect labor (supervisory and clerical costs), indirect materials (fuels, abrasives, lubricants), depreciation, insurance, and power.

Administrative Overhead

Included are salaries of executives, staff personnel, secretarial and clerical personnel, and other nonfactory administrative expenses.

Sales Overhead

Expenses related to the marketing of the product, such as advertising and sales promotion, transportation and storage costs, and salaries paid to sales personnel.

Direct material and labor costs are by definition directly related to the production of a particular product. Such costs can generally be computed and charged from material requisition forms and employee time tickets. However, the cost accountant cannot always assume that such raw data are accurate. Behavioral studies indicate that factory supervisory and operating personnel sometimes deliberately distort information to protect and pursue individual and group interests. A number of methods and formulas are used to distribute factory, administrative, and other overhead expenses. The problem is to find a common factor that varies with the amount of overhead that can be properly assigned to particular products. Variations in direct labor costs, direct labor hours, direct material costs, and machine hour costs are often used to distribute factory overhead or burden. For example, if the total factory overhead is the same as total direct labor costs, one dollar would be added to every dollar of direct labor costs to cover factory overhead expenses. The basic logic of such techniques is to allocate overhead costs to products on an equitable or fair share basis. The intended result is an average unit cost that incorporates some or all elements of actual or historical costs.

Historical cost information can be helpful in determining the profitability of operations. However, distortions in the raw data, the problems of distributing overhead, and classification and computational difficulties can make such information highly inaccurate. The information provided by cost accounting, like other kinds of accounting information, cannot be understood without a knowledge of the nature of the data, the logic used in compilation, and the operations to which the data relate. Executives should also recognize that historical costs, developed by the techniques described in the previous paragraph, are not useful for some purposes. One problem is that the kind of cost information required for planning is not directly provided by historical cost data. A simple projection of past costs into the future, like a projection of past sales data, is generally inadequate. Changes in the resource markets, technological innovations, motivational factors, and changes in plant utilization are factors that may significantly influence future costs. The uncertainties of a dynamic economy can cause estimating errors of great magnitude. Another difficulty is that planning involves a consideration of alternative strategies and combinations of strategies. Estimating the cost consequences of the various alternatives presents difficult measurement and forecasting problems. The executive should not expect a high degree of accuracy in the cost information that can be derived about such matters. A rough approximation is about the best that can be achieved even with the most sophisticated mathematical and statistical techniques.

A number of techniques have been developed by accountants, economists, and statisticians to adapt actual and estimated costs to particular managerial problems. Some companies develop *standard costs* to measure efficiency, to serve as a guide for pricing and estimating bids, and for analytical purposes. Standard costs represent management's conception of what cost ought to be under certain assumptions. They are derived from analyses of past cost behavior, time study data, material specifications, and estimates of output level, prices, wages, and overhead expenses. A comparison of actual and standard costs (variance analysis) can be helpful in determining problem areas that require corrective action. Cost data are frequently classified by the degree to which they vary with changes in output for budgeting and planning purposes. Such classifications (fixed, semifixed, and variable costs) are used to construct flexible budgets (discussed earlier in this chapter) and break-even charts. A break-even chart shows the relationship between total sales income and costs at outputs ranging from zero to full plant capacity.

Figure 15-3 presents a simplified version of the break-even charts used in business and other organizations. The sales line indicates the expected total income or revenue at different output levels and the total cost line shows expected total expenses over the same output range. The intersection point of the sales and cost lines is the break-even point or the point at which profits are zero. Total profits or losses for different output levels are also indicated

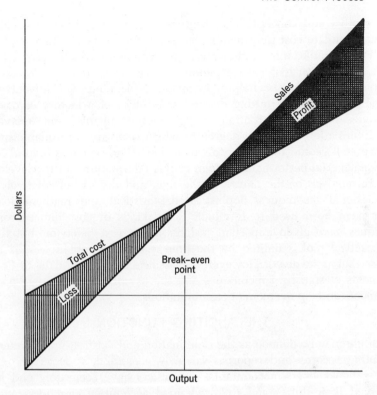

FIGURE 15-3. A simplified break-even chart.

on the chart. The need to absorb fixed costs is the primary reason for the losses that are shown for output levels to the left of the break-even point. Some of the break-even charts used by business concerns are constructed to show the manner in which particular factors may influence the total income and expense picture.[11] For example, a series of total cost lines can be used to indicate the manner in which changes in wages, material costs, and more efficient operations affect the profit situation. Break-even charts emphasize that planning involves incremental changes in the total program and that each change should be evaluated in terms of its contribution to profits. They can be used to estimate the income and cost consequences of particular planning alternatives, such as product line additions, changes in plant capacity, price changes, sales promotion programs, and changes in particular cost factors. However, executives should recognize that difficult estimating and measurement problems place limitations on the validity of the data that make up break-even charts.

[11]The data on break-even charts can also be expressed in algebraic form.

Many other cost concepts, classifications, and computational techniques are used to formulate cost information that relates to particular managerial problems. For example, information about the extent to which costs are out-of-pocket (require current cash expenditures) as opposed to book costs (such as depreciation) may be helpful in financial planning. The advantages that may be derived from shutting down a sales office or a factory can be partly determined from a classification of costs into "escapable" and "unavoidable" costs. Information about the degree to which costs are controllable by a particular executive and the extent to which they could be cut is helpful in measuring managerial performance. Much of this information can be developed by a careful analysis of the nature of the data and the use of relatively simple computational techniques. Sophisticated statistical and mathematical techniques have been used to formulate some kinds of cost information. Such techniques have given important insights about cost behavior, but their use as a practical tool is limited by the time required to obtain results and the expense that is involved. However, a classification of cost data to fit the requirements of statistical techniques and the use of electronic data-processing equipment can help overcome these limitations.

THE AUDITING FUNCTION

Auditing may be defined as the examination and verification of financial and accounting records and reports. Narrowly construed, it seeks to determine whether bookkeepers, accountants, and others have accurately and honestly performed their duties and followed good accounting practices. A broader view is that the auditing function also involves a check on managerial performance in the light of appropriate and established policies, plans, standards, and procedures. Thus, the peering eye of the auditor may be focused upon matters that range from the moving hand of a clerk who dips into the till to a decision by a vice-president to buy copper from Alpha Company rather than Beta Company. Some organizations employ auditing personnel to conduct internal audits of financial, accounting, and related activities. Others rely exclusively on external auditing by independent certified public accounting firms, and still others use both internal and external auditing facilities. In addition to factors relating to internal managerial control, external audits are particularly important when management is required to present financial statements and reports to private and public interest groups. For example, the management of a corporation is legally obligated to the stockholder; may be compelled under certain conditions to provide financial information to creditors, customers, suppliers, and unions; and is forced to contend with a vast array of governmental informational requirements. A professional stamp of approval by independent auditors has become an important factor in authenticating the financial statements and reports required for such purposes.

BUDGETING AND ACCOUNTING

Budgeting is concerned with the *expected* consequences of planning and operations, and accounting with the *actual* consequences measured in monetary and other quantitative terms. Quantitative variations between expected and actual results can be used to gauge planning and operating efficiency. An analysis of such variations is frequently useful in determining the kind of problem that may be involved. But a quantitative approach is inadequate without an understanding of the nature of accounting and budgeting systems and the manner in which they relate to environmental and organizational conditions. Why did the organization or a departmental unit fail to meet or more than meet the expectations set forth in the budget? The answer may involve a diversity of considerations that cannot generally be reduced to a simple cause-and-effect analysis. Forecasting and estimating errors, deliberate and nondeliberate distortions in the information, communication and motivational difficulties, technological factors, inflexibilities evolving from past planning failures, and inadequacies in current planning represent major categories into which causal factors can be placed. Appropriate corrective action is impossible if the behavior of budget and accounting information cannot be related to dynamic forces that they are supposed to represent.

16

LOGISTICAL CONTROL SYSTEMS

This chapter directs attention to logistical control systems. Such systems are concerned with the flow of materials and products through the organization and encompass the functions of procurement, production, and distribution. Consideration is also given to informational systems required for the control of personnel.

Logistical and Personnel Control Systems

PRODUCTION CONTROL

Production control is concerned with these functions: (1) the *routing* of parts and subassemblies through an appropriate sequence of machine and human operations, (2) *scheduling* or designating the time sequences for the performance of various amounts and kinds of work, and (3) *dispatching* or assigning work in a manner that results in the best possible utilization of machines, equipment and tools, materials, and manpower in line with the requirements set forth by routing and scheduling. These functions may be handled on an informal and nonspecialized basis in small and simple production systems. In large and complex systems, they are generally performed by specialized personnel in production planning and control departments.

Informational Requirements and Interrelationships

Production planning translates a variety of information into the information required for manufacturing operations. Sales forecast and inventory information is used to formulate the overall (master) production schedule. Mechanical drawings of the product and its various components are used to determine the proper sequence of operations (production routing) and the types and amounts of necessary materials. Machine and manpower requirements can be derived from production routing information and time study data. Such information can be used to formulate other data needed for systematic planning. Machine load information can be developed to determine the adequacy or inadequacy of existing capacity. A lack of machine capacity can cause changes in the master production schedule, result in the purchase of additional facilities, bring about overtime or multishift operations, and other planning adjustments. Information about personnel and material requirements is ultimately translated into personnel requisitions (or layoffs) and purchase orders.

The Gantt Chart

A number of specialized informational and analytical devices have been developed to facilitate production planning and control. A highly useful device is the Gantt Chart, which was developed by Henry L. Gantt in 1917. The Gantt Chart has been called "the most notable contribution to the art of management made in this generation."[1] The innovation of the Gantt Chart was that it presented facts in their relation to time. Each division of space along the horizontal axis simultaneously represents: (1) equal divisions of time, (2) varying amounts of work scheduled, and (3) varying amounts of work completed. The vertical axis shows the human and machine capacities to which production and other activities can be assigned. The manner in which these variables are portrayed on a Gantt Chart is illustrated in Figure 16-1. The use of the Gantt Chart requires a plan of operations that can be expressed in quantitative terms. The plan is recorded along the horizontal axis of the chart in relation to increments of time (days, weeks, months). Actual progress is posted on the same axis, and the reasons for variations between plan and performance can be indicated by symbols denoting such factors as machine breakdown, lack of materials, power failure, absence of operator, and lack of tools. Gantt Charts can be designed to plan and control production activities by operations, machines, groups of machines, departments, or factories. They can also be used to schedule purchasing activities, personnel recruitment, transportation facilities, and many other activities.

PERT: A New Planning Technique

The last few years have brought into being a number of planning instruments which offer important advantages over the Gantt Chart for some pur-

[1]Wallace Clark, *The Gantt Chart* (New York: The Ronald Press, 1922), p. 3. This book was translated into French, Italian, Polish, Czechoslovakian, German, Spanish, Russian, and Japanese. In Russia alone 100,000 copies were printed and, according to some reports, the first "Five-Year Plan" was completely plotted on Gantt Charts.

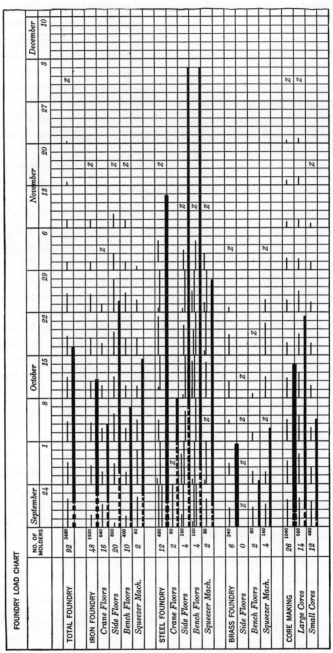

FIGURE 16-1. Gantt Chart for a foundry. (Reproduced with permission from Charles A. Koepke, *Plant Production Control*, 2nd ed. New York: John Wiley and Sons, Inc. 1949.)

poses.[2] The new techniques have been particularly useful in programming large and complex atomic, military, and space projects. They have also proven useful in planning advertising campaigns, introducing new products, publishing books, constructing homes, and preparing theatrical productions. Probably the most noted of the many recent planning innovations is Program Evaluation Review Technique (PERT), which was developed in 1958 by the U.S. Navy's Special Projects Office. Two parallel planning techniques are the Critical Path Method (CPM), developed by the Du Pont Company, and Program Evaluation Procedure (PEP), which came from the U.S. Air Force.

The first step in building a PERT network is to prepare a list of the activities that will be necessary to complete a project. An activity may encompass the work performed by a single operator, a departmental unit, or an entire organization. Activities must have definite starting and stopping points if they are to be plotted into a PERT network. Such points are called milestones or events, which represent a clearly identifiable achievement. A PERT event is the beginning or the end of an activity; it does not consume time or resources. Events are represented in the network by circles, squares, or other appropriate geometric devices.

A PERT network shows the interrelationship of the events and activities that are required to achieve an objective. Figure 16-2 represents a highly simplified PERT network. The events, represented by circles, are numbered

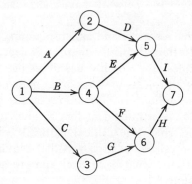

FIGURE 16-2. A simplified PERT network.

[2]The following references provide a comprehensive analysis of PERT and related planning techniques: Federal Electric Corporation, *A Programmed Introduction to Program Evaluation, and Review Technique* (New York: John Wiley & Sons, Inc., 1963); Robert W. Miller *Schedule, Cost, and Profit Control with PERT* (New York: McGraw-Hill Book Company, Inc., 1963); Richard A. Johnson, Fremont E. Kast, and James E. Rosenzweig, *The Theory and Management of Systems* (New York: McGraw-Hill Book Company, Inc., 1963).

for purposes of identification. The lines between the events denote activities, which are labeled by letters. Activities are the time-consuming aspects of the PERT network; they involve the expenditure of resources. The arrows in the network shown in Figure 16-2 indicate the order of events or the sequence in which the work must be done. Events must take place in a proper sequence—a house cannot be finished before the foundation is laid, an airplane cannot be flown before its engines are installed, and a television play cannot be presented until it has been written. In Figure 16-2, event 5 cannot take place until events 2 and 4 have been completed, event 7 cannot take place until events 5 and 6 are completed, and so on.

After the PERT network has been built, the next step is to make estimates of the time (days, weeks, months, etc.) it will take to complete each activity.

The expected elapsed times t_e for the activities can be used to calculate the earliest possible time T_E the events in the network can be expected to occur. (See Figure 16-3). The t_e data can also be used to compute the T_L or the latest allowable date an event can occur without causing a delay in the project. The difference between the latest allowable time T_L and the earliest expected time T_E is the amount of slack in the project. Slack may be positive (ahead of schedule), zero (on schedule), and negative (behind schedule). The measurement of slack can be used to determine the critical path or the longest path in a network. The critical path, as the term implies, represents the sequence of events and activities that are most apt to upset the scheduled date of completion. All other paths in the network have more slack (time) or resources to achieve the objective.

PERT, like operations research and other planning techniques, forces all levels of management to think logically about a project and to give consideration to pertinent variables. It is highly useful in handling the uncertainties involved in nonrepetitive projects and has proven to be almost indispensable in planning the massive military and space programs of recent years. PERT directs constant attention to strategic factors through the information it provides about "slack time" and "the critical path." It can significantly reduce costs by indicating those aspects of a project that require attention. Resources can be shifted from activities that have slack time to activities on the critical path. As one executive noted:

"In years past, when a program was in trouble, it was assumed that the *entire* program was in trouble, and most often everyone on the project was put on overtime. PERT now clearly shows that close to 90% of this crash effort was wasted, since it was applied to activities which were on slack paths where there was already time to spare."[3]

[3]Quoted in *News Front*, June 1963, p. 32.

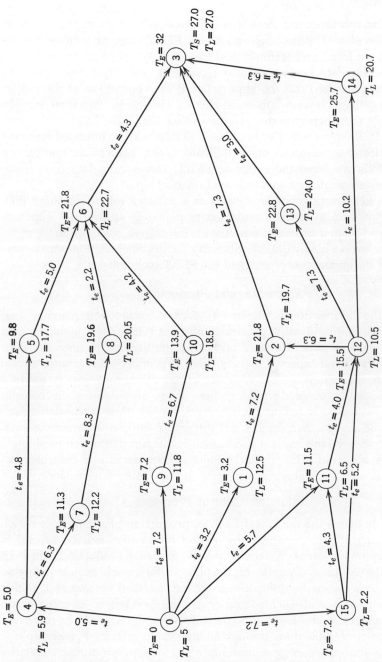

FIGURE 16-3. A PERT network with time estimates.

Management can often use slack time information to make necessary modifications in the plan. The time schedules in a PERT network assume a given level of resource input and technological capacity. A lack of sufficient time to meet a particular date can often be overcome by additional resources. The additional costs involved may be appropriate if the completion of the project is highly important. However, in some cases a change in objectives may be more desirable than higher costs. Variables other than time have been incorporated into PERT networks. For example, cost data may be obtained for many of the activities in a project. A major difficulty is that present accounting systems do not always serve the needs of PERT. Inadequate data often force highly tenuous assumptions about time-cost relationships.

PERT should obviously not be viewed as a panacea for all planning difficulties. It provides a systematic approach to planning; it does not eliminate uncertainty and related managerial problems. Executives must still make many decisions that involve highly illusive subjective factors. Such decisions make possible much of the apparent objectivity of the PERT technique.

Paperwork and Production

Many of the informational instruments used in production planning and control simulate the production process in abstract terms. One might say that production occurs on paper before it takes place on the factory floor. A Gantt-type chart portrays the expected consequences of production over some period of time. Route sheets indicate the sequence of operations necessary to produce a part, subassembly, or product. Operation sheets give detailed instructions about operation methods, tooling requirements, specifications, and related matters. These and many other devices are integrated into an informational system that activates the mechanical and human forces through which production objectives are achieved. The physical results are translated into control information that is used to evaluate managerial and operating performance.

Production Control Problems

Variations between the norms set forth in production planning information and the actual results as measured by control information can be helpful in determining problem areas. A failure to meet planned production schedules can be attributed to a diversity of possible factors, such as unanticipated shortages of raw materials, difficulties in hiring qualified personnel, a higher than average incidence of machine and equipment breakdown, or a slowdown by factory workers. A problem in one part of the production system can cause a chain reaction of difficulties throughout the whole system. For example, a shortage of a strategic part or subassembly can disrupt production activities generally and play havoc with planned schedules. Production failures can also be attributed to informational and communication difficulties. The information used in the planning process presents a highly abstract picture of the realities of the production process. Mechanical drawings, operation sequence information, standard time data, purchasing specifications, personnel requisitions, raw material and work-in-process inventories, and machine load data do not always provide completely adequate or accurate information for planning and operating purposes. The preciseness with which these devices seem to measure future requirements and results is partly a property of the measuring stick rather than what the stick measures. The data used in production planning contain assumptions and estimates that may be repudiated by actual events. Furthermore, some degree of deliberate and nondeliberate distortion of information results from processing and transmission activities. For example, an inventory of work-in-process may include defective subassemblies and parts because an inventory clerk failed to note this fact or because a supervisor wanted to cover up a mistake.

QUALITY CONTROL

An important planning problem is to determine quality standards for products and services. A primary consideration in solving this problem is the relationship between revenues and costs. Additional quality must produce sufficient revenues to compensate for the costs that are incurred. Thus, the solution is not to achieve the highest possible quality but to meet the quality criteria implied by market forces. Furthermore, such factors as company, product, and management reputation may be more important than short- or long-run profit considerations. Governmental legislation, such as the Pure Food and Drug Act, and standards developed by industry associations also play a part in the quality picture.

Operational Definitions

Quality may be defined in subjective terms, as: "we give the best service," "we strive for quality, not quantity," and "built by craftsmen who know quality." However, such definitions of standards are subject to a variety of interpretations by managerial and operating personnel. Quality information should convey exact meanings and, if possible, should be expressed in language systems that define in operational terms. For example, the size of the product should be specified by the metric or other measurement system, its form should be shown by scaled drawings, color should be indicated by formula or samples, etc. Precise quality definitions or specifications are particularly important in manufacturing operations involving the assembly of interchangeable parts and subassemblies.

Specifications and Tolerances

The quality problem is a fundamental factor in the production control process. Thus, product specifications indicated by mechanical drawings and other information are translated into processing, equipment, tooling, purchasing, and personnel specifications. The totality of production plans contains a diversity of implicit or explicit quality specifications or norms. However, physical and human factors preclude perfect uniformity in the things that flow from the production line. In other words, every item in a given quantity of items manufactured on the same production line will be somewhat different. For this reason, quality specifications must set forth an acceptable range of variation from norm. Specifications should indicate tolerances in precise terms.

Inspection

Quality control involves a comparison of planning specifications with actual results by inspection and other techniques. Inspection may amount to little more than a visual scrutiny of manufactured items by production or inspection personnel. However, it generally requires the use of predetermined tests and measuring instruments. The inspection process may be concerned only with finished products or it may include a number of inspections throughout the production process. Many companies check all purchased materials, inspect parts and subassemblies at various stages of production, and subject finished products to a final inspection. Inspection may involve a check of every item, or it may be restricted to a limited percentage of items. Statistical techniques are sometimes used to predict and control the range of variability that will result from a given process. Corrective action is taken whenever a sampling of items shows too much deviation from a predetermined distribution.

Control Considerations

One purpose of quality control is to keep substandard products out of the market. Another is to gauge the performance of managerial and operating personnel. Quality control can also be used to indicate planning deficiencies and techniques that can be used to overcome them. An evaluation of actual results may pinpoint technical and human problems that were not anticipated during the planning phase. Such problems sometimes result in a revision of quality specifications to meet the realities of the production situation. The quality control function is frequently given departmental status outside the production department. Quality and quantity objectives are not always in accord; the pressures of production schedules sometimes give rise to laxity in the enforcement of quality standards. However, the responsibility for quality planning and control cannot be completely centralized in a separate department. The ultimate responsibility rests with the people who plan and perform the physical acts of production.

Nonmanufacturing Areas

Quality planning and control have become specialized areas of endeavor in industrial management and engineering. The degree of specialization is indicated by university courses and professional literature that focus upon particular aspects of the quality control area, such as statistical quality control and specification writing. The theories and techniques of quality control specialists have found their greatest application in the manufacturing and purchasing fields. An important reason is that the technology of things is much more susceptible to precise measurement than the psychology of people, but this fact should not lead to the idea that quality is less important in other areas of endeavor. The problem of quality is an implicit or explicit property of almost every executive decision. A restaurant or a department store manager who instructs personnel on "proper" techniques for waiting on customers is dealing with a quality problem. However, there is no one set of techniques that will give the best results or fit every situation. Furthermore, such standards cannot be as precisely measured and communicated as the specifications that should be used in a lathe operation. Performance information may also be subject to a diversity of meanings. For example, customer complaints about a particular waitress or sales employee may indicate below-standard performance, but it could also reflect peculiar personality traits of a few customers who happened to sit at a particular table or shop in the lingerie department. Every other customer may have been more than satisfied by the service accorded them.

PROCUREMENT CONTROL

Procurement or purchasing is concerned with the acquisition of merchandise, materials, supplies, and equipment required for managerial and operating activities. Narrowly construed, purchasing is the act of buying items at a price. More broadly defined, purchasing is an important aspect of managerial planning and involves activities other than buying. Some of the activities that may be included are:

"The research and development required for the proper selection of materials and sources from which those materials may be bought; the follow-up to insure proper delivery; the inspection of incoming shipments to insure both quantity and quality compliance with the order; the development of proper procedures, methods, and forms to enable the purchasing department to carry out established policies; the coordination of the activities of the purchasing department with such other internal divisions of the concern as traffic, receiving, storekeeping, and accounting so as to facilitate smooth operations; and the development of a technique of effective communication with top management of the company so that a true picture of the performance of the purchasing function is presented."[4]

[4]J. H. Westing, I. V. Fine, and others, *Industrial Purchasing: Buying for Industry and Budgetary Institutions*, 2nd ed. (New York: John Wiley and Sons, Inc., 1961), p. 2.

Informational Instruments

The procurement process begins with a receipt of information from a user department or the stores department that various kinds and quantities of items are required at a particular time or over a period of time. An important informational device is the purchase requisition, which indicates the nature of requirements and authenticates the request by an appropriate signature. Requisitions may be routed to the stores department to determine whether existing stocks can fill the demand and then to purchasing if stocks are inadequate or lacking. Purchase requirements may also evolve from the production planning process and be derived from bills of materials, production scheduling information, and inventory data. In retail establishments, the managers of merchandising and selling departments frequently determine purchase requirements and perform the buying function, sometimes with guidance from specialists in such areas as market research and fashions. Budgetary systems can impose limitations on the amounts and types of items that can be purchased. The lack of budgeted funds may prevent the purchase of needed materials and equipment even though more than enough money is available for other things.

The Quality Problem

The problem of quality standards, discussed in the previous section, is a highly important element in purchasing. Quality requirements may be designated through brands or trade names, physical or chemical specifications, market grade, use or purpose, samples, and the names of vendors. They may be determined by operating departments (such as manufacturing or merchandising departments), the quality control department, the purchasing department, or through the joint efforts of two or more departments.

The Selection of Suppliers

The selection of companies from which purchases will be made is another important aspect of the purchasing process. The number of potential suppliers may range from one for some things to hundreds for others. The final selection depends on such factors as price, quality, capacity to meet delivery schedules, transportation costs, and the supplier's reputation. Actual purchases are made on a purchase order form which stipulates quantities, delivery dates, price, discounts, shipping instructions, and other information. Copies are retained by the purchasing department and distributed to other departments requiring them, such as accounting and receiving. The ordering transaction is formally completed after acceptance is received from the supplier. Many companies follow up orders with written reminders and personal consultations to assure prompt delivery. Shipments made by vendors are generally inspected to determine whether quantitative and qualitative standards have been met. Invoices, bills of lading, and other pertinent forms are compared with inspection information and the original purchase order.

Other Informational Requirements

An efficient purchasing system develops and maintains a large amount of information about such matters as sources of supply, prices and discounts, market and economic trends, past performance of suppliers, product specifications, and shipping costs. Informational techniques are also devised to facilitate a follow-up of quotation requests and purchase orders. The letters, forms, and other information relating to completed transactions are generally filed for a period of time.

INVENTORY CONTROL

The time required to produce goods and services makes necessary an inventory or stock of merchandise, raw materials, work-in-process, manufactured products, tools and equipment, and supplies. However, inventories increase operating expenses and should not exceed whatever level is necessary to adequately perform organizational functions. Inventory strategy evolves from a consideration of such factors as the length of purchase, production, and merchandising cycles, the nature of technological processes, expected market and price trends, storage capacity, and anticipated shortages in market supplies. Inventory planning and control should be viewed as a dynamic problem involving a continuous inflow and outflow of stock as a result of operating activities. Changes in the relative rates at which items are purchased, produced, shipped, or sold will affect the level of physical inventories. Thus, higher sales will reduce inventories unless the amounts purchased are increased correspondingly. Such imbalances cannot always be immediately corrected, which means that inventory levels may fluctuate considerably in the short run. This problem also gives emphasis to the relationship between inventory planning and marketing, production, and purchasing programs. Planning inadequacies in other areas can impede attempts to develop efficient inventory plans.

Systematic Handling and Storage

Inventory planning and control require a systematic approach toward the handling and storage of merchandise and materials. The location and layout of storage space and the arrangement of stock on shelves, counters, and other storage devices should be carefully planned for efficient operations. Everything should have a place and be in place to facilitate the production and sales process and the identification and enumeration involved in a physical inventory. The things that make up inventories must be brought under physical control if the informational devices that measure inventories are to have any meaning.

Identification Systems. The translation of the facts of physical inventory into information requires a language system for identification purposes. Items are sometimes identified by the names that are ordinarily used such as hammers, hosiery, shoes, rivets, bolts, and tires. However, specialized identification systems are frequently used when inventories are large and complex. The following are some basic systems.

1. *Alphabetical*: the use of a letter or a group of letters according to some predetermined scheme.

2. *Mnemonic*: the use of letters in some such combination that they suggest the classification name of the particular item. Numbers may be combined with letters in the mnemonic system, particularly to suggest size or some generally accepted standard.

3. *Numerical*: the use of numbers to identify the particular item.

4. *Sign*: the use of symbols or signs to indicate items or operations. These have been extensively used in motion-study techniques.

5. *Combination*: the use of any of the foregoing systems in combination with any other one or all others to identify a particular item, service, or operation.[5]

Perpetual Inventory

Most organizations use some kind of perpetual inventory to provide information about changes in inventories. Such a system involves a corresponding informational adjustment when merchandise or materials flow into or out of storage. Balance-of-stores forms are commonly used to record the basic information required for this kind of inventory control. A separate form is maintained for each inventory item with information about such matters as the quantities ordered by purchase requisition, the quantities received by storage, the quantities issued by department or production requisition, and the quantities not issued but apportioned to production orders. The balance on hand and the number of items that have not been apportioned are generally computed after each transaction. A minimum inventory level or the ordering point together with the quantity that should be ordered is frequently indicated. The ordering point takes into account the time required to purchase the item and the amount that will be required during that period. In other words, the level of inventory must be sufficient to supply the needs of production, merchandising, and other departments during the purchasing cycle. The appropriate ordering quantity or the economic lot size is determined by balancing purchasing costs with the costs of maintaining inventory. For example, the costs involved in holding larger inventories are often justified by the lower cost of

---

[5]William R. Spriegel and Richard H. Lansburgh, *Industrial Management*, 5th ed. (New York: John Wiley and Sons, Inc., 1955), p. 32.5.

quantity purchases. Information about the value of the items in stock is also maintained on perpetual inventory forms for costing and other purposes. The data about inventory items can be combined and classified to meet the varied informational requirements of purchasing, production, budgeting, accounting, and marketing.

Physical Inventory

A perpetual inventory system would theoretically seem to eliminate the need for a physical count of inventory. However, the problem of information distortion cannot be completely avoided. A periodic physical inventory is necessary to correct the errors that arise in the informational system. Also important is that tax legislation requires verification of inventory information by actual count.

PERSONNEL CONTROL

The personnel or industrial relations department accumulates and maintains a diversity of information for planning and control purposes. Some of this information is concerned with the qualities of applicants for managerial and operating positions. Application forms, interview rating sheets, test results, recommendations, and medical reports can be placed in this category. Other information is concerned with the induction of personnel, providing them with facts about their position, the company, wages or salaries, promotion policy, rules relating to conduct, and other matters. Still other information deals with the performance of past and present personnel and includes reports and records on merit and performance ratings, transfers and promotions, wage and salary increases, disciplinary action, accidents and sickness, and termination of employment.

Job Information

Personnel recruitment and training require information about the nature of the positions that are to be filled. Position or job specifications are generally prepared by the personnel department with the help of information from industrial engineering and operating departments. Another problem is to evaluate positions or jobs for promotion and wage or salary administration purposes. Job evaluation is a systematic technique for measuring the relative importance of positions in terms of content. The job, not the person, is the focal point of the evaluation. The first step in the job evaluation process is to determine and define the nature of duties required for each position. The next is to select factors that are common to the positions being evaluated, such as the skill required (education, experience, etc.), effort requirements(physical and mental), the responsibility that is involved (equipment, material, safety of others), and job conditions (working conditions and hazards). Quantitative values are then assigned to various degrees or gradations of skill, effort, responsibility, and working conditions. For example, one year of education may be worth more than two years of experience, heavy physical labor may be valued higher than work requiring little physical effort, work under hazardous conditions may rate higher than work in comparative safety, etc. Each position is rated in terms of common factors and the extent to which factor values apply to it. The end product is a system of comparative values or rankings that can be used as a basis for planning wage and salary schedules and promotion policy. However, market conditions and collective bargaining play an important part in the final solution given to the problem.

Personnel Data and Reports

The administration of safety programs, suggestion systems, grievance systems, and personnel service activities have many informational requirements. Personnel departments also compile data and prepare reports on such matters as labor supply and wage trends, productivity, labor turnover, and absenteeism. Other informational needs evolve from collective bargaining, public relations, and government legislation.

Subjective Factors

Much of the above information contains implicit assumptions about the nature and predictability of individual and social behavior. For example, application forms and testing materials are based on the assumption that there is a measurable relationship between various specific stated or tested qualities and future performance. Some of the assumptions that are made in this respect evolve from highly tenuous logic. The meaning of such performance measures as merit ratings and disciplinary actions is frequently open to question. The apparent objectivity of some of this information may conceal subjective factors that were involved in the evaluation process. A similar statement can be made about job evaluation information. The values that persons with different backgrounds assign to such factors as working conditions and job hazards may vary a great deal. Since information concerned with the dynamics of human behavior is generally less reliable than information about things, psychologists and sociologists have not made as much progress in developing predictive theories as physicists. Executives should recognize the limitations of information that deals with individual, social, and institutional (such as unions) behavior. But they are also faced with planning and control problems that demand some kind of an answer. Many of the informational techniques developed by the behavioral scientists provide better results than a purely subjective approach. Thus, while it would be foolish to contend that psychological testing and other selection devices give perfect results, they undoubtedly are more reliable than phrenology.

17

COMPUTERIZED INFORMATIONAL SYSTEMS

The present and potential contribution of electronic computers to the informational process is now considered. The first part of the discussion deals with the nature of electronic computers and the manner in which they function. The section that follows describes the basic processes of computerized systems development and the kinds of systems that have been developed. Attention is then given to the problem of organizing for computers after which some conclusions are made about present achievements and future prospects.

Computer Functioning

What can electronic digital computers do? Fundamentally, they can read, remember, do arithmetic, make simple logical choices, and write. But they do not perform these tasks in a manner that can be called human. Computers do not read with eyes or write with fingers. An electronic data-processing system is composed of integrated or separate components that can be categorized as follows: (1) information input or "reading" devices, (2) memory or information storage instruments, (3) arithmetical and logical facilities, (4) information output or "writing" devices, and (5) operator control panels or consoles. The following briefly surveys the nature of some of the hardware that make up the above categories.

INPUT DEVICES

A number of devices can be used to feed instructions and data into a computer. One is a keyboard attached to the computer, which can be used either as the primary input mechanism or only to make modifications or corrections.

Another is punch cards that can be converted through intermediate devices into paper or magnetic tape. Paper tape containing serially arranged perforated characters is another important input device. The fastest input medium is magnetic tape, which can hold several hundred characters per inch of length. Each of the above input devices has advantages and disadvantages from a business point of view. Thus, magnetic tape can be read by the machine at a rate that may approach several hundred thousand characters per minute, but it is subject to breakage and deterioration. Punch cards are read at a much slower pace but provide a better permanent record of business information.

INFORMATION STORAGE DEVICES

Information may be stored on instruments external to the computer, such as punch cards, paper tape, and magnetic tape. It may also be stored within the machine on such devices as magnetic drums, magnetic cores, cathode-ray tubes, and vacuum tubes or transistors. Internal devices store bits or units of information in particular locations or addresses in much the same manner as mail is stored in numbered postal boxes. Computers can put information into storage addresses, delete existing storage information, and transfer information to other addresses or into an output device. Storage facilities are used to store instructions to the machine, data received from external input devices, intermediate computing results, and the final answers derived from the computing process. A large enough internal storage system could theoretically maintain all information relating to past and present business operations. Files and other external storage instruments would no longer be a part of the office scene. Although such a state of affairs may prevail at some future time, technical imperfections and business requirements provide good arguments for a more tangible permanent storage instrument. A technical failure in the computer might destroy a large amount of vital and irreplaceable company records. Furthermore, legal, regulatory, and tax requirements place limitations upon the use that can be made of electronic storage. Extensive use is still being made of punch cards because they represent a compromise between technical and business requirements. Punch cards are reasonably efficient in feeding information into intermediate and internal input and storage devices. They also provide a type of permanent storage that is well adapted to present business practices and purposes.

ARITHMETIC AND LOGICAL DEVICES

Computers perform arithmetic operations by a flow of electrical current through electronic on-off switching devices. As current enters the system, numbers are accumulated in a series of electronic storage devices. The process is sequenced by off-on gates or switches that open when an appropriate state of computation has been achieved. Gating results in a transfer of totals in one accumulator to higher order accumulators. Computers can only add and subtract but, by repeated additions and subtractions, can also multiply and divide. Their computational capacity is no greater than an ordinary mechanical-type desk calculator with one important difference. Electronic on-off switching devices operate in terms of a thousandth (millisecond) or millionth (microsecond) of a second. Computers can make hundreds or thousands of arithmetic computations in less than a second.

Most computers use a binary (base 2) number system rather than a decimal (base 10) system in making arithmetic computations. A binary system, using the numbers 0 and 1, is well adapted to the on-off (off equals 0; on equals 1) switching devices that make up a computer. Computers generally convert a decimal number input into binary numbers and back again into an output of decimal numbers. Thus, the user can work in terms of a decimal system even though the machine uses a binary system internally.

Computers have the capacity to make logical choices automatically with proper instructions. That is, they can select the appropriate operation from the logical relationship that exists between two or more conditions. For example, if two sums are equal or their difference is zero, the computer will automatically select a particular sequence of operations. A different sequence will be selected if one number is larger than another or if a quantity is plus or minus. In other words, the computer automatically sequences operations in terms of such logical forms as: if "a" is true, then "b" is true; if "a" is true, then "b" is false. This built-in logical capacity is necessary because the exact values that may be fed into the computer and derived from various stages of computation are not known. The computer automatically selects alternative instructions on the basis of logical relationships in the information.

OUTPUT DEVICES

Electric typewriters can be used to print the output of the computer, but their lack of speed makes them inadequate for many purposes. Greater efficiency is sometimes obtained by recording the results on paper or magnetic tape and then feeding tapes into a number of electric typewriters and other printing devices. A great deal of attention has been given to the development of faster printing facilities. Printing speeds as high as 30,000 lines per minute have been made possible through a variety of mechanical and electronic innovations.

CONTROL DEVICES

Computers have both internal and external control devices. Internal control is essentially concerned with the sequencing, timing, and coordination of computer operations. External control involves direct communication between the computer and a human operator. The operator can start and stop the computer, perform particular operations, determine values in storage or memory locations, put data into or take data out of internal storage facilities, regulate input and output devices, and control other aspects of computer functioning. The computer can also be designed or instructed to transmit information to the operator. For example, computers can indicate internal breakdowns or computational errors by printing the information, by flashing lights, by stopping, and in other ways. They can even point out the nature of the difficulty and identify the internal component that requires attention. Facilities may also be provided for checking out the adequacy or correctness of the instructions given to the computer. Some computers have the capacity to automatically bypass defective components and make periodic checks on the accuracy of computation.

The Development of Computerized Informational Systems

The development of computerized information is viewed from a dual perspective in the pages that follow. The first relates to the basic processes that begin with computer systems design and end with computer operations. The second is concerned with the kinds of computerized informational systems that may be developed in an organization. Figure 17-1 portrays the nature of these interrelationships.

THE DESIGN OF INFORMATIONAL SYSTEMS

The design of informational systems involves an analysis of informational needs of a department or an entire organization and a determination of the manner in which a computerized system can meet these needs. The basic problem is to translate informational requirements into a form that can be effectively handled by an electronic computer. The conversion to a computerized system may impose limitations that were not present in an existing noncomputerized system. In some instances, a systems study will result in the conclusion that computerization cannot solve the informational problem. But a computerized system can provide information that would not otherwise be possible.

The systems designer is obviously concerned with the capacities of the computer in designing an informational system. But this requirement does not mean that the systems designer must be able to perform the detailed steps involved in computer programming. A broad knowledge of computer capacities is adequate for most purposes. It is generally more important for the systems designer to understand the nature of the specialized field for which the informational system is being developed. Systems personnel should have a good background in accounting, economics, finance, marketing, production, and

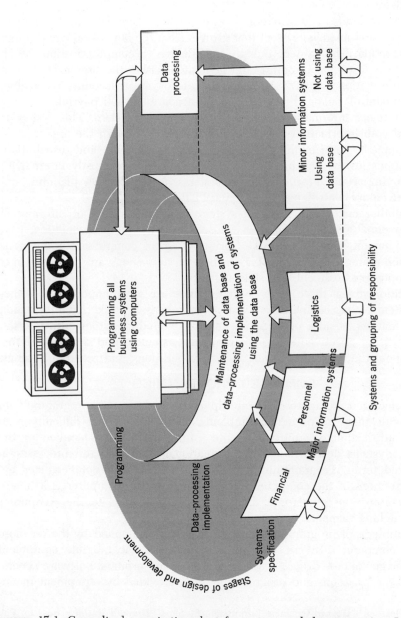

FIGURE 17-1. Generalized organization chart for systems and data processing. John Dearden, "How to Organize Information Systems," *Harvard Business Review*, Vol. 43, No. 2, March–April 1965, pp. 71 (with permission).

personnel before they attempt to design a computerized informational system for such fields.

Three major kinds of informational systems can be found in most organizations.[1] One is the financial system that evolves from the flow of dollars through the organization. This system is highly conducive to computerization. Much of the data is historical in nature and generated within the organization. Important informational subsystems are accounts payable, accounts receivable, budgetary control, financial reports, general accounting, and payroll.

Another major informational system is the logistics system. This system is concerned with information about the flow of goods through the organization and encompasses the functions of procurement, production, and distribution. The functions involve the processing of large amounts of mostly internal information. Important informational subsystems are production planning and control, inventory control, purchasing, and PERT.

Still another major informational system involves the flow of information about personnel.[2] Such information is used for purposes of promotion, pay, work assignment, and transfer. The primary use of computer equipment is information storage and retrieval. Examples of subsystems are personnel records, manpower assessment, and skills inventory.

In addition to the three major systems, there are other important informational systems. Many companies maintain comprehensive marketing information on such matters as sales performance, customer credit, customer inventories, and advertising effectiveness. Some companies assemble and distribute information about the economic system, industry conditions, and research findings.

COMPUTER PROGRAMMING

Most electronic computers are multipurpose and can be programmed to solve a wide range of particular problems. The programming difficulty is to translate informational requirements into a form that can be handled by the machine. Systems design indicates informational objectives and processes in generalized terms. Programming sets forth the necessary, detailed, step-by-step instructions to the computer. The language of the computer is a binary code (combinations of zeros and ones) that corresponds to the computer's off-on switching elements.

The problems of programming have been greatly simplified by the development of computer software. Computer hardware is the tangible equipment such as magnetic tape drives, central processors, and printers. Software is composed of the programs and programming aids provided by equipment manu-

[1]John Dearden, "How to Organize Information Systems," *Harvard Business Review*, Vol. 43, No. 2, March–April 1965, pp. 65–73.

[2]Richard T. Bueschel, *EDP and Personnel*, Management Bulletin 86 (New York: American Management Association, 1966).

facturers and developed by users. Software is an important ingredient for efficient hardware utilization.

A number of different techniques to assist the programmer can be noted. One is the assembly program that enables the programmer to use mnemonic designations in writing a program. In other words, one set of codes becomes another with the same or a similar meaning. The programmer must still think in terms of each machine operation, but he can write the specific instruction in something other than binary code. For example, he can write ADD or SUBTRACT instead of long sequences of zeros or ones. An assembly program will automatically translate mnemonic programming codes into machine or binary code.

Another important programming aid is the compiler program. An assembly program is a one-for-one translation device. For each machine instruction there is a corresponding mnemonic type code. Compiler programs are macro in the sense that they translate into many micromachine instructions. The programmer can set forth what needs to be done in much broader terms. He needs to be less concerned with the details of machine operation and can give more attention to the information procedure with which he is concerned.

Compiler programs through which the computer itself can be used to fill in the details have made possible programming languages that have greatly facilitated computer programming. A good example is COBOL (Common Business Oriented Languages), which can be used for a wide variety of organizational and managerial applications. Another example is FORTRAN (Formula Translation), which is a scientific and engineering language. Other important languages could be noted, but the basic idea is the same. They all use macro symbols relating to the fields concerned, which can be translated into micromachine instructions through compiler programs. A word of caution is probably in order at this point. These languages have not made programming an amateur pursuit. Precise and complicated procedures must be followed in using them and the programmer must still have extensive knowledge about computer operations.

Still another important advance in the software area is the development of standardized application programs that can be used by many organizations. Computer manufacturers have developed programs of this kind for sales forecasting, capital investment, PERT, linear programming, production line balancing, inventory control, and many other systems. Such programs can often be used with a slight amount of modification to meet particular needs.

COMPUTER OPERATIONS

A computer installation produces a large variety of information through hardware and software components. Hundreds of people may be employed in large data-processing departments. Some of the basic functions performed in such departments are the following. The preparation of input data for machine operations involves such activities as key punching cards with round or rectangular holes so that they can be "read" by machine input equipment. Punched cards may be duplicated, collated, and sorted in order to arrange or rearrange data for machine operations and other purposes. They are also important information storage devices. Punched card information cannot be directly read by the computer; it must be first transferred to magnetic tape.

Computer programs and operating data are generally fed into the computer through magnetic tapes. The program is first put into the computer memory after which the data are inserted for operations. The computer console operator monitors the processing to check for programming errors, incomplete or incorrect data input, and other problems. The results of computer operation are recorded on magnetic tape, punched cards, or paper; high speed printers are used to provide much of the data output.

The problems that face other production facilities are also pertinent in data-processing departments. Production planning and scheduling, quality control, maintenance problems (hardware and software), software storage, personnel supervision and training, and customer (user departments) relations are highly important managerial responsibilities.

REAL-TIME COMPUTER SYSTEMS

A great deal has been written in recent years about real-time systems that can supply completely up-to-date information about company operations. Information in such a system is updated as operations occur and is immediately available in an appropriate form at output stations. Airline reservation systems and railroad traffic control systems are good examples of real-time systems in action.

Some companies are beginning to use something approaching a real-time system to provide relatively up-to-date inventory, production, and sales information. Strictly speaking, most such systems are not real time because they involve batching of input data and lengthy delays in output transmission. Sales personnel, for example, transmit sales data at the end of the day to the computer system for processing. This information is made available to management in an appropriate form the next morning. Such a system has a lag of about a day that could be reduced by a number of relatively simple techniques, but there would be little purpose in doing so. Management does not need to have the information on a "real-time" basis. Much of the data required for planning and control does not need to be up to the minute. A lag of a day, a week, or even a month is not too long for many managerial purposes.

Real-time systems require expensive hardware and software. The reservation system (SABRE) developed for American Airlines, for example, involved about 10 years of experimentation and development at a cost of approximately

$30 million. The cost of such a system is an important limiting factor at the present time. But even if costs are significantly reduced, there is still the question of whether real-time information is required for every kind of informational need. Indeed, real-time information may have little value for some management purposes. Professor John Dearden has suggested that the real-time concept can generally be better applied to logistical than to financial or personnel informational systems.[3]

SHARED-TIME COMPUTER SYSTEMS

Shared-time computer systems evolve from technological and economic considerations. The tremendous speed at which the electronic computer performs computational and other functions means that a large volume of operations is necessary if there is to be no unused capacity. Large computer systems are generally more economical if they are fully utilized and have much more problem-solving and processing capacity than smaller systems. The difficulty is that many organizations are able to use only a small proportion of the potential of a large system. A solution is to share a large computer with other organizations. One approach is a joint venture in which several organizations participate. Another is to acquire a larger computer and lease a portion of its capacity to other organizations. Still another is to lease computer time from a company set up for that purpose in the manner of telephone, electric power, and other public utilities. Shared time systems have already shown that they can be successful, and there are good reasons for believing they will become more popular in the future.

Organizing for Computers

This section is concerned with the problem of organizing for computerized informational systems. The nature of the informational systems department and the manner in which it relates to other departments is briefly discussed. Particular attention is given to ways in which business and government have solved such organizational problems.

THE INFORMATION SYSTEMS DEPARTMENT

Departments concerned with computerized informational systems are generally referred to by such names as the Electronic Data Processing Department, the Business Systems Department, and the Electronic Computer Department. They are generally organized on a functional basis with the following primary units: (1) Systems Analysis and Design; (2) Computer Program-

---

[3]John Dearden, "Myth of Real-Time Management Information," *Harvard Business Review*, Vol. 44, No. 3, May–June 1966, pp. 123–132.

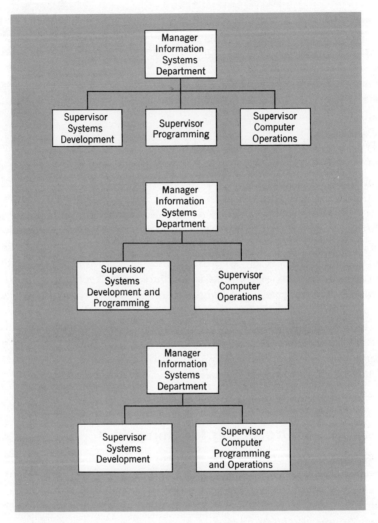

FIGURE 17-2. Alternative organizational structures for an information systems department.

ming; and (3) Data Processing or Computer Operations. Other possible subsidiary units have responsibility for such functions as program maintenance and storage, planning, education and training, scheduling, and quality control.

A basic organizational structure for an information systems department and some variations of this basic structure are shown in Figure 17-2.[4] In some in-

---

[4]*Administration of Electronic Data Processing*, Studies in Business Policy No. 98 (New York, N.Y.: National Industrial Conference Board, Inc., 1961), pp. 57–67.

stances, systems development and programming are combined in the same departmental unit. One argument for such an arrangement is that informational systems should be designed so that they can be efficiently programmed. Another is that programmers cannot perform their functions properly unless they understand the purpose and logic of the system. Still another is that parts of the system can be programmed and checked to insure greater compatibility between the needs of the system and the programming problem.

Other organizations contend that systems design should be done in a separate departmental unit. The argument is that programmers might be too inclined to modify informational systems to simplify computer programming and operations. Some organizations have segmented the computer organization by placing the informational systems design function in a broader systems and procedures department. A possible difficulty is that systems design can become too far removed from the computer side of the schema. The result can be a lack of coordination and failures in cooperation.

Computer programming and operations are sometimes combined into one departmental unit. (See Figure 17-2.) The rationale is that efficiency in programming is an important prerequisite for efficient computer performance. Computer operations can then indicate the manner in which an informational system can be more efficiently programmed.

Future Prospects and Problems

This section attempts to build a bridge between present computer applications and future prospects. Computers have been tested on the firing line and have shown that they can solve important planning and informational problems. There is every indication that much more progress will be made in the future. But recognition should also be given to possible limitations and problems.

MORE TIMELY INFORMATION

Computerized informational systems have made possible more rapid communication of information about environmental and organizational conditions to management. The increased speed of information processing has given organizations a greater capacity to adapt to change. The planning period can in some instances be significantly shortened. However, more timely information is useful only if executives take advantage of it. The benefit of high speed processing can be negated by sluggishness in the planning and control process. A further consideration is that the costs of more timely information may more than offset their value. Also important is that instant information (such as real time) is by no means always necessary or even desirable.

THE PROBLEM OF INFORMATIONAL INPUT

Electronic computers are essentially errorproof as far as the technical aspects of operations are concerned. They do exactly what they are directed to do by their programs. But they cannot correct inputs of incomplete or inaccurate information. As one data processing executive put it, "The feeding of bad in-puts into faster and more capable equipments will only generate more bad information at a faster pace."[5] Production or sales personnel who deliberately or nondeliberately distort the data they provide are much the same problem they were before computerized informational systems were introduced.

TOWARD INTEGRATED INFORMATIONAL SYSTEMS

There is little indication that organizations will soon have totally integrated informational systems. But a significant amount of integration has occurred within such functional areas as marketing and production.[6] In one survey of over 100 companies, a sizable number expect to have informational systems that tie together two or more functional areas. All of the companies in the survey expect their computer systems to be integrated to some significant degree in the future. Many companies reported that they are investigating the possibility and potential of a total informational system, but they do not intend to go that far in the immediate future.

PREDICTIVE INFORMATION AND MODELS

A great deal of effort will undoubtedly be expended during the next decade to develop predictive and planning models. The high speeds at which computers perform their operations have probably improved the quality of accounting and statistical data. But the fact remains that such data are historical. Predictive and planning models are concerned with what will happen in the future. The human behavior reflected in data about the past can change significantly in a relatively short period of time. Computers have the capacity to provide a more accurate and complete history of human behavior, and they may well improve prediction of future behavior through their tremendous speed and computational capacity. But there is little likelihood that they will soon be able to improve upon the logical formulations that are presently employed by human behavioral scientists. The speed with which computers can solve logical and computational problems will not eliminate some of the more critical assumptions of predictive and planning models.

[5]Norman J. Ream, "Developing a Long-Range Plan for Corporate Methods and the Dependence on Electronic Data-Processing," presented at the Western Joint Computer Conference, San Francisco, California, March 3–5, 1959.

[6]Neal J. Dean, "The Computer Comes of Age," *Harvard Business Review*, Vol. 46, No. 1, January–February 1968, pp. 89–90.

SOCIOPSYCHOLOGICAL PROBLEMS

Some informational subsystems can be entirely controlled by computers, but man-machine interface cannot be avoided unless factories and offices are completely automated. The impact of machine-derived messages on human receivers can have important psychological implications. Communicating with a machine can create problems that impede the communication process. In some cases communication may be blocked; in others, it may be improved.

The tremendous rate of technological change that characterizes the computer revolution has had a profound impact on educational requirements. There is much more emphasis on continuing education at all age and experience levels. Further education is for fathers and mothers as well as sons and daughters. A man can become as obsolete as a machine in a relatively short period of time.

PART VI

The Responsibility of Management

18

THE RESPONSIBILITY OF MANAGEMENT

This chapter begins with a brief analysis of legal, economic, and other conceptions of managerial responsibility. Consideration is then given to particular interest groups that relate to this aspect of organizational dynamics.

Concepts of Managerial Responsibility

THE LEGAL THEORY OF RESPONSIBILITY

Under corporation law, management is required to manage in the best interests of the stockholder. This narrow conception of management responsibility has not been unchallenged. Those opposing this view advance the idea that management should also assume responsibility to the public, the consumer, labor, and other groups. A difficulty with this argument is that of legally enforcing the broader responsibility. The fear of those who oppose an abandonment of the theory of sole legal responsibility to the stockholders is that it will eliminate the only existing legal means for enforcing responsibility.[1] To expand the theory to include responsibility to other groups presents the danger of eliminating legal responsibility until a practical scheme of enforcement can be devised.

---

[1] A. A. Berle, Jr., "For Whom Corporate Managers Are Trustees: A Note," *Harvard Law Review*, Vol. 45, No. 8, June 1932, pp. 1365–1372. Berle has written more recently that the argument has been settled, at least for the time being, in favor of the broader approach to responsibility. *The 20th Century Capitalist Revolution* (New York: Harcourt, Brace and Company, Inc., 1954), p. 169.

Is the assumption of a broader organizational and social responsibility compatible with the legal theory of management responsibility? One answer to this question is that the acceptance of a broader responsibility is merely an enlightened view of the interests of the stockholder. Another view is that the legal responsibility to the stockholder does not exclude the assumption of a responsibility to other groups and to the common enterprise. What is the purpose of the legal responsibility theory? It is designed to protect the stockholder's property from an irresponsible management that might seek to divert that property into its own pockets or the pockets of some other group. Its purpose is to prevent irresponsibility; it was not formulated to impede the development of a more constructive and comprehensive philosophy of management responsibility.

ECONOMIC THEORY AND MANAGERIAL RESPONSIBILITY

In the theory developed by the classical economists, the problem of managerial responsibility is "solved" by product and resource markets which are assumed to be competitive. The individual firm plays a passive role in the determination of market values because it does not produce or purchase a large enough quantity to influence the market. The discretion of the entrepreneur or manager is limited by the requirements of the system. Competition forces productive efficiency and adaptation to the values of the market. The planning problem is solved by a series of adjustments or "decisions" which are essentially mathematical in nature. The symmetry and simplicity of classical economic theory should not delude students of management into thinking it had nothing to say about the problem of managerial responsibility. The theory was philosophically oriented toward the consumer even though other participants in the production process were not actually ignored. The primary purpose of the firm and of the economic system in which it plays a part was assumed to be the satisfaction of consumer wants. Every other aspect of the process was viewed as a means to this ultimate end.

LABORISTIC PHILOSOPHY AND MANAGERIAL RESPONSIBILITY

The proponents of unionism and collective bargaining generally assume that the traditional market does not give the worker his proper share in the distribution of income.[2] They contend that the employer has too much power under the usual state of economic affairs. A major consideration of the Congress in passing labor legislation favorable to union organization was that there existed an unfavorable balance of power between property and labor. Unionism and collective bargaining do not necessarily conflict with the conceptions of managerial responsibility developed in corporation law and eco-

[2]This idea is usually stated in terms of the short run rather than the long run.

nomic theory. However, they present a potential area of conflict both in a philosophical and a practical sense. Powerful labor unions can make inroads into the income that might otherwise be paid to the stockholder. The unorganized stockholder seems to have become somewhat of an "underdog" in the total scheme of things.[3] The consumer may also have suffered some of the fate ascribed to the stockholder. Urwick has drawn the following picture of the situation.

"Over the last century, man has developed a complex of organisational forms for representing his interests as a producer, while his interests as a consumer have remained relatively unorganised save in so far as they could be protected by government or by the action of business managers. . . . The business manager . . . has found himself a trustee for the interests of man as a consumer under an increasing fire of criticism from the organisations designed to protect man's interests as a producer."[4]

A highly productive industrial system may well be able to afford some shift from the traditional emphasis on consumption. But, too much "consumption on the job" by a portion of the total population (unionized workers or others) may significantly affect the welfare of those who are not organized for power.

MANAGEMENT RESPONSIBILITY: A BROADER VIEW

Many managers contend that they should assume responsibility to the organization itself and to all of the interest groups of which it is composed. Other interest groups, such as customers, creditors, suppliers, and workers, are placed on an essentially equal plane with stockholders. The fact that workers are included represents some kind of challenge to the philosophical position of unions. Such a conception of managerial responsibility represents a major shift in the philosophy of management. They reflect a historical evolution toward management by professionals who are psychologically oriented toward the organization as a cooperative system. The organization is viewed as something apart from the personal motives of its constituents. The problem of distributing the product of the cooperative process to the interest groups becomes less concerned with social ideology and more with organizational efficiency.

Some people have contended that the business manager should place his duty to society above his duty to his company and above his private interest. This sort of thing is difficult to translate into practical terms. There is no unified theory of social welfare to determine what kind of decision will best serve

[3] J. A. Livingston has presented this thesis in *The American Stockholder* (Philadelphia: J. B. Lippincott Company, 1958).

[4] L. Urwick, *The Load on Top Management—Can It Be Reduced?* (London: Urwick, Orr, & Partners Ltd., 1954), pp. 7–8.

the society. The lack of such a theory gives considerable license for irresponsibility because there are no norms to indicate the nature of responsible behavior. Much of the difficulty is removed by making management primarily responsible to the organization. Such a conception pinpoints responsibility and provides a focal point for control.

It should not be assumed that the interests of the organization and those of the society are always in conflict. They tend to be compatible in the long run although the mechanism by which this is brought about is highly illusive. The society is not in danger of being destroyed by the organizations that live in its domain. The management of today seems generally less inclined than some of its forebears to profit at the expense of society. Organizations may modify markets and other aspects of their environment, but they would not long survive if they failed to adapt to important economic, political, and social forces. Management cannot ignore the interests of consumers, stockholders, employees, creditors, suppliers, and society. Its discretionary powers are by no means absolute. It is forced to adapt to environmental forces as presently constructed, but it is also threatened by potential politically imposed restrictions if discretion is used without wisdom.

The Interest Groups: Management Strategies

Previous chapters have given a great deal of attention to the problem of interest groups. Interest group representation on boards of directors and other committees was considered in Chapter 8. The chapters concerned with environmental factors and dynamic planning (Chapters 4 and 5) indicated the manner in which labor, creditors, customers, suppliers, and government influence organizational objectives. This section gives brief attention to some of the strategies that may be appropriate in dealing with the major interest groups. No significance is intended by the order in which they are considered.

THE STOCKHOLDERS

The number of stockholders in a corporation may range from a few to well over a million. The interests of majority and large minority stockholders are generally well protected through either direct participation in the management or the real power to intervene if necessary. The millions of small stockholders who collectively own a large percentage of the total investment in corporate enterprises are in a much less favorable position in this respect. Such stockholders are generally content to collect dividends and let management do the managing. They take an active interest in what management is doing only if their dividends or assets begin to dwindle. In spite of the rights afforded by the law, the actual power of the small stockholder to protect himself from managerial actions detrimental to his interests is limited. Some managements may be inclined to take advantage of the situation, but such a policy tends in the long run to be contrary to the best interests of the organization. However, it should not be assumed that the best intentions will keep every stockholder happy. The interests of different stockholders are not the same, and some stockholders may prefer a policy not preferred by others. Thus, stockholders who want income in the short run may not like a policy of plowing back a large part of earnings, but the interests of stockholders who think in terms of future equity and income prospects might be enhanced by such a policy.

Recent years have witnessed a trend toward a more positive approach to stockholder relations. Stockholders are invited to the annual meetings and are given a great deal of consideration if they do attend. The large majority who stay at home are remembered through letters from executives and publications informing them about company policy, products, profit, and potential. Every effort is made to make them feel they are important to and a member of the organization. But management should not assume that the techniques of Madison Avenue can really put a silver lining on what are really dark clouds. No amount of advertising copy can hide the fact that the postman failed to deliver a dividend check or that values have declined on the Exchange. People generally respond well to the hard facts if they are honestly presented, and they may even forgive an honest error in judgment.

THE EMPLOYEES

The rise of powerful labor unions can be partly attributed to past failures by management to properly represent the interests of employees. Union organizers generally consider good employee relations as an important obstacle to their goals. However, no amount of speculation as to what might have happened can help when the union becomes firmly established. Management should remember that union members are also company employees and that harsh measures may show up in employee and community relations for many years. There is no point in unnecessarily antagonizing company employees. Executives should negotiate forcefully and oppose demands they cannot accept, but they should not neglect employee relations even during a long strike. They should also recognize that union leaders may be helpful in advancing the company program. Management-union cooperation on many matters is possible under some circumstances and can bring important rewards.[5] Such cooperation has been practiced in such problem areas as accident prevention, labor turnover, job evaluation, methods improvement, and technological change.

Management should not neglect its responsibilities to unorganized factory and office workers. Unions will eventually fill the gap if management fails to act. Management must make employees feel that it is genuinely interested in

[5]Ernest Dale, *Greater Productivity Through Labor-Management Cooperation*, Research Report, No. 14 (New York: American Management Association, 1949).

their welfare and views. A perfunctory or a paternalistic approach to employee relations is not adequate. Furthermore, management should not assume that the loyalty of the employee can be bought by a give-away program. Employees want a "fair" wage and other benefits, but they also want to retain their self-respect.

CUSTOMERS

Customers play a vital part in maintaining business and industrial organizations. Barnard includes customers in his scheme of organization and places them on a par with employees, stockholders, creditors, and suppliers.[6] Whyte has given emphasis to the manner in which customers may influence human relations within an organization.[7] Something more is involved in defining the term "customer" than the act of buying a company's products or services. A customer may be broadly defined as a person who has a favorable impression of a company and its products or services. A person may be categorized as a customer even though he has not committed the act of buying. Someone who owns a company product or has used its services may not properly be called a customer if he now has a negative attitude toward the company. Thus, a customer is as much a potential as an actual purchaser. He has a cooperative attitude toward the company and its products or services and represents an important company asset generally called "good will." The value of good will is frequently far greater than the evaluation given in the accounting records.

A variety of techniques is used to induce people to become a company's customers. Advertising and sales promotion programs, the use of trade names, price policies, product innovation, quality control, credit purchase plans, and customer servicing represent some of the more obvious techniques. The problem should be viewed in terms of a total approach that involves a combination of many techniques. People tend to develop an image of a company and its products or services that may be influenced by many direct and indirect ways. The techniques noted above are some of the more direct approaches to the problem, but management should also recognize the importance of actions not directly oriented toward customer relations. Thus, a speech on world affairs by the company president, the conduct of executives during a labor dispute, and participation or lack of participation in community affairs can significantly influence the situation.

The customer becomes an important variable in the human relationships that make up an organization. Whyte has noted, "when workers and customers meet, in the service industries, that relationship adds a new dimension to the

---

[6]Chester I. Barnard, *Organization and Management* (Cambridge: Harvard University Press, 1952), pp. 111–133.

[7]William Foote Whyte, *Human Relations in the Restaurant Industry* (New York: McGraw-Hill Book Company, 1948), and *Industry and Society* (New York: McGraw-Hill Book Company, 1946), pp. 123–147.

pattern of human relations in industry."[8] Customers in banks, retail stores, restaurants, night clubs, barber shops, and many other types of enterprises come into direct face-to-face contact with employees. Planning and controlling the behavior of the customer frequently becomes an important area of management action. Customers are "trained" to accept specific behavior patterns in the manner of employees. For example, the customers of a bank are taught the accepted procedures for making out deposit slips, endorsing checks, and packaging small change. Restaurant patrons may be directed to a specific table by a hostess, are restricted by menus in what they can order, and may even be asked to leave if they insult the waitress. Customers in self-service laundries, grocery stores, automats, and drugstores become almost literally company employees. Many of the techniques that pertain to the supervision of employees apply with equal validity to customers.

The customer has become an especially significant social force through the efforts of people like Ralph Nader. Consumers have sometimes been neglected in the interests of powerful producer groups, such as big business and big unions. Nader's crusade has caused even the largest corporations to review their policies, although sometimes reluctantly, to demands for better and safer products. The economic need to serve the consumer has been reinforced by political and social demands for greater responsibility on the part of business enterprise.

CREDITORS, SUPPLIERS, AND OTHER INTERESTS

Some of the ideas expressed about stockholders, employees, and customers are also pertinent in the relationships involving creditors, suppliers, and other interests. Thus, a company might be ill-advised to take advantage of its suppliers in a buyer's market. The good will of suppliers and creditors is an important asset that should generally not be dissipated in the interests of short-run gains. Companies should have a similar attitude toward the communities in which their plants and offices are located. They should make an effort to gain the support of the community, and the executives should behave like good neighbors rather than bosses from the outside. Good will with respect to an interest group may reap many indirect rewards. Customers represent fertile ground for the sale of securities; stockholders frequently become buyers and boosters of company products and services; employees are potential customers and stockholders.

THE MORAL RESPONSIBILITY OF MANAGEMENT

Moral responsibility involves more than conformity. Management does and should play a positive role in man's quest for the better life. Management should become concerned about such major social issues as environmental pol-

[8]Ibid., p. 123.

lution, racial discrimination, and poverty. The people who do the managing are the product of the society in which they work and should understand the traditions and customs of that society, not only for purposes of conformity but also as a starting point for its further ethical development. Managers should not be content merely to provide the means for social goals pronounced by consumers, politicians, labor leaders, or educators. Management becomes a creative force in society through the achievements of organized endeavor. It should give thought to the ethical implications of such achievements and become creative in the ethical sense to the same degree that it has demonstrated an ability to produce efficient techniques.

INDEX